CW00957193

CUSTOM WOODWORKING

Outdoor Projects
Deck, Lawn & Garden

CONVERSION CHART

WEIGHT EQUIVALENTS
(ounces and pounds / grams and kilograms)

US	METRIC
$\frac{1}{4}$ oz	7 g
$\frac{1}{2}$ oz	14 g
$\frac{3}{4}$ oz	21 g
1 oz	28 g
8 oz ($\frac{1}{2}$ lb)	227 g
12 oz ($\frac{3}{4}$ lb)	340 g
16 oz (1 lb)	454 g
35 oz (2.2 lb)	1 kg

CONVERSION FORMULA
ounces x 28.35 = grams
1000 grams = 1 kilogram

TEMPERATURE EQUIVALENTS
(fahrenheit / celsius)

US	METRIC
0° F (freezer temperature)	-18° C
32° F (water freezes)	0° C
98.6° F (normal body temp.)	37° C
180° F (water simmers)*	82° C
212° F (water boils)*	100° C

*at sea level

CONVERSION FORMULA
degrees fahrenheit minus 32, divided by 1.8
= degrees celsius

LINEAR EQUIVALENTS
(inches and feet / centimetres and metres)

US	METRIC
$\frac{1}{4}$ in	0.64 cm
$\frac{1}{2}$ in	1.27 cm
1 in	2.54 cm
6 in	15.24 cm
12 in (1 foot)	30.48 cm
1 ft^2	929.03 cm^2
39$\frac{1}{2}$ in	1.00 m
1 yd	91.44 cm
1 yd^2	0.84 m^2

CONVERSION FORMULA
inches x 2.54 = centimetres
100 centimetres = 1 metre

VOLUME EQUIVALENTS
(fluid ounces / millilitres and litres)

US	METRIC
1 tbsp ($\frac{1}{2}$ fl oz)	15 ml
$\frac{1}{2}$ cup (4 fl oz)	120 ml
1 cup (8 fl oz)	240 ml
1 quart (32 fl oz)	960 ml
1 quart + 3 tbsps	1 L
1 gal (128 fl oz)	3.8 L
1 in^3	16.39 cm^3
1 ft^3	0.0283 m^3
1 yd^3	0.765 m^3

CONVERSION FORMULA
fluid ounces x 30 = millilitres
1000 millilitres = 1 litre

DISCLAIMER

Readers should note that this book was initially intended for publication in the United States of America, and the existence of different laws, conditions and tools means that it is the reader's' responsibility to ensure that they comply with all safety requirements and recommended best practices in the European Economic Area.

The improper use of hand tools and power tools can result in serious injury or death. Do not operate any tool until you have carefully read its instruction manual and understand how to operate the tool safely. Always use all appropriate safety equipment as well as the guards that were supplied with your tools and equipment. In some of the illustrations in this book, guards and safety equipment have been removed only to provide a better view of the operation. Do not attempt any procedure without using all appropriate safety equipment or without ensuring that all guards are in place.

Neither August Home Publishing Company nor Time-Life Books assume any responsibility for any injury, loss or damage arising from use of the materials, plans, instructions or illustrations contained in this book. However, nothing here is intended to exclude or limit liability for death or personal injury if, and to the extent that, such exclusion or limitation would be contrary to public policy or otherwise be unenforceable.

CUSTOM WOODWORKING

Outdoor Projects
Deck, Lawn & Garden

By the editors of Time-Life Books
and *Woodsmith* magazine

Time-Life Books, Alexandria, Virginia

CONTENTS

CUSTOM WOODWORKING

Outdoor Projects
Deck, Lawn & Garden

LAWN FURNITURE 6

Redwood Bench

GARDEN ACCENTS 50

Bird Feeder

With its copper roof and real cedar shingles, this project looks complex. But using pre-cut shingles and copper foil simplifies construction.

It's easy to customize this planter to fit your deck or below a window. And the box joints aren't glued together — they're pinned.

Making this cylindrical birdhouse doesn't require a lathe. Whether it's built to house birds or just for show, there are lots of ways to customize it.

Large projects don't have to be complicated. This arbor is built in sections with very basic joinery. Then the sections are taken outside and assembled.

PATIO, DECK & PORCH 86

Picnic Table

With four different sizes and two unique side panels to choose from, there are a lot of ways to customize these beautiful boxes.

As sturdy as it is good looking, this Picnic Table features splined miter joints that keep the table top and bench tops flat.

It's not just the shape of this table that's unique. A few of the techniques used to build it are similar to what you'd use for an indoor table.

This swing can be built with a traditional curved back and slats or with straight rails and a slatted panel back with decorative diamond cut-outs.

LAWN FURNITURE

For someone new to woodworking, building lawn furniture has always been a fun way to get started. The garden seat is a great beginning project. It's simple to build, yet it offers some interesting challenges.

The Adirondack chair can be the centerpiece of an outdoor set. Other pieces include a settee with room for two, and an Adirondack table or side table.

The chaise lounge and redwood bench each provide comfortable ways to relax outdoors. Both are beautiful pieces that will test your skills and are sure to last for many years.

Garden Seat

The Garden Seat is designed to be built in a weekend. For a more traditional look, you can add an arched back and arm rests. Either way, this economical, easy-to-build seat fits any outdoor setting.

Building most garden benches is no walk in the park. The back legs are typically angled, and the joinery connecting the arms, legs, and back can get a bit complicated. But I decided on a simpler approach. This garden "seat" doesn't have a back or arms. So it not only has a simple look — it's much easier to build, too.

And there's another benefit to this approach. You don't need to have a large formal garden to justify building this Garden Seat. It will be right at home on a front porch, beside a flower bed, or even in the backyard.

If you choose to build a formal garden bench, plans for adding an arched back and arm rests can be found in the Designer's Notebook on pages 14 and 15.

GIVE IT A REST. This Garden Seat is simple enough to build in a weekend.

But you don't want to go out to buy your lumber one day and start building it the next, especially if you're working with dimensional lumber ("two-by" and "one-by" stock — I used Douglas fir).

Dimensional lumber can be pretty "wet" when you buy it, and it needs a chance to dry. I like to let it sit in my shop for a couple weeks. After that time, there are usually small checks in the ends of a few of the boards, and some of the boards will have warped. Waiting allows me to "see" these problems before they get built into the seat.

OUTDOOR SUPPLIES. Because this seat is going to spend significant time outdoors, you'll want to take care in

selecting your supplies. When it came to the glue and hardware, I used a water-resistant glue and galvanized exterior screws.

Note: If your seat is going to be outside all year long (as opposed to keeping it on a porch or storing it away during the winter), you may want to use a waterproof glue like plastic resin or polyurethane glue.

FINISH. The finish will require some extra care, too. I used a semi-transparent finish (see the Finishing Tip on page 12). Of course, you have several options for finishing the Garden Seat. For instance, if you want to show off the wood's grain, an outdoor oil may be a better choice. Another option is to paint the bench with an alkyd primer and latex.

EXPLODED VIEW

OVERALL DIMENSIONS:
48L x 20⁵⁄₈D x 18H

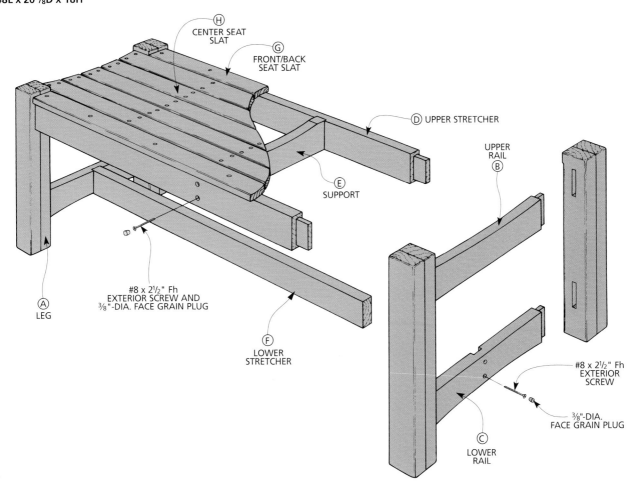

H CENTER SEAT SLAT

G FRONT/BACK SEAT SLAT

D UPPER STRETCHER

UPPER RAIL B

E SUPPORT

A LEG

#8 x 2½" Fh EXTERIOR SCREW AND ⅜"-DIA. FACE GRAIN PLUG

F LOWER STRETCHER

#8 x 2½" Fh EXTERIOR SCREW

⅜"-DIA. FACE GRAIN PLUG

C LOWER RAIL

CUTTING DIAGRAM

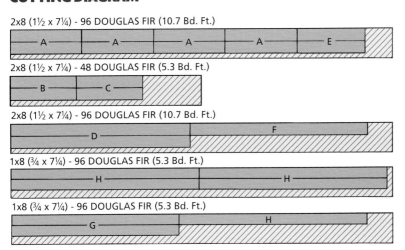

2x8 (1½ x 7¼) - 96 DOUGLAS FIR (10.7 Bd. Ft.)

A   A   A   A   E

2x8 (1½ x 7¼) - 48 DOUGLAS FIR (5.3 Bd. Ft.)

B   C

2x8 (1½ x 7¼) - 96 DOUGLAS FIR (10.7 Bd. Ft.)

D   F

1x8 (¾ x 7¼) - 96 DOUGLAS FIR (5.3 Bd. Ft.)

H   H

1x8 (¾ x 7¼) - 96 DOUGLAS FIR (5.3 Bd. Ft.)

G   H

MATERIALS LIST

WOOD

A	Legs (4)	3 x 3 - 18
B	Upper Rails (2)	1½ x 3 - 16⅝
C	Lower Rails (2)	1½ x 3 - 16⅝
D	Upper Stretchers (2)	1½ x 3 - 45
E	Supports (2)	1½ x 3 - 17⅛
F	Lower Stretcher (1)	1½ x 2½ - 44½
G	Fr./Bk. Seat Slats (2)	¾ x 2⅝ - 42
H	Center Seat Slats (5)	¾ x 2⅝ - 47¼

HARDWARE SUPPLIES

(12) No. 8 x 2½" Fh exterior screws
(52) No. 8 x 1½" Fh exterior screws
(64) ⅜"-dia. face grain plugs

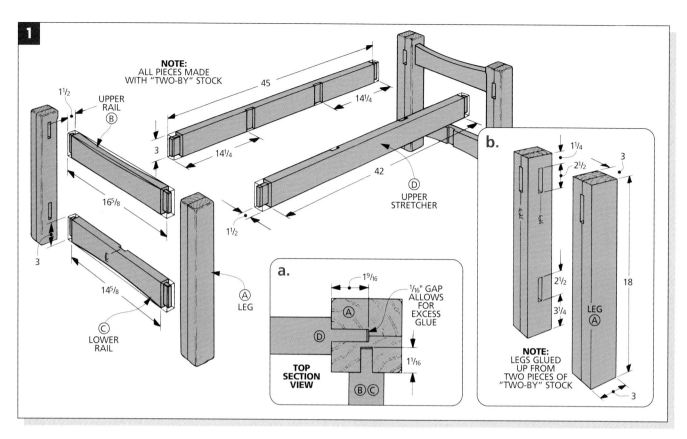

1

NOTE: ALL PIECES MADE WITH "TWO-BY" STOCK

UPPER RAIL Ⓑ

$1^{1}/_{2}$

45

$14^{1}/_{4}$

3

$14^{1}/_{4}$

$16^{5}/_{8}$

42

Ⓓ UPPER STRETCHER

3

$14^{5}/_{8}$

Ⓒ LOWER RAIL

$1^{1}/_{2}$

Ⓐ LEG

3

b.

$1^{1}/_{4}$

$2^{1}/_{2}$

3

$2^{1}/_{2}$

$3^{1}/_{4}$

18

LEG Ⓐ

3

NOTE: LEGS GLUED UP FROM TWO PIECES OF "TWO-BY" STOCK

a.

$1^{9}/_{16}$

Ⓐ

$^{1}/_{16}$" GAP ALLOWS FOR EXCESS GLUE

Ⓓ

$1^{1}/_{16}$

TOP SECTION VIEW

Ⓑ Ⓒ

LEGS

To make the legs (A), I glued up two pieces of "two-by" stock and ripped them 3" square *(Figs. 1 and 1b)*. They can be cut to length at this point, too (18").

LEG MORTISES. With the legs cut to size, three mortises can be cut in each leg: two for the rails and one for the stretcher *(Fig. 1b)*.

When laying out these mortises, the trick is to make sure that the four legs can be assembled later into a complete frame for the seat. This means the legs on each end of the seat should end up with mortises that mirror each other *(Fig. 1b)*.

I drilled these mortises on the drill press *(Figs. 2 and 2a)*. They're the same width and length, but the depths are different. On each leg, the two mor-

tises for the rails are only $1^{1}/_{16}$" deep, while the one for the stretcher is $1^{9}/_{16}$" deep *(Fig. 1a)*.

ROUT ROUNDOVERS. Now to complete the legs, I routed a $^{1}/_{4}$" roundover on all the edges except the inside edge *(Figs. 3 and 3a)*. Here you want to stop the roundover $1^{1}/_{4}$" from the top of the leg *(Fig. 3b)*. This allows the outside slat to be flush with inside edge of the leg.

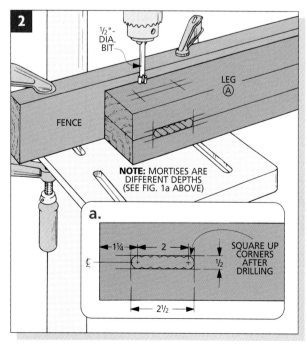

2

$^{1}/_{2}$"-DIA. BIT

LEG Ⓐ

FENCE

NOTE: MORTISES ARE DIFFERENT DEPTHS (SEE FIG. 1a ABOVE)

a.

$1^{1}/_{4}$

2

$^{1}/_{2}$

$2^{1}/_{2}$

SQUARE UP CORNERS AFTER DRILLING

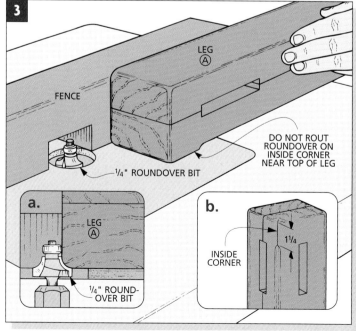

3

LEG Ⓐ

FENCE

$^{1}/_{4}$" ROUNDOVER BIT

DO NOT ROUT ROUNDOVER ON INSIDE CORNER NEAR TOP OF LEG

a.

LEG Ⓐ

$^{1}/_{4}$" ROUND-OVER BIT

b.

$1^{1}/_{4}$

INSIDE CORNER

The rails connect the legs and create end assemblies. The upper stretchers will be added later to connect the two end assemblies *(Fig. 1)*.

CUT TO SIZE. Start by ripping the upper (B) and lower rails (C) and the upper stretchers (D) to finished width *(Fig. 1)*. Then cut the two pairs of rails and both of the stretchers to length.

CUT TENONS. Next cut the tenons on each piece *(Fig. 4)*. They're identical, except for their lengths *(Fig. 4a)*.

CUT DADOES. Once the tenons have been added, the next thing to do is cut the dadoes in the lower rail (C) and the upper stretchers (D) *(Fig. 5)*. These dadoes hold the seat supports and the lower stretcher to be added later (refer to *Fig. 6* on page 12).

The dadoes are cut 1/2" deep *(Fig. 5a)* and they require multiple passes over a dado blade. An easy way to do this is to use the rip fence as a stop, flipping the pieces between passes. This way you can sneak up on the width of the dadoes by adjusting the fence.

On the lower rails (C) this technique centers the dadoes perfectly. I like to start with the rails roughly centered. Then I make multiple passes until the dado is cut in the pieces to match the thickness of the stock *(Figs. 5 and 5a)*. (Mine ended up being 1½" wide.)

For the upper stretchers (D), start by making the cut on the outside shoulder of each dado. This way flipping the pieces locates the dadoes the same dis-

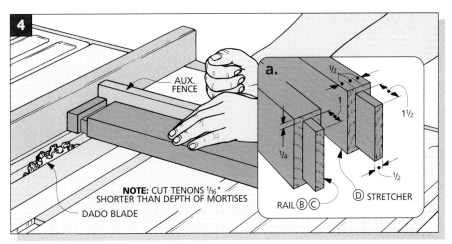

NOTE: CUT TENONS 1/16" SHORTER THAN DEPTH OF MORTISES

DADO BLADE

AUX. FENCE

a.

RAIL B C   D STRETCHER

1/2   1/2   1   1½   1/4   1/2

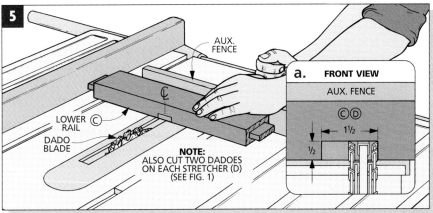

AUX. FENCE

LOWER RAIL C

DADO BLADE

NOTE: ALSO CUT TWO DADOES ON EACH STRETCHER (D) (SEE FIG. 1)

a. **FRONT VIEW**

AUX. FENCE

C D   1½   1/2

tance from each end and allows you to sneak up on the width.

CUT CURVES. Next, cut the curves on the upper and lower rails *(Fig. 1)*. The curve creates a more comfortable surface for sitting. The same arc is cut on the bottom edge of the lower rails so they will match the upper rails.

Lay out the curves using a simple template (see the Shop Tip below). Then cut just outside the line with a band saw or jig saw and sand it smooth.

END ASSEMBLIES. Now the legs and rails can be glued together. But don't glue the stretchers yet. There are a couple more pieces to add first.

SHOP TIP .... *Curve Template*

This garden seat requires six curves in all: one curve on each of the upper and lower rails and another curve on each of the seat supports. These curves are identical, so to make it easier to lay out and cut them, I created a hardboard template. This way all the pieces will end up being exactly the same.

You can draw graph lines and plot points on the blank to lay out the curve. Or you can bend a straightedge and trace it onto the template blank.

Once the curve is laid out on the blank, cut it out with a band saw or jig saw and then sand it smooth. Do the same for each of the rails and the seat supports.

1

1/2

2

CURVE TEMPLATE FOR UPPER (B) AND LOWER RAILS (C) AND SEAT SUPPORTS (E)

14⅝

The seat supports strengthen the slats that are added later. To determine the final length of these pieces, dry-assemble the frame of the seat *(Fig. 6)*.

SUPPORTS. The supports (E) are ripped 3" wide and are cut to length to fit between the dadoes in the upper stretchers *(Fig. 6)*.

CUT CURVES. Once the supports are cut to fit between the stretchers, it's time to form a curve on the top edge of each. This curve is the same as the one on the rails. But there is one difference. On the rails, the curves span from shoulder to shoulder, but the seat supports are slightly longer. So now the template is centered side-to-side, leaving a flat spot at each end of the support *(Fig. 7)*.

ASSEMBLY. After the curves have been cut and sanded smooth, the seat supports can be glued and screwed between the two stretchers. To do this, I drilled counterbored shank holes in the upper stretchers *(Fig. 6a)*.

LOWER STRETCHER. Finally, after gluing the end assemblies in place, all that's left to complete the frame is to add the seat supports and the lower stretcher (F). The lower stretcher is ripped to width to match the lower rail at the center *(Fig. 6)*. (Mine was 2$\frac{1}{2}$" wide.) Then I cut it to length to fit between the dadoes in the lower rails. Along with the supports, it's glued and screwed in place *(Fig. 6a)*.

Note: Plug the counterbores in the stretchers, lower rails and seat slats later.

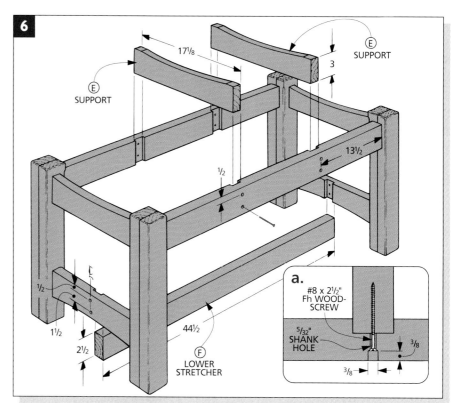

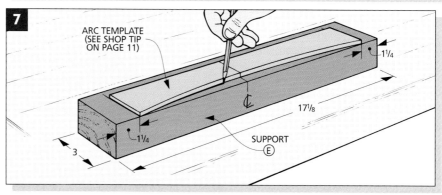

FINISHING TIP............ *Semi-Transparent Stain*

When it's time to apply a finish on an outdoor project like this, you have several options from which to choose. It all depends on what kind of wood you used to build the project.

If I'd wanted to let the grain of the wood stand out as much as possible, I could have used an oil finish formulated for outdoor use. This is a good choice with a more expensive wood, like redwood or teak. But you'll want to

renew the finish every year by applying an additional coat of oil.

Another option is to paint the bench with an alkyd primer and a couple of coats of a quality latex paint. This, of course, covers up all that beautiful wood grain, but paint will protect the wood better (and longer) than any other finishing option.

When it came right down to it, I couldn't bring myself to paint the Garden

Seat. But I was willing to sacrifice a little of the wood grain for more protection. So I applied a semi-transparent stain (see photo).

You'll want to follow the instructions for the stain you pick out. But I found that when it came to staining the vertical sec-

tions of the seat (like the legs) a dry foam brush was helpful for removing the excess so I didn't end up with any runs.

SEAT SLATS

At this point, the only pieces left to add are the slats for the seat *(Fig. 8)*. The seat slats are $3/4$" thick, so if necessary, resaw and plane thicker material down to size.

CUT TO SIZE. I started by ripping seven seat slats to finished width ($2^5/8$") *(Figs. 8 and 8b)*. Then I cut them to final length. The front and back seat slats (G) are cut to fit between the two legs. (Mine were 42".) The center seat slats (H) are cut to set back $3/8$" from the outside face of each leg. I measured the overall length of the seat (48") and subtracted $3/4$" *(Fig. 8b)*.

ROUND OVER EDGES. Before attaching the slats, soften the edges by routing $1/8$" roundovers on the top edges of each *(Fig. 9)*. The center slats (H) are routed on all four edges *(Fig. 9a)*. But since the ends of the front and back slats (G) butt up against the legs, only the long edges are routed.

ASSEMBLY. Now the slats can be glued and screwed to the frame of the seat *(Fig. 10)*. Again, they're counterbored $3/8$" deep and will be plugged later *(Fig. 8a)*.

I added the front and back slats (G) first. Position them flush with the inside edge of the legs *(Fig. 8b)*. Next I centered one center slat between the legs. Then use spacers to add the remaining slats *(Figs. 10 and 10a)*.

Once the slats have been added, all that's left is to plug the screw holes and apply the finish (see the Finishing Tip on the opposite page). ■

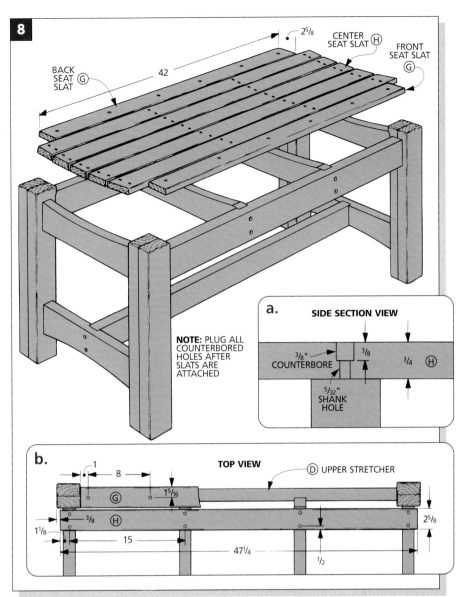

8

BACK SEAT SLAT — G
$2^5/8$
CENTER SEAT SLAT — H
FRONT SEAT SLAT — G
42

NOTE: PLUG ALL COUNTERBORED HOLES AFTER SLATS ARE ATTACHED

a. SIDE SECTION VIEW
$3/8$" COUNTERBORE
$3/8$
$3/4$ — H
$5/32$" SHANK HOLE

b. TOP VIEW
D — UPPER STRETCHER
1
8
$1^5/16$
G
$3/8$ — H
$1^1/8$
15
$47^1/4$
$2^5/8$
$1/2$

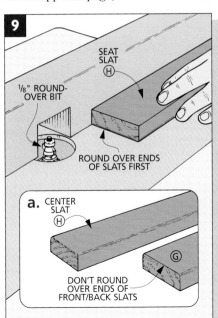

9

SEAT SLAT — H
$1/8$" ROUND-OVER BIT
ROUND OVER ENDS OF SLATS FIRST

a. CENTER SLAT — H
DON'T ROUND OVER ENDS OF FRONT/BACK SLATS
G

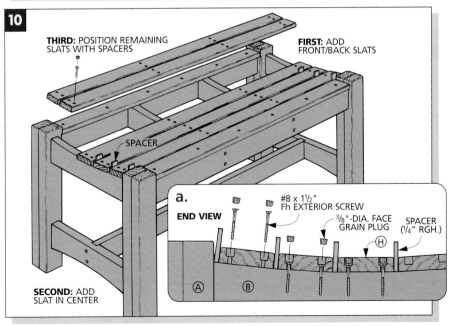

10

THIRD: POSITION REMAINING SLATS WITH SPACERS
FIRST: ADD FRONT/BACK SLATS
SPACER

SECOND: ADD SLAT IN CENTER

a. END VIEW
#8 x $1^1/2$" Fh EXTERIOR SCREW
$3/8$"-DIA. FACE GRAIN PLUG
SPACER ($1/4$" RGH.)
H
A
B

DESIGNER'S NOTEBOOK

The addition of arms and a low, arched back give this garden seat a more traditional look. But it remains easy to build, thanks to the post and rail construction of the arms and back.

CONSTRUCTION NOTES:

■ Everything from the original version of the Garden Seat will be used for this version, except for the legs (A). The new legs are longer to accept arm rests (M) and back rails (K, L). Begin by gluing up the pieces of "two-by" stock for the front legs (I) and back legs (J). Then rip each of them into 3"-square posts *(Fig. 2)*.

■ Next, cut the posts to length. The front legs (I) should now be 24¼" and the back legs (J) should now be 28¾" *(Fig. 1)*.

■ With the legs cut to size, lay out the original mortises for the upper stretchers (D), upper rails (B) and lower rails (C) *(Figs. 1 and 2)*.

■ Next, a new mortise for the arm rests (M) is added to the back face of each of the front legs (I) *(Fig. 2)*.

■ Also lay out three new mortises on each back leg (J). One in the front face of each leg will accept the arm rests. Two more on the inside face of each leg will accept the upper back rail (K) and lower back rail (L) *(Fig. 2)*.

■ Cut the mortises on the drill press and clean them up with a chisel.

   Note: As with the Garden Seat, all of the mortises are centered side to side

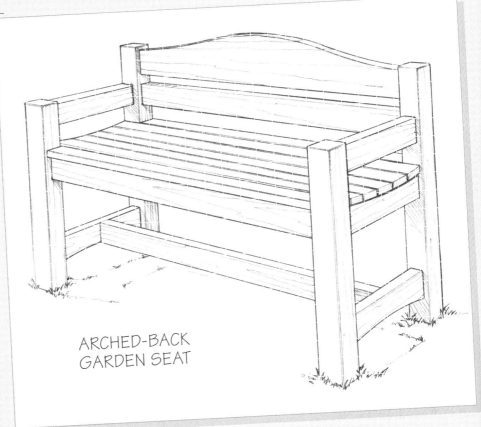

ARCHED-BACK
GARDEN SEAT

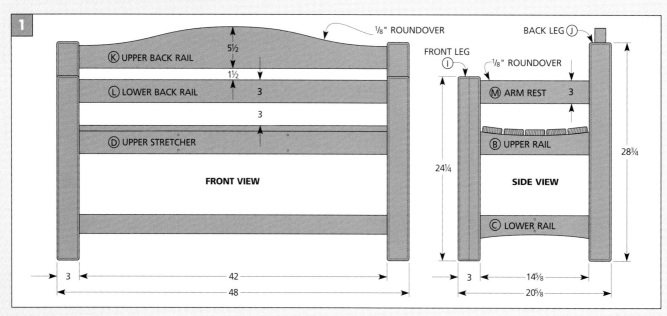

on the posts and all are the same width and length, but the depths are different. The mortises for the rails (B, C) and arm rests (M) are only 1¹/₁₆" deep, while the ones for the stretchers (D) and the upper and lower back rail (K, L) are drilled 1⁹/₁₆" deep (Fig. 2).

■ Rout ¹/₄" roundovers on all edges of the front and back legs.

Note: If you choose, a short section of each leg can be left square where the front and back seat slats meet the edge of the leg. To do this, the roundover on the inside face of each leg should be stopped 16³/₄" from the bottom edge of the legs and begin again at 18".

■ Now you're ready to begin work on constructing the arm rests (M), the upper back rail (K), and lower back rail (L). The arm rests and the upper and lower back rails are all ripped to finished width from "two-by" stock (Figs. 3 and 4).

■ Cut the two arm rests to 16⁵/₈" long (Fig. 4) and each of the back rails to 45" long (Figs. 3 and 4).

■ Next, lay out and cut the ¹/₂"-thick tenons for the upper back rail (Fig. 3). The tenons are centered on the ends of the piece and the offset allows for the waste removed for the arched portion.

■ To lay out the curves for the arch, first draw a 1" grid on the workpiece (Fig. 3). Next, cut the curves slightly oversize on the band saw or with a jig saw.

■ Then to finish the curve, sand up to the line (Fig. 3). I also soften the top edges of the upper back rail using a ¹/₈" roundover bit in the router.

■ Finally, lay out and cut the tenons on each of the arm rests (M) and on the lower back rail (L) (Fig. 4).

Note: All tenons are ¹/₂" thick and centered on the end of the stock.

■ To lessen the risk of splinters, soften the top edges of the arm rests by again adding ¹/₈" roundovers.

■ Construct the garden seat as before, except now add the arm rests (M) to the end assembly. The upper and lower back rails (K, L) are added when connecting the two end assemblies.

MATERIALS LIST

NEW PARTS

I	Front Legs (2)	3 x 3 - 24¹/₄
J	Back Legs (2)	3 x 3 - 28³/₄
K	Upper Back Rail (1)	1¹/₂ x 5¹/₂ - 45
L	Lower Back Rail (1)	1¹/₂ x 3 - 45
M	Arm Rests (2)	1¹/₂ x 3 - 16⁵/₈

Note: Do not need part A.

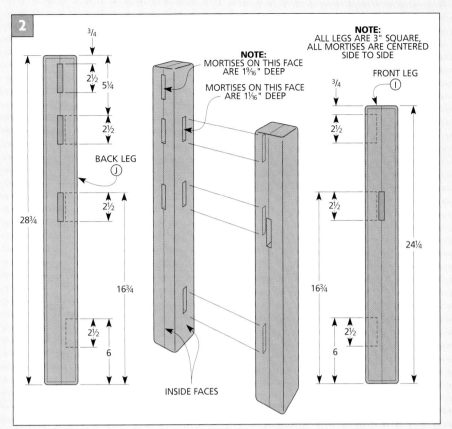

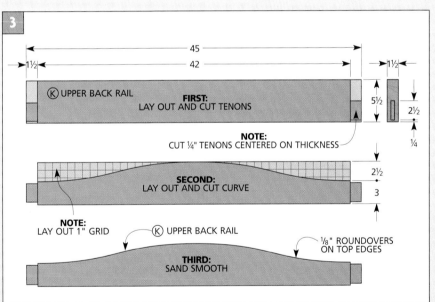

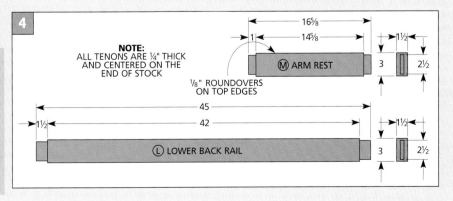

Adirondack Chair

The centerpiece in our set of customizable Adirondack furniture, this chair features a classic design and — like all the pieces in the set — simple construction with straightforward joinery.

When you sit in an Adirondack Chair, it's so easy to get comfortable that you may not want to get up. And in some designs, the angle of the seat makes it difficult to get out, even if you want to.

This Adirondack Chair is designed with a contoured seat and a slightly angled back. The angle I used lets you rest naturally in the chair. But even after you get comfortable, it's not difficult to get back on your feet.

TEMPLATES. Laying out the angles and curves on the contoured pieces of the chair (the back legs and arms) isn't hard to do. The patterns on the opposite page show you how.

While your pieces don't have to match the patterns exactly, it is important that the curves and angles on each leg are identical. One way to do this is to make a hardboard template of the legs. Using the template with a flush trim bit guarantees an identical set of legs. And if you decide to add another chair in the future, the template will make it easy to duplicate the curves.

MATERIALS. The first chair I built was made from regular "one-by" pine lumber and painted white. Later, I decided to make an entire Adirondack set, only this time using Clear All Heart redwood. This grouping includes the settee in the Designer's Notebook on page 23 and the table beginning on page 24. (All three pieces are shown on the cover of this book.) The leg template I'd made for the first chair saved me a good amount of time and effort when making these additional pieces.

JOINERY. Most of the joints on the chair are butt joints fastened with screws or glue — not the strongest way to secure two pieces of wood. So to strengthen the leg joints, I added corner blocks. These are just triangular pieces under the seat at each corner. They are cut from a 2x4 and help brace

the corners by providing extra gluing surface and better "grip" for the screws.

I also used a different type of glue on all the joints. Regular yellow glue wouldn't last long outdoors. So instead, I used waterproof construction adhesive. It's a bit unusual, but the bond is strong and weatherproof. (See the Shop Info box on pages 48-49 for more about outdoor materials and glues.)

I also chose brass screws instead of the regular zinc-coated type. Brass screws won't rust, but you do have to take care when driving them to avoid breaking them. (See page 79 for more information about outdoor screws.)

EXPLODED VIEW

OVERALL DIMENSIONS:
31³/₄W x 37D x 38³/₄H

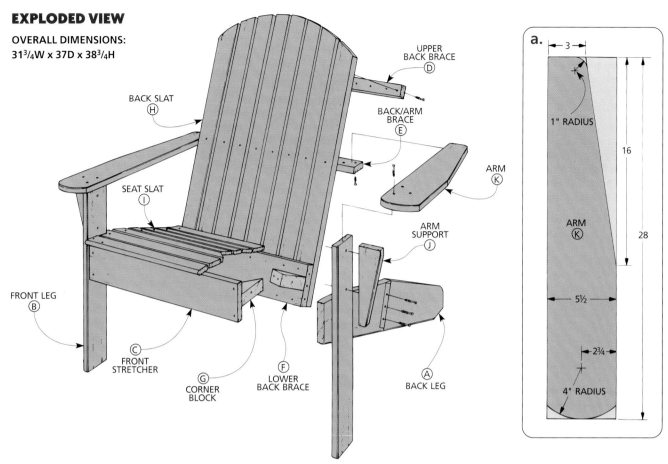

BACK SLAT
(H)

SEAT SLAT
(I)

FRONT LEG
(B)

FRONT
STRETCHER
(C)

CORNER
BLOCK
(G)

LOWER
BACK BRACE
(F)

UPPER
BACK BRACE
(D)

BACK/ARM
BRACE
(E)

ARM
(K)

ARM
SUPPORT
(J)

BACK LEG
(A)

a.

3

1" RADIUS

16

ARM
(K)

28

5½

2³/₄

4" RADIUS

b.

LAY OUT
1" GRID

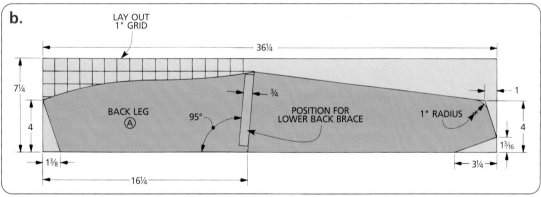

36¼

7¼

4

BACK LEG
(A)

95°

³/₄

POSITION FOR
LOWER BACK BRACE

1" RADIUS

1

4

1³/₁₆

1³/₈

16¼

3¼

MATERIALS LIST

WOOD

A	Back Legs (2)	³/₄ x 6½ - 36¼
B	Front Legs (2)	³/₄ x 3½ - 22
C	Front Stretcher (1)	³/₄ x 4¼ - 22¼
D	Upr. Back Brace (1)	³/₄ x 2³/₈ - 19³/₄
E	Back/Arm Brace (1)	³/₄ x 2³/₈ - 24³/₄
F	Lwr. Back Brace (1)	³/₄ x 5½ - 20³/₄
G	Corner Blocks (4)	1½ x 3 - 4¼
H	Back Slats (8)	³/₄ x 2³/₈ - 35⁷/₈
I	Seat Slats (7)	³/₄ x 2³/₈ - 23³/₄
J	Arm Supports (2)	³/₄ x 2⁷/₈ - 8
K	Arms (2)	³/₄ x 5½ - 28

HARDWARE SUPPLIES

(60) No. 8 x 1¼" Fh brass woodscrews
(28) No. 8 x 2" Fh brass woodscrews

CUTTING DIAGRAM

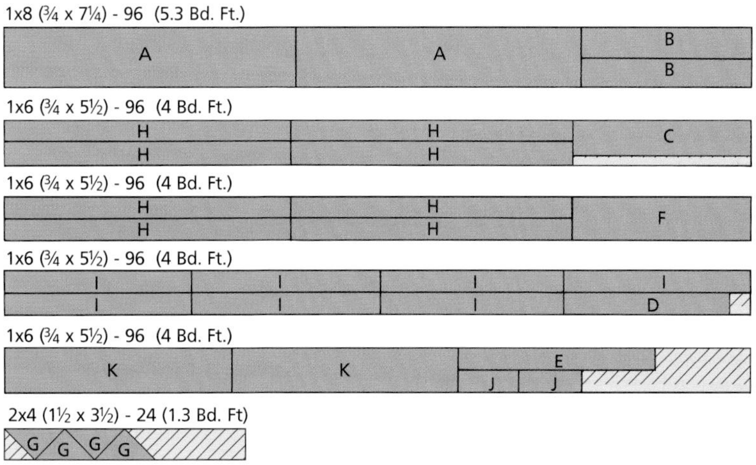

1x8 (³/₄ x 7¼) - 96 (5.3 Bd. Ft.)

| A | A | B |
| | | B |

1x6 (³/₄ x 5½) - 96 (4 Bd. Ft.)

| H | H | C |
| H | H | |

1x6 (³/₄ x 5½) - 96 (4 Bd. Ft.)

| H | H | F |
| H | H | |

1x6 (³/₄ x 5½) - 96 (4 Bd. Ft.)

| I | I | I | I |
| I | I | I | D |

1x6 (³/₄ x 5½) - 96 (4 Bd. Ft.)

| K | K | E |
| | | J | J |

2x4 (1½ x 3½) - 24 (1.3 Bd. Ft)

| G | G | G |

BACK LEGS

I started work on the Adirondack Chair by making the base. The base consists of the front and back legs connected by a front stretcher and a lower back brace (refer to *Fig. 7*).

ROUGH CUT LEGS. The front and back legs can be cut from one 8-foot-long 1x8. To do this, first cut two blanks for the back legs (A) to a rough length of 37" *(Fig. 1)*. Then cut two front legs (B) to a finished size of $3^1/2$" x 22" *(Fig. 2)*.

LAY OUT BACK LEGS. To shape the back legs, first draw an outline of the leg onto a leg blank. (Work from detail 'b' on page 17.)

Note: If you plan to make several Adirondack Chairs or the Settee on page 23, you may want to make a template from $1/4$" hardboard. Then you can use the template with a flush trim bit in the router to rout all the back legs to identical shape *(Fig. 1a)*.

With the outline laid out on the blank, use a jig saw to trim to within $1/16$" of the line. Then fasten the hardboard template to the blank with double-sided carpet tape and trim the leg to final shape *(Fig. 1a)*.

Now repeat the process to shape the other leg blank.

ROUND OVER. With a $1/8$" roundover bit in the router table, soften all the edges of the front and back legs, except the tops of the front legs and the front ends of the back legs.

BASE ASSEMBLY

The base assembly consists of two mirror-image sides. Each side has a back leg (A) and a front leg (B). The sides are connected by a front stretcher (C), which is installed now, and a lower back brace (installed later).

REFERENCE LINES. Before assembling the legs, mark reference lines on the inside face of each *front* leg to indicate where the back legs will be attached *(Fig. 2)*. Also mark reference lines on the *back* legs to indicate where the lower back brace will be attached later *(Fig. 2b* and detail 'b' on page 17).

SCREW HOLES. Before screwing the legs together, several holes have to be drilled in the back legs. First, drill three countersunk shank holes on the inside face of each back leg *(Fig. 2a)*.

Then drill three shank holes for the lower back brace *(Fig. 2b)*. The coun-

tersinks for these holes are drilled on the outside face of each back leg.

JOINING LEGS. Now you can begin assembling the sides one at a time. First spread some construction adhesive where the front leg laps the back leg. (Keep the adhesive well inside the layout lines. It will spread out as the two pieces are pressed together.)

Position the back leg against the pencil marks and drive in one of the screws *(Fig. 2)*. Then stand the front leg upright on a flat surface and adjust the leg members so the feet of each are resting perfectly flat on the table. Now drive in the other two screws.

After the first side is assembled, join

the other two legs in the same way, so the second side mirrors the first side.

FRONT STRETCHER. Once the sides are complete, the next step is to make the front stretcher (C) that connects the two sides.

To do this, first cut the piece to length ($22^1/4$") from a 1x6 *(Fig. 3)*. Then rip it to final width ($4^1/4$"). Now drill two countersunk shank holes near each end *(Fig. 3a)*.

Next, clamp the front stretcher between the leg assemblies and drill pilot holes through the shank holes and into the back legs (A) *(Fig. 3)*. Apply adhesive to the front ends of the back legs and screw the stretcher in place.

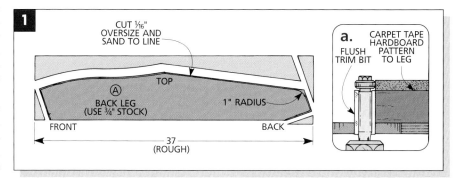

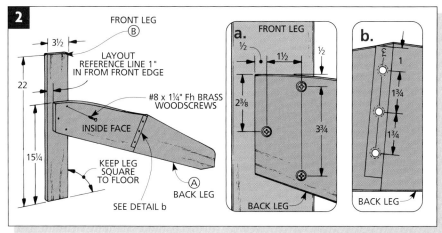

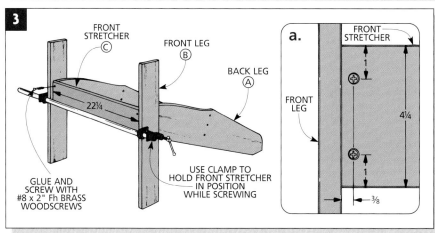

BACK BRACES

The last piece needed for the base is the lower back brace (F) (refer to *Fig. 7*).

At this time, I also cut the other two braces that support the back slats (refer to *Fig. 10* on page 20).

Begin by cutting the upper back brace (D) to length and width *(Fig. 4)*.

BACK/ARM BRACE. Next, cut the back/arm brace (E) to a rough width of $2^1/2$" and $24^3/4$" long *(Fig. 4)*. Since the back slats are angled, this piece has to be beveled along its front edge to support them. So tilt the saw blade to 25°, and rip the back/arm brace (E) to a finished width of $2^3/8$" *(Fig. 4a)*.

LOWER BACK BRACE. The lower back brace (F) is wider than the other braces ($5^1/2$") *(Fig. 4)*. To determine its length, measure the distance between the back legs at the front of the assembled base ($20^3/4$") (refer to *Fig. 7*).

SLAT LINES. After the lower back brace is cut to length, lay out the position of the back slats on it *(Fig. 5)*.

First, draw a line centered on the length of the piece *(Fig. 5)*. Then, to determine the position of the edges of the middle two slats, draw lines $1/8$" on either side of the centerline. Now mark the positions of the remaining $2^3/8$"-wide slats, allowing $1/4$" between them.

The next step is to transfer all the lines from the lower back brace to the upper back brace. To do this, mark a centerline on the upper back brace (D) and align it with the centerline on the lower back brace (F) *(Fig. 6)*. Then use a square to transfer the lines.

SCREW HOLES. Next, mark the position of the screw holes centered on the slat positions on each piece *(Fig. 5)*. Now drill countersunk shank holes in the lower back brace and the upper back brace at the marks.

ROUND OVER EDGES. With the screw holes drilled, rout $1/8$" roundovers on all the edges of the three braces, except the beveled edge of the back/arm brace (E), and the top edge and ends of the lower back brace (F).

LOWER BACK BRACE

After all three of the back brace pieces are rounded over, the lower back brace (F) can be installed between the back legs on the assembled base *(Fig. 7)*.

To do this, first apply a bead of con-struction adhesive to the ends of the lower back brace. Then position the brace so that the countersunk holes are facing toward the front of the chair.

Now clamp the piece in position between the pencil marks on the insides of the back legs. The front edge of the lower back brace should meet the top edge of each back leg *(Fig. 7a)*.

Then drill pilot holes into the brace through the holes already drilled in the back legs *(Fig. 7)*. To secure the brace, drive No. 8 x 2" brass flathead wood-screws through the back leg.

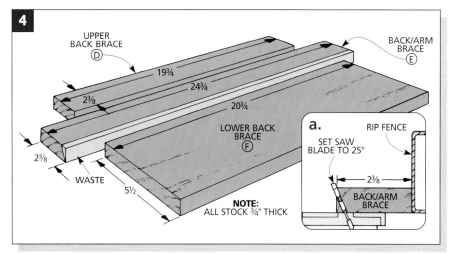

4 UPPER BACK BRACE (D) — BACK/ARM BRACE (E) — $19^3/4$ — $24^3/4$ — $2^3/8$ — $20^3/4$ — LOWER BACK BRACE (F) — $2^3/8$ — WASTE — $5^1/2$ — NOTE: ALL STOCK $3/4$" THICK

a. RIP FENCE — SET SAW BLADE TO 25° — $2^3/8$ — BACK/ARM BRACE

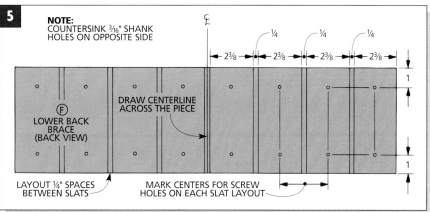

5 NOTE: COUNTERSINK $3/16$" SHANK HOLES ON OPPOSITE SIDE — $1/4$ — $1/4$ — $1/4$ — $2^3/8$ — $2^3/8$ — $2^3/8$ — $2^3/8$ — 1 — (F) LOWER BACK BRACE (BACK VIEW) — DRAW CENTERLINE ACROSS THE PIECE — 1 — LAYOUT $1/4$" SPACES BETWEEN SLATS — MARK CENTERS FOR SCREW HOLES ON EACH SLAT LAYOUT — 1

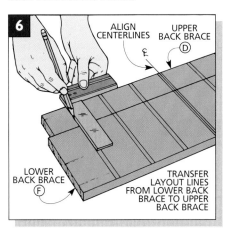

6 ALIGN CENTERLINES — UPPER BACK BRACE (D) — LOWER BACK BRACE (F) — TRANSFER LAYOUT LINES FROM LOWER BACK BRACE TO UPPER BACK BRACE

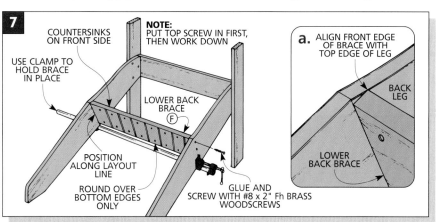

7 COUNTERSINKS ON FRONT SIDE — NOTE: PUT TOP SCREW IN FIRST, THEN WORK DOWN — USE CLAMP TO HOLD BRACE IN PLACE — LOWER BACK BRACE (F) — POSITION ALONG LAYOUT LINE — ROUND OVER BOTTOM EDGES ONLY — GLUE AND SCREW WITH #8 x 2" Fh BRASS WOODSCREWS

a. ALIGN FRONT EDGE OF BRACE WITH TOP EDGE OF LEG — BACK LEG — LOWER BACK BRACE

CORNER BLOCKS. To help strengthen the chair base, I cut four corner blocks (G) from a length of 2x4. Refer to the Technique box on the opposite page for tips on cutting corner blocks properly.

MOUNT BLOCKS. Once the blocks are cut and the holes are drilled, they are glued and screwed to the inside corners of the base *(Figs. 8 and 9)*. (Since the lower back brace is angled, the back corner blocks will also be angled.)

BACK ASSEMBLY

Now that the base of the chair has taken shape, it's time to make the back slats.

CUT TO SIZE. First, cut eight back slats (H) $2^3/8$" wide and $35^7/8$" long. Then soften all four edges of each slat using a $1/8$" roundover bit in the router.

INSTALL OUTSIDE SLATS. Assembling the back starts by installing the two outside slats *(Fig. 10)*. To do this, first apply adhesive to the back side of the lower back brace (F). Then align the slats to the reference marks on this brace, and flush with the bottom edge.

After the slats are in position, screw them in place from the front *(Fig. 11)*.

REFERENCE LINES. Next, draw two lines on each outside slat to indicate the location of the other two back braces (D, E) *(Fig. 10)*. Draw the first line $30^1/2$" up from the bottom of each slat to indicate the top edge of the upper back brace (D) *(Fig. 11)*.

Then draw the second line $17^5/8$" up

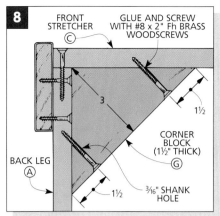

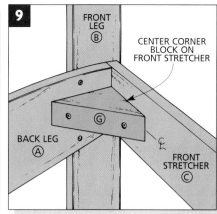

from the bottom of each slat to indicate the top edge of the back/arm brace (E) *(Fig. 11)*. (This reference line should be level with the top of the front leg.)

INSTALL UPPER BACK BRACE. Now, glue and screw the upper back brace (D) to the back of the two outside slats, aligning it with the reference lines you just drew *(Fig. 10)*.

Then glue and screw the rest of the back slats to both braces, making sure they are aligned with the reference marks on the braces *(Fig. 10)*.

BACK/ARM BRACE. Next, the back/arm brace (E) is screwed to the back slats, driving the screws from the front of the chair. To locate the position of these screw holes, first transfer the reference lines from the back of the two outside slats around to the front with a square *(Fig. 11a)*.

Then make a second reference mark

$3/16$" down from the lines you just transferred. Now connect these second reference marks with a pencil line across the front of the slats.

Working from the front of the chair, drill a series of countersunk shank holes on this line, centering the holes on the width of each slat. Once the holes are drilled, you can attach the back/arm brace (E) behind the slats, screwing from the front.

SEAT SLATS

The next step in the process is to cut and install the seat slats.

First, rip six slats (I) to a finished width of $2^3/8$", and one slat to a rough width of $2^1/2$". (This last slat will be ripped to finished width later.)

To determine the length of the slats, add $1^1/2$" to the width of the base to

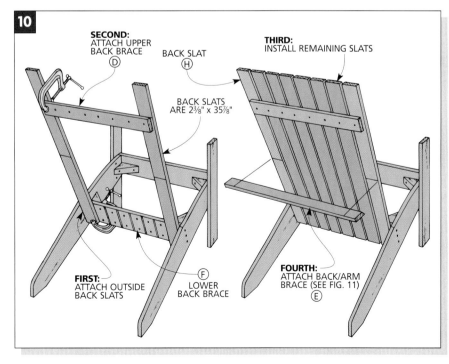

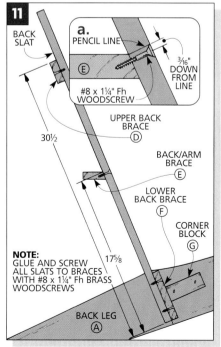

The butt joints at the corners of the Adirondack Chair (and also on the Adirondack Table on pages 24-28) need some beefing up to help resist racking. That's why I added corner blocks to strengthen these joints.

Although there's nothing difficult about making corner blocks, there are a couple of things to consider.

STOCK. The two most important considerations are the size of the block and the way the grain runs on it. I like to use thick blocks to provide the most gluing surface. On the Adirondack furniture, I made the corner blocks from a 24" length of 2x4 cut 3" wide *(Fig. 1)*.

CUTTING THE BLOCKS. The easiest way to make a corner block is to cut a 45° triangle off the *end* of the board. That's the easiest way, but not the best.

The problem is the direction of the grain. When the block is screwed in place, the screws are almost in line with the grain *(Fig. 1a)*. This means they can split off the corners as they're tightened. And that makes your corner block useless.

It's better to have the grain run *across* the screw holes. This is done by laying out triangles as shown in *Fig. 1*. This way the grain runs parallel to the long side of the triangle *(Fig. 1b)*.

SCREW HOLES. To drill the screw holes, I set up a simple jig on the drill press table *(Fig. 2)*. To make this jig, first miter a piece of scrap at 45° to produce a stop block. Then clamp the angled stop block to the front of another board (or to a fence). Finally, clamp them both to the drill press table.

The corner block is pressed against the fence and stop block with the long edge up. (I drilled the holes with a countersink bit.)

GLUE. Since the screws might loosen as the furniture is racked, I applied construction adhesive to the blocks before screwing them in place.

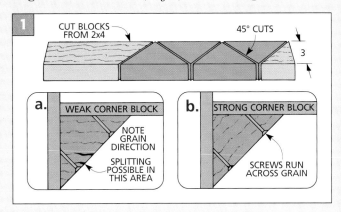

1 CUT BLOCKS FROM 2x4 — 45° CUTS — 3

a. WEAK CORNER BLOCK — NOTE GRAIN DIRECTION — SPLITTING POSSIBLE IN THIS AREA

b. STRONG CORNER BLOCK — SCREWS RUN ACROSS GRAIN

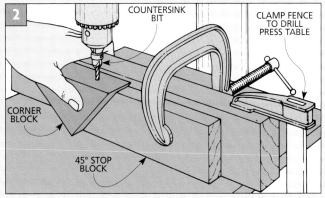

2 COUNTERSINK BIT — CLAMP FENCE TO DRILL PRESS TABLE — CORNER BLOCK — 45° STOP BLOCK

allow for a $3/4$" overhang at each end. Cut six slats to this length. The remaining slat is cut to fit between the front legs *(Fig. 12)*. Finally, cut a notch at each end of the second slat where it meets the front leg *(Fig. 12)*.

Next, rout $1/8$" roundovers on all four edges of each slat, except for the front edge and the ends of the front slat. A $1/2$" roundover is routed on the front edge of the front slat to make it more comfortable on the back of your legs *(Fig. 12a)*.

SCREW HOLES. Before securing the slats to the chair, drill countersunk shank holes centered on the width of each slat, $1^1/8$" from each end *(Fig. 12)*.

Also drill four countersunk shank holes along the front edge of the first slat where it attaches to the front stretcher *(Figs. 12 and 12a)*.

SPACER STRIPS. Starting from the front, install the slats, separating them with $1/4$" spacers. The last slat (the $2^1/2$"-wide one) will need to be bevel ripped to final width so it fits flush against the lower edge of the back slats *(Fig. 12b)*.

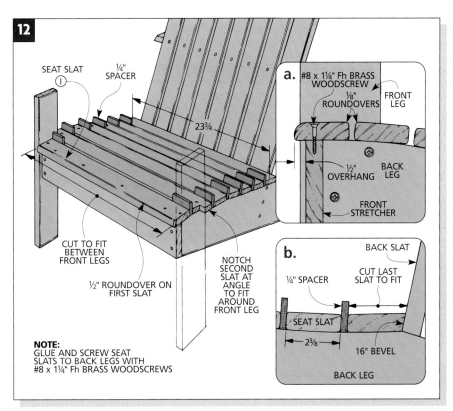

12 SEAT SLAT — $1/4$" SPACER — 23¾ — CUT TO FIT BETWEEN FRONT LEGS — $1/2$" ROUNDOVER ON FIRST SLAT — NOTCH SECOND SLAT AT ANGLE TO FIT AROUND FRONT LEG

a. #8 x 1¼" Fh BRASS WOODSCREW — $1/8$" ROUNDOVERS — FRONT LEG — $1/2$" OVERHANG — BACK LEG — FRONT STRETCHER

b. BACK SLAT — CUT LAST SLAT TO FIT — $1/4$" SPACER — SEAT SLAT — 2⅜ — 16° BEVEL — BACK LEG

NOTE: GLUE AND SCREW SEAT SLATS TO BACK LEGS WITH #8 x 1¼" Fh BRASS WOODSCREWS

One of the last steps is to add the arms and arm supports. First cut the two arm supports (J) to final length (8") and width (2⅞"). Then lay out and cut the angle on the supports *(Fig. 13)*. Now round over only the outside and bottom edges of the supports. (The edges that go against the arm and front leg should remain square.)

Next, center an arm support on the outside of each front leg and drill countersunk shank holes from the inside of the leg *(Fig. 13)*. Then glue and screw the supports in place.

ARMS. Once the arm supports are in place, you can cut the two arms (K) to shape (refer to detail 'a' on page 17). Next lay out and drill countersunk shank holes for the screws that attach the arms to the legs *(Fig. 14)*. Then round over all the edges of both arms.

To attach the arms, start by spreading adhesive on the top of the front leg, arm support, and back/arm brace. Then screw the arm to the front leg and arm support *(Fig. 16)*.

Now adjust the "tilt" of the back slats so the back end of the arm is flush with the rear edge of the back/arm brace. Clamp the arms in place, then drill and screw them to the back/arm support from underneath *(Fig. 15)*.

RADIUS BACK SLATS. Finally, lay out and cut the 16"-radius arc on the top

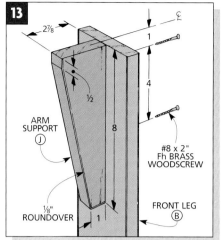

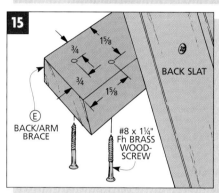

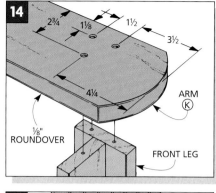

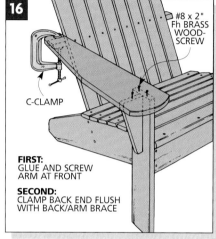

ends of the back slats (refer to the Exploded View on page 17). To do this, I used a simple beam compass to lay out the arc (see the Shop Tip below). Then I made the cut with a jig saw.

Easing the edges of the back slats

takes some hand work. I used a file instead of a router to prevent chipout.

FINISH. After priming my pine chair, I used a latex spray paint to reach between the slats. The redwood version received an oil/varnish finish. ∎

SHOP TIP . . . . *Drawing an Arc*

To make a simple beam compass, cut a piece of ⅛" hardboard or heavy poster board to a width of 1" and to a rough length

of 18" *(Fig. 1)*.

Next, mark two points 16" apart on the compass. Drive a finish nail through one point *(Fig. 1a)*. Then

drill a hole just big enough to fit a pencil lead at the other point *(Fig. 1b)*.

To use the compass, you'll need to fasten a

piece of scrap across the two center back slats to serve as the pivot point *(Fig. 2a)*. Then strike the arc on the chair *(Fig. 2)*.

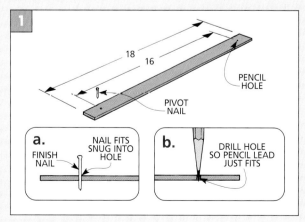

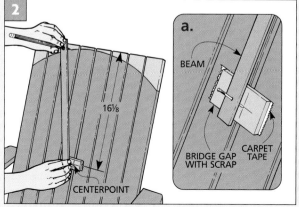

DESIGNER'S NOTEBOOK

The Adirondack Chair for one can be made as a Settee for two quite easily. Most of the parts are the same, except that a few are longer. Then just add some more back slats and a support under the seat.

CONSTRUCTION NOTES:

▪ The only additional part needed for the Settee is the center support (L) (refer to *Fig. 3*). It's just a chopped-off version of one of the back legs (A). Start by cutting an 18"-long blank from a 1x8.

▪ Then lay one of the completed back legs (or your leg template) on the blank so the bottom edges are flush *(Fig. 1)*.

▪ Now trace the curved top edge and the angled front end from the back leg onto the blank.

▪ Cut the top and front edge now, but wait until after the base is assembled to cut the support to final length.

▪ Several pieces for the Settee have to be made longer than they are on the Adirondack Chair. When cutting the front stretcher (C), back braces (D, E, F), and seat slats (I), refer to the measurements in the materials list below. (But cut the seat slats to fit.)

▪ Since the Settee has twice as many back slats (16) as the chair, you will need to mark and drill more holes in the upper and lower back braces.

▪ After the base is assembled, you can get back to the center support (L). The back edge of the center support is cut at a 95° angle to fit against the lower back brace (F). To do this, lay out a mark for the back edge $14^1/_8$" from the front bottom corner *(Fig. 2)*. Cut the support a little long and test fit in the base. Then sneak up on the final length.

▪ When the center support fits, mount it by drilling countersunk holes through

SETTEE

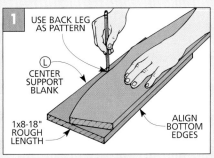

1 USE BACK LEG AS PATTERN

CENTER SUPPORT BLANK

1x8-18" ROUGH LENGTH

ALIGN BOTTOM EDGES

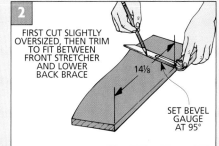

2 FIRST CUT SLIGHTLY OVERSIZED, THEN TRIM TO FIT BETWEEN FRONT STRETCHER AND LOWER BACK BRACE

$14^1/_8$

SET BEVEL GAUGE AT 95°

the front of the front stretcher (C) and the back of the lower back brace (F) *(Fig. 3)*. Then glue and screw the center support in place.

▪ When the seat slats are added, screw them to the top of the legs and to the top of the center support.

▪ After the Settee is assembled, lay out and cut a double arc on the back. I used a jig saw to cut both 16"-radius arcs.

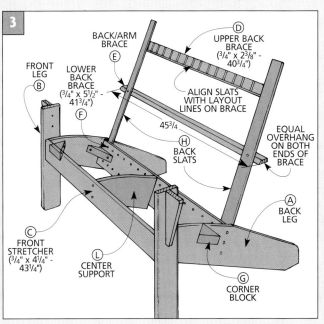

3

BACK/ARM BRACE (E)

FRONT LEG (B)

LOWER BACK BRACE ($^3/_4$" x $5^1/_2$" - $41^3/_4$") (F)

UPPER BACK BRACE ($^3/_4$" x $2^3/_8$" - $40^3/_4$") (D)

ALIGN SLATS WITH LAYOUT LINES ON BRACE

$45^3/_4$

EQUAL OVERHANG ON BOTH ENDS OF BRACE

BACK SLATS (H)

BACK LEG (A)

FRONT STRETCHER ($^3/_4$" x $4^1/_4$" - $43^1/_4$") (C)

CENTER SUPPORT (L)

CORNER BLOCK (G)

MATERIALS LIST

CHANGED PARTS

C	Front Stretcher (1)	$^3/_4$ x $4^1/_4$ - $43^1/_4$
D	Upr. Back Brace (1)	$^3/_4$ x $2^3/_8$ - $40^3/_4$
E	Back/Arm Brace (1)	$^3/_4$ x $2^3/_8$ - $45^3/_4$
F	Lwr. Back Brace (1)	$^3/_4$ x $5^1/_2$ - $41^3/_4$
H	Back Slats (16)	$^3/_4$ x $2^3/_8$ - $35^7/_8$
I	Seat Slats (7)	$^3/_4$ x $2^3/_8$ - $44^3/_4$

NEW PART

L	Center Support (1)	$^3/_4$ x $6^1/_2$ - 18 rough

HARDWARE SUPPLIES

(102) No. 8 x $1^1/_4$" Fh brass woodscrews
(32) No. 8 x 2 " Fh brass woodscrews

Adirondack Table

Whether part of a set or on its own, this Adirondack Table looks great on any patio or deck.
Like the Adirondack Chair and Settee, it features wide, sturdy legs and simple glue and screw joinery.

After building the Adirondack Chair and Settee (pages 16-23), I decided to complete the set by building a small patio table in a matching style. Like the chair and settee, the table is built using simple glue and screw joinery.

Should you want to add to the set or if you need a table for a small area, the Side Table shown in the Designer's Notebook on page 28 offers another version.

LEGS. The actual construction of this table is fairly easy. The tricky part was making the legs look right. I wanted them to appear sturdy — without using thick stock. (All of the stock for the

chair, settee, and table is $^3/_4$" thick, except for the corner blocks.)

To do this, I cut the legs $3^1/_2$" wide and screwed them to the outside of the aprons. Because of this width, when they're viewed from the side you get the impression that they're made from thick stock — maybe from a 4x4. Of course, when the table is viewed from the end you can see they're not that thick. But when stretchers are added between the legs, they're strong enough to support the table easily without any racking.

WOOD AND SCREWS. I built the table from Clear All Heart redwood (not con-

struction grade) to match the chair and settee. (For more on redwood grades, see the Shop Info article on page 35.) But you could use pine and paint it.

To avoid rust stains on the table, I used brass screws and countersunk them slightly below the surface.

FINISH. Finally, to protect the Adirondack Table without hiding the beauty of the Clear All Heart redwood, I finished it with two coats of a 50/50 mixture of tung oil and spar varnish.

For more information on finishes, wood, and supplies appropriate for outdoor furniture, see the Shop Info article on page 48.

EXPLODED VIEW

OVERALL DIMENSIONS:
20³/₄W x 46³/₄L x 16H

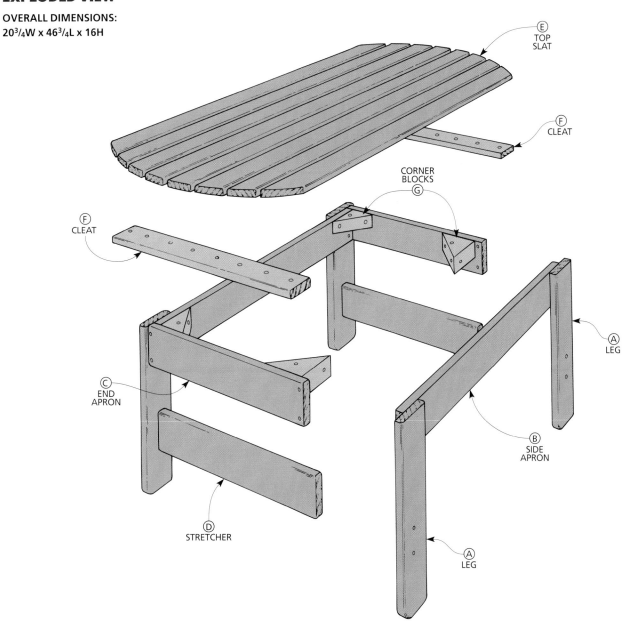

E
TOP
SLAT

F
CLEAT

CORNER
BLOCKS
G

F
CLEAT

A
LEG

C
END
APRON

B
SIDE
APRON

D
STRETCHER

A
LEG

MATERIALS LIST

WOOD

A	Legs (4)	³/₄ x 3¹/₂ - 15¹/₄
B	Side Aprons (2)	³/₄ x 3¹/₂ - 31
C	End Aprons (2)	³/₄ x 3¹/₂ - 17³/₄
D	Stretchers (2)	³/₄ x 3¹/₂ - 17³/₄
E	Top Slats (8)	³/₄ x 2³/₈ - 47
F	Cleats (2)	³/₄ x 2 - 19³/₄
G	Corner Blocks (4)	1¹/₂ x 3 - 4¹/₄

HARDWARE SUPPLIES

(24) No. 8 x 1¹/₄" Fh brass woodscrews
(32) No. 8 x 2 " Fh brass woodscrews

CUTTING DIAGRAM

1x8 (³/₄ x 7¹/₄) - 48 REDWOOD (2.6 Bd. Ft.)

B	A
B	A

2x4 (1¹/₂ x 3¹/₂) - 24 REDWOOD (1.3 Bd. Ft.)

1x8 (³/₄ x 7¹/₄) - 48 REDWOOD (2.6 Bd. Ft.)

C	A	
C	A	

1x8 (³/₄ x 7¹/₄) - 48 REDWOOD (2.6 Bd. Ft.)

D	F	
D	F	

1x6 (³/₄ x 5¹/₂) - 48 REDWOOD (Four Boards @ 2 Bd. Ft. Each)

E
E

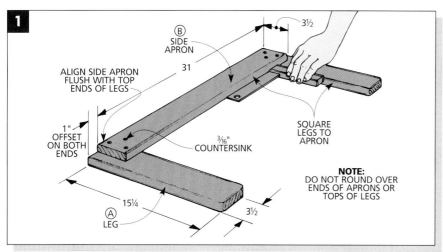

1 ③ SIDE APRON
ALIGN SIDE APRON FLUSH WITH TOP ENDS OF LEGS
31
3½
SQUARE LEGS TO APRON
1" OFFSET ON BOTH ENDS
³⁄₁₆" COUNTERSINK
NOTE: DO NOT ROUND OVER ENDS OF APRONS OR TOPS OF LEGS
15¼
Ⓐ LEG
3½

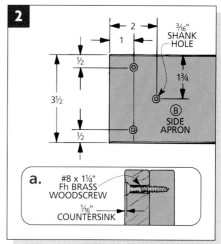

2 2 / 1 / ³⁄₁₆" SHANK HOLE
½ / 1¾
3½
½
Ⓑ SIDE APRON
a. #8 x 1¼" Fh BRASS WOODSCREW
¹⁄₁₆" COUNTERSINK

LEGS & SIDE APRONS

I started building the table by making two side units. Each side unit consists of two legs connected with a side apron *(Fig. 1)*. Later, the side units are connected with end aprons to form the base

of the table (refer to *Fig. 4*).

CUT PIECES TO SIZE. To make a side unit, cut the four legs (A) to a width of 3¹⁄₂" and length of 15¹⁄₄". Then cut two side aprons (B) 3¹⁄₂" wide and 31" long.

RADIUS LEGS. Next, I sanded ¹⁄₂" radii on the bottom corners of the legs. This helps prevent the corners from chipping if the table is dragged across a rough surface. See the Shop Tip at left for a way to lay out this radius.

ROUND OVER. Once the bottom corners have been shaped, rout ¹⁄₈" round-overs on all four edges of the legs and aprons and the bottom ends of the legs.

Note: Don't round over the tops of the legs or the ends of the aprons.

SCREW HOLES. After all of the edges are rounded over, the next step is to drill countersunk ³⁄₁₆"-dia. shank holes on the inside face of each side apron (B) near the ends *(Fig. 2)*.

ASSEMBLY. Now the side units can be assembled. Use construction adhesive and brass woodscrews to attach them. Make sure you position the top edge of the apron flush to the top of each leg, keeping the end of the apron 1" from the outside edge of each leg *(Fig. 1)*.

END APRONS & STRETCHERS

Once the side units are completed, they can be connected with end aprons and stretchers to form the base.

CUT TO SIZE. Begin by cutting two end aprons (C) and two stretchers (D) to the same size, 3¹⁄₂" x 17³⁄₄" *(Figs. 3 and 5)*. Next, round over the edges (but not the ends) of the aprons and stretchers with a ¹⁄₈" roundover bit.

SCREW ON APRONS. Now the end aprons can be glued and screwed to the ends of the side aprons. To do this, first drill two countersunk shank holes near each end of the end aprons (C) *(Fig. 3a)*.

Then begin assembly by laying one of the side units on its side *(Fig. 3)*. Screw one end apron (C) to the end of the side apron with No. 8 x 2" flathead brass woodscrews and construction adhesive. Check that the pieces are flush across the top. Then screw the other end apron to the opposite end of the unit.

Stand up both side units, apply adhesive, and clamp them together *(Fig. 4)*. Check that the aprons are flush at the top, and that the base is square. Then the screws can be tightened into place.

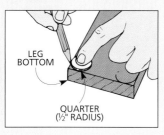

SHOP TIP
Quick Radius

An easy way to mark a ¹⁄₂" radius (like the one on the bottoms of the legs of the Adirondack Table) is simply to trace around a quarter.

LEG BOTTOM
QUARTER (¹⁄₂" RADIUS)

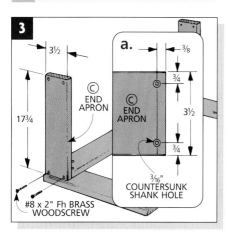

3 3½
a. ³⁄₈
¾
Ⓒ END APRON
Ⓒ END APRON
3½
17¾
¾
³⁄₁₆" COUNTERSUNK SHANK HOLE
#8 x 2" Fh BRASS WOODSCREW

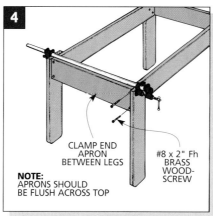

4 CLAMP END APRON BETWEEN LEGS
#8 x 2" Fh BRASS WOODSCREW
NOTE: APRONS SHOULD BE FLUSH ACROSS TOP

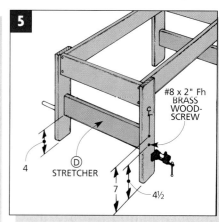

5 #8 x 2" Fh BRASS WOODSCREW
4
Ⓓ STRETCHER
7
4½

ADD STRETCHER. With the legs and aprons screwed together, the stretchers (D) can be added. Start by drilling countersunk shank holes $4^1/_2$" and 7" up from the bottom of each leg *(Fig. 5)*. Center the holes on the width of the leg.

Finally, glue and clamp the stretchers between the legs with their bottom edges 4" up from the bottom. The stretchers should be centered on the width of the legs. Once they're in place, screw the legs to the stretchers with brass woodscrews.

TOP

After the base is complete, the top can be made to fit on it. The top consists of eight top slats (E) held together by two cleats (F) fastened underneath.

SLATS. Start by cutting the eight top slats (E) from $3/_4$"-thick stock to a width of $2^3/_8$" and a length of 47" *(Fig. 6)*.

To soften the edges of the slats, I rounded all four edges on the router table using a $1/_8$" roundover bit.

CLEATS. Next, cut two cleats (F) from $3/_4$" stock to a width of 2" and length of $19^3/_4$" *(Fig. 6)*. Rout $1/_8$" roundovers on the edges of these as well.

The cleats are screwed to the bottom of the slats. To do this, first drill $3/_{16}$" countersunk shank holes centered on the width of the cleats at the locations shown in *Fig. 6*. (These hole locations will center the screws on the slats.)

The slats are positioned with $1/_4$" gaps between them. To create uniform gaps during assembly, I placed $1/_4$"-thick spacers between the slats and clamped the whole assembly together with pipe clamps *(Fig. 6)*.

POSITION CLEATS. With the slats clamped together, the cleats are now positioned on top of the slats *(Fig. 6)*. To determine where to position the cleats, set the base upside down on the slats so it's centered on the length of the top (refer to *Fig. 9*). Then position the cleats $1/_{16}$" outside the legs on both ends.

After the cleats are centered on the length of the table top, center them on the width of the top so there's an even overhang on both sides *(Fig. 6)*.

SCREW TOGETHER. When the location of the cleats is determined, screw the cleats to the slats *(Fig. 6a)*.

RADIUS ENDS. Once the top is assembled, lay out a 16"-radius arc on each end, centered on the width of the table. (See the Shop Tip on page 22 for an easy way to do this.) Then cut the arcs with a jig saw *(Fig. 7)*. Finally, soften the edges on the ends of the slats with a file.

CORNER BLOCKS

The final step in assembly is to add the corner blocks. These blocks prevent the base from racking and provide a means for screwing the top to the base.

The triangular-shaped corner blocks (G) are cut from a length of 2x4 *(Fig. 8)*. (For more on making the corner blocks, see the Technique article on page 21.)

After the corner blocks are cut to size, drill three countersunk $3/_{16}$" shank holes in each one *(Fig. 8a)*. The first two holes are drilled in the long edge of the block and are used to screw the block to the table base.

The other hole is drilled through the face of the block for mounting the top.

Once the holes are drilled, the blocks are glued (with construction adhesive) and screwed in place to the inside of the base *(Fig. 8)*.

FINISH. Before adding the top, finish all the pieces with a 50/50 combination of tung oil and spar varnish.

ATTACH TOP. Once the finish dries, the top is mounted to the base. To do this, turn the top upside down and position the base between the cleats so the base is centered on the width of the top *(Fig. 9)*. Then drive screws through each block into the top *(Fig. 9a)*. ■

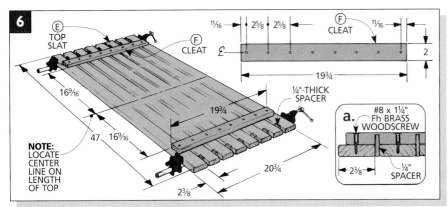

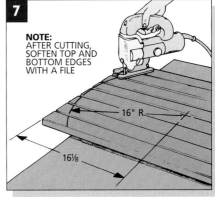

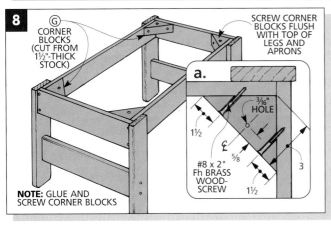

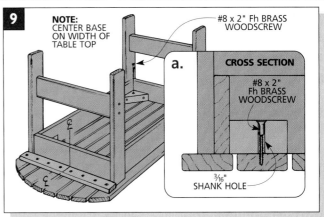

DESIGNER'S NOTEBOOK

In a small setting, such as a garden patio, where a full-size table is too big, this Side Table fits perfectly. It's still made of redwood and has sturdy legs, but it's taller and not as long as the Adirondack Table.

CONSTRUCTION NOTES:

■ Construction of the Side Table hasn't changed from that of the Adirondack Table. The main difference between the two is the length of the top slats and the side aprons. They've both been shortened. The shorter side aprons make the table base square (see the Side Table drawing at right).

The same traditional-looking curves have been added to the table top. In addition, the legs are taller than before, making the table easier to reach while sitting in the low Adirondack Chair.

Finally, a gentle curve has been cut from the bottom edge of the stretchers. It closely matches the radius of the table top ends, giving the base a more graceful look.

■ Start construction by building the two side units. Each side unit consists of two legs (A) and a side apron (B). The legs and side aprons should still be ripped to $3^1/2$" wide, but now each should be cut to a length of $17^1/4$" *(Fig. 1)*.

■ Add the radii and the roundovers to these pieces as before and assemble the side units with glue and screws.

■ Next, cut the end aprons and the stretchers (D) to size *(Fig. 1)*.

■ Before assembling the base, lay out and cut a 15" radius centered on the bottom edge of each stretcher *(Fig. 1)*.

■ The end aprons and stretchers can now be attached to the side units with glue and screws. Again, be sure that the aprons and side units are flush at the top and that the base is square.

■ Finally, cut the top slats (E) to length, then lay out and cut the radius on each end *(Fig. 2)*.

Note: The center point of the radii is still centered on the top slats, so I made the top $32^1/4$" long and I kept the radius arc at 16" *(Fig. 2)*.

MATERIALS LIST

CHANGED PARTS

A	Legs (4)	$^3/_4$ x $3^1/_2$ - $17^1/_4$
B	Side Aprons (2)	$^3/_4$ x $3^1/_2$ - $17^1/_4$
D	Stretchers (2)	$^3/_4$ x $3^1/_2$ - $17^3/_4$
E	Top Slats (8)	$^3/_4$ x $2^3/_8$ - $32^1/_4$

SIDE TABLE

1

SIDE APRON B — LEG A — **SIDE VIEW** (CROSS SECTION) — $17^1/4$ — $3^1/2$ — $3^1/2$ — 4

END VIEW — STRETCHER D — END APRON C — $17^3/4$ — $1^1/2$ — 15" RADIUS

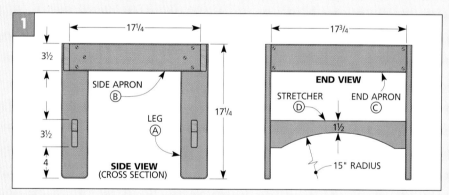

2

$16^1/8$ — $2^3/8$ — E TOP SLAT — 16" RADIUS — $19^3/4$ — $20^3/4$ — WASTE — 2 — $9^{11}/16$ — $9^{11}/16$ — $32^1/4$

Chaise Lounge

*Built from redwood, the Chaise Lounge is designed with comfort and convenience in mind.
Its unusual shop-made wheels can be adapted to lots of other outdoor projects.*

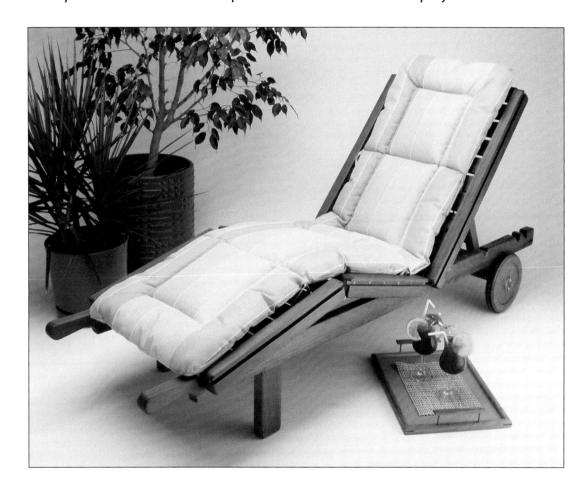

T he Chaise Lounge is so comfortable that you may be tempted to try it without a cushion. That's because I designed the chaise to accommodate the human body — and it does just that. It provides you with some well-deserved comfort and relaxation.

But don't worry. I didn't sacrifice convenience for comfort. To get all this to work, the chaise consists of two assemblies — a lounging platform (with a backrest, seat, and leg rest) and a support frame with handles at one end and a set of wheels at the other for easy transport.

REDWOOD. The chaise lounge I built is made of redwood, which seems right at home out in the sun. Redwood is an ideal material to use on outdoor projects, because it has a natural resistance to both insects and decay. (For more information on redwood and other outdoor woods, as well as glues and finishes, see the Shop Info articles on pages 35 and 48.)

COMFORT. Whether you want to fully recline, raise the back a little for sunning, or raise it upright for reading (see the photo above), the lounging platform is easy and simple to adjust. And you can also raise the leg rest to a comfortable angle. A series of holes, notches and dowels allow various adjustments.

WHEELS. Another interesting challenge in building this project is making the wheels. They allow you to move the chaise wherever you want it. But, they need to be sized and shaped correctly for the chair to roll smoothly.

Once I got started, I realized that making the wheels wasn't going to be that difficult — it just takes a few simple holding jigs and a router. (For more on how to do this, see the Technique article on page 37.)

Of course, you don't have to build your own wheels. For sources of ready-made wheels, as well as other supplies and hardware, see page 126.

EXPLODED VIEW

OVERALL DIMENSIONS:
78L x 23½D x 12H

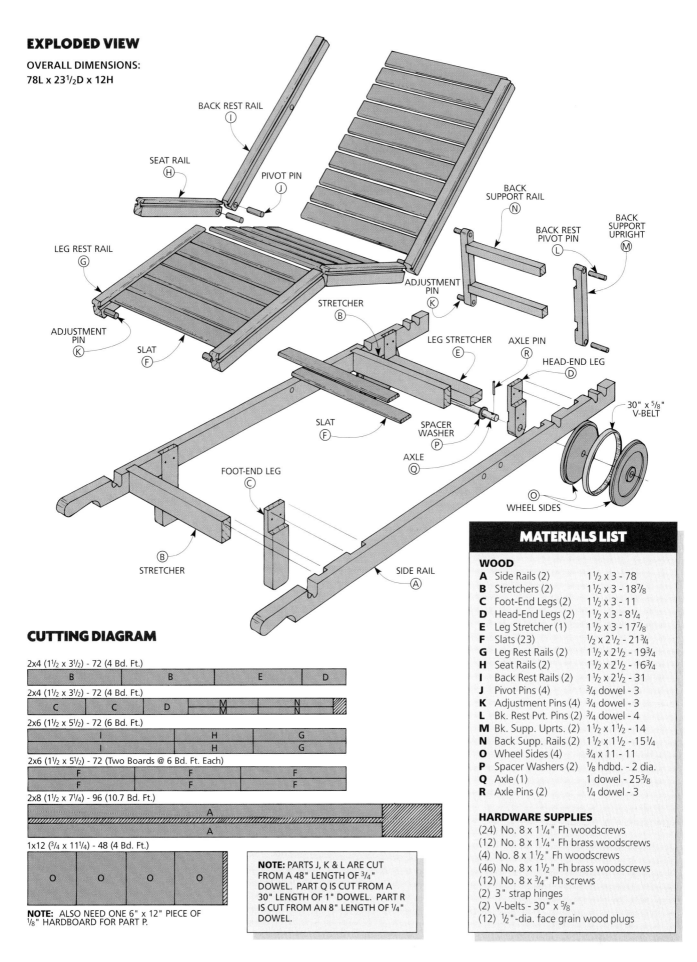

BACK REST RAIL
I

SEAT RAIL
H

PIVOT PIN
J

LEG REST RAIL
G

ADJUSTMENT PIN
K

SLAT
F

BACK SUPPORT RAIL
N

BACK REST PIVOT PIN
L

BACK SUPPORT UPRIGHT
M

ADJUSTMENT PIN
K

STRETCHER
B

LEG STRETCHER
E

AXLE PIN
R

HEAD-END LEG
D

SLAT
F

SPACER WASHER
P

AXLE
Q

30" x ⅝" V-BELT

FOOT-END LEG
C

WHEEL SIDES
O

STRETCHER
B

SIDE RAIL
A

CUTTING DIAGRAM

2x4 (1½ x 3½) - 72 (4 Bd. Ft.)

| B | B | E | D |

2x4 (1½ x 3½) - 72 (4 Bd. Ft.)

| C | C | D | M / M | N / N |

2x6 (1½ x 5½) - 72 (6 Bd. Ft.)

| I | H | G |
| I | H | G |

2x6 (1½ x 5½) - 72 (Two Boards @ 6 Bd. Ft. Each)

| F | F | F |
| F | F | F |

2x8 (1½ x 7¼) - 96 (10.7 Bd. Ft.)

| A |
| A |

1x12 (¾ x 11¼) - 48 (4 Bd. Ft.)

| O | O | O | O |

NOTE: ALSO NEED ONE 6" x 12" PIECE OF ⅛" HARDBOARD FOR PART P.

NOTE: PARTS J, K & L ARE CUT FROM A 48" LENGTH OF ¾" DOWEL. PART Q IS CUT FROM A 30" LENGTH OF 1" DOWEL. PART R IS CUT FROM AN 8" LENGTH OF ¼" DOWEL.

MATERIALS LIST

WOOD

A	Side Rails (2)	1½ x 3 - 78
B	Stretchers (2)	1½ x 3 - 18⅞
C	Foot-End Legs (2)	1½ x 3 - 11
D	Head-End Legs (2)	1½ x 3 - 8¼
E	Leg Stretcher (1)	1½ x 3 - 17⅞
F	Slats (23)	½ x 2½ - 21¾
G	Leg Rest Rails (2)	1½ x 2½ - 19¾
H	Seat Rails (2)	1½ x 2½ - 16¾
I	Back Rest Rails (2)	1½ x 2½ - 31
J	Pivot Pins (4)	¾ dowel - 3
K	Adjustment Pins (4)	¾ dowel - 3
L	Bk. Rest Pvt. Pins (2)	¾ dowel - 4
M	Bk. Supp. Uprts. (2)	1½ x 1½ - 14
N	Back Supp. Rails (2)	1½ x 1½ - 15¼
O	Wheel Sides (4)	¾ x 11 - 11
P	Spacer Washers (2)	⅛ hdbd. - 2 dia.
Q	Axle (1)	1 dowel - 25⅜
R	Axle Pins (2)	¼ dowel - 3

HARDWARE SUPPLIES

(24) No. 8 x 1¼" Fh woodscrews
(12) No. 8 x 1¼" Fh brass woodscrews
(4) No. 8 x 1½" Fh woodscrews
(46) No. 8 x 1½" Fh brass woodscrews
(12) No. 8 x ¾" Ph screws
(2) 3" strap hinges
(2) V-belts - 30" x ⅝"
(12) ½"-dia. face grain wood plugs

The support frame consists of two side rails (A) connected by two stretchers (B) (refer to *Fig. 8* on page 32). This frame rests on four legs that are half-lapped into the side rails and joined with a third stretcher. All frame parts are made from "two-by" redwood lumber.

SIDE RAILS. To start construction on the chaise lounge, I laid out the dadoes for the stretchers and legs. Since the two rails are mirror images of each other, I found it easier to cut all the dadoes on a single 2x8, cross-cut to 78" long *(Fig. 2)*. (Before starting, I ripped just a hair off each edge to make sure it would be straight and square. Then later I ripped this 2x8 piece to form the two side rails.)

Note: To make it easier to keep the ends straight, I marked a "head" end and a "foot" end before laying out the dadoes and locations for the holes.

CUT DADOES. When marking the width of the dadoes, the two for the legs are 3" wide, but the two for the stretchers are cut to equal the actual thickness of the stock for the stretchers. After marking their positions, cut all four dadoes $^3/_4$" deep.

LOCATE HOLES. Next, a series of holes are drilled for the pivot pins and support notches. Holes "d" and "e" *(Fig. 3)* are for pivot pins (J) for the back rest and seat *(Fig. 1)*. Holes "a", "b", "c" *(Fig. 4)* and "f", "g"*(Fig. 5)* are formed into notches to support the back and leg rests while in the up position.

Again, work from the head end of the board to locate the positions of these holes along the board *(Fig. 3)*.

Next, mark the center of the holes $^3/_4$" from each edge — except for hole "f" *(Figs. 4 and 5)*. This hole is located $1^1/_8$" from the edge. When all the holes have been located, bore each of them with a $^3/_4$" Forstner bit.

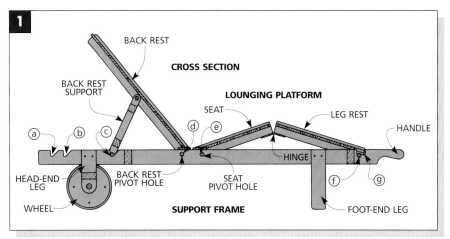

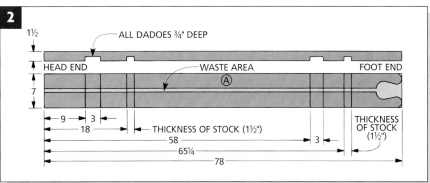

CUT NOTCHES. Now the notches can be formed. I used a jig saw to cut out V-shaped notches at holes "a", "b", and "c" *(Fig. 4)*. I also cut the double notch at holes "f" and "g" *(Fig. 5)*.

RIP RAILS. After the notches have been cut, the rails can be ripped to their final width *(Fig. 3)*.

CUT OUT HANDLES. To complete the rails, mark the shape of the handles on the foot end of the support frame *(Fig. 6)*. Cut the outline with a jig saw, sawing just outside of the lines. Then smooth the edges with a drum sander.

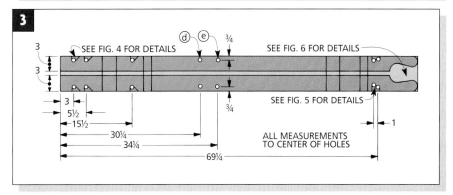

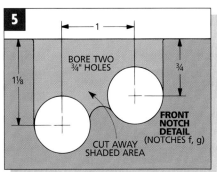

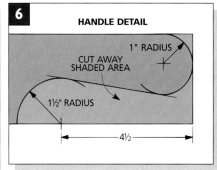

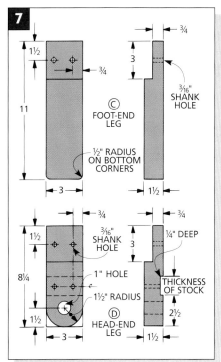

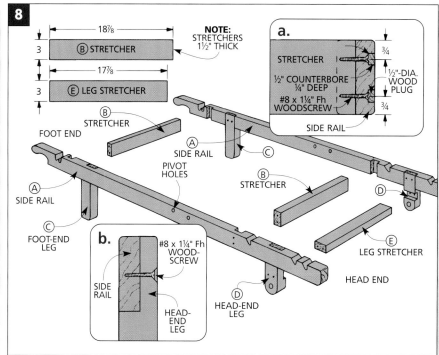

LEGS

Now that the support frames are finished, the legs are ready to be made. I started by ripping four legs from 2x4 stock to a width of 3". (Rip a little from each side of the 2x4s so both edges are nice and square.)

Now cut the legs (C) that go at the foot end 11" long, and the legs (D) at the head end 8¼" long *(Fig. 7)*. (These legs are shorter so they can accommodate the wheels.)

MAKE HALF LAPS. The legs are joined to the rails using half laps. To make sure the surfaces of the joints are flush, cut the half laps on the legs so the thickness matches the depth of the dadoes already cut in the rails *(Fig. 8b)*.

After the half laps are cut on all four legs, a dado is cut in each head-end leg (D) for a leg stretcher (E) *(Fig. 7)*.

To complete the head-end legs (D), mark the location of the axle hole 1½" up from the bottom of the leg *(Fig. 7)*. Before drilling the hole, draw a semicircle with a 1½" radius on the bottom of each leg. Then bore the axle hole and round the ends of the legs. Also, round the bottom corners of the foot-end legs (C) to a ½" radius *(Fig. 7)*.

MAKE STRETCHERS. Finally, make the three stretchers (B, E) that hold the support frame together. I ripped them 3" wide from 2x4 stock. Then cut all three stretchers to length *(Fig. 8)*.

SUPPORT FRAME ASSEMBLY

After all the parts are cut to size, the frame can be assembled. I used epoxy and brass screws for this.

ATTACH LEGS. Start the support frame assembly by attaching the legs to the rails with glue and flathead screws, countersinking the heads *(Fig. 8b)*.

ATTACH STRETCHERS. Before attaching the three stretchers, round over all edges of the rails and legs with a ¼" roundover bit. Then drill counterbores for the stretchers, glue and screw them in place, and plug the holes with ½"-dia. face grain plugs *(Fig. 8a)*.

Once the support frame has been completed, the three-part lounging platform can be assembled.

LOUNGING PLATFORM

I've designed the lounging platform to be comfortable in all positions. So there are actually three frames that make up the platform — the back rest, the seat, and the leg rest. The back rest can be adjusted to three positions. And the seat and leg rest are attached with hinges, letting you raise and lower them to a comfortable position.

There's not much to these frames — each is just a series of ½"-thick slats held together with two outside rails (refer to *Fig. 14* on page 34).

SLATS. To make the slats (F), I resawed 2x6 material down to size. First, rip the 2x6 into two 2½"-wide pieces (Step 1 in *Fig. 9*). Then turn these pieces

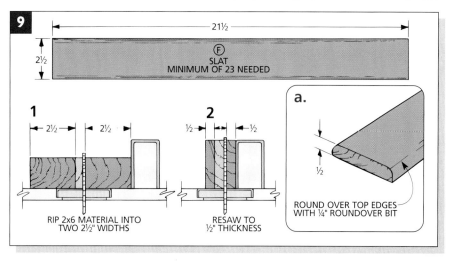

on edge to resaw them to a thickness of $1/2$" (Step 2 in *Fig. 9*). (You need 23 slats in all, but I made a few extra just in case.)

Now cut the slats to a length of $21^{1}/_{2}$". (This should equal the outside width of the assembled support frame, plus $1^{1}/_{8}$" for the $1/2$" grooves in the frame rails and $1/8$" clearance.) And finally, round over the top edges of the slats with a $1/4$" roundover bit *(Fig. 9a)*.

RAILS

The slats are joined to three sets of rails (G, H, I) to form the leg rest, seat, and back rest. To make these rails, begin by ripping 2x6 stock to a width of $2^{1}/_{2}$" *(Fig. 10a)*. Then cut the six rails to final length *(Fig. 10)*.

PRE-DRILL HOLES. Next, I pre-drilled the shank holes for the screws used to mount the slats to the rails. On each rail, start by marking the first hole $3^{1}/_{4}$" from one end of the rail and centered $3/4$" down from the top edge *(Figs. 10 and 10a)*.

Then mark off holes every 3" along the rail *(Fig. 10)*. After the positions of the holes are marked, drill shank holes all the way through at each point.

GROOVES. Next, I cut $1/2$" grooves on both sides of the rails. (The inside groove is used to hold the slats in place, and the outside groove is a way to recess all the screw heads.)

Cut these grooves $1/2$" deep on both sides of the rails so they're centered over the shank holes (Step 1 in *Fig. 11*). Then use a drill bit to countersink the holes in the outside groove (Step 2 in *Fig. 11*).

PIVOT HOLES. These rails also have $3/4$"-dia. holes for the dowels that fit in the pivot holes and notches in the support frame *(Figs. 10 and 12)*. I've found that the trick to getting the precise location of these holes is to partially assemble the platforms and then use the holes in the side rails as a guide.

Begin by drilling a pivot hole on the inside face at the end of the rails of the seat rail (H) and the back rest rail (I) *(Figs. 10 and 10a)*. These holes are the ones that correspond with pivot holes "d" and "e" on the support rails *(Fig. 12)*.

Then in order to locate the other two holes (that correspond with notches "c" and "g"), you have to partially assemble the platforms. To do this, insert two slats between the ends of each pair of rails and put $3/4$" dowels (which serve as pivot pins) in the two holes that have

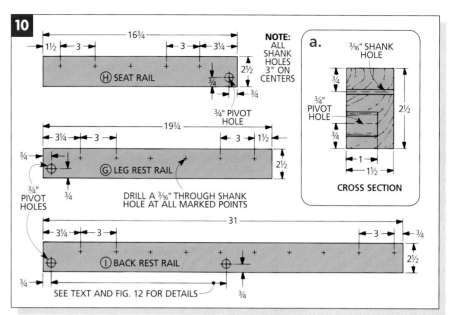

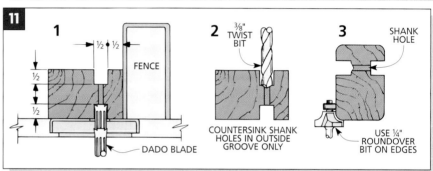

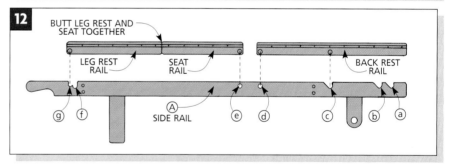

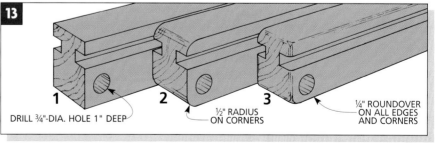

already been drilled.

Now place the platforms over the side rails with the pins in holes "d" and "e." Butt the ends of the leg rest and seat together and mark the location of the hole that corresponds with notch "g." Then mark the hole in the back rest that

corresponds with notch "c" *(Fig. 12)*.

When these holes are marked, drill $3/4$"-dia. holes 1" deep (Step 1 of *Fig. 13*).

ROUND EDGES. Then round the ends of all of the rails (Step 2 in *Fig. 13*). And finally, round over all of the rail edges (Step 3 in *Figs. 11 and 13*).

Putting the platform together is tricky. You want the slats evenly spaced, and there will also be some special spacing requirements for the outside slats at both ends of all three platforms *(Fig. 14)*.

LEG REST. I started assembly with the leg rest. Place six slats between the rails and loosely clamp the rails against the ends of the slats. Now tap the two outside slats into final position *(Fig. 14)*.

At the foot end of the leg rest, space the slat 2" from the end *(Fig. 14b)*. Then at the other end space the slat $1/4$" from the end *(Fig. 14a)*. Now it's just a matter of jogging the four interior slats to get them evenly spaced — about $1/2$" apart.

SEAT. The same basic procedure is followed on the seat. Loosely clamp five slats between the rails. Then adjust the slat at the foot end so it's $1/4$" from the end of the rails *(Fig. 14a)*. And adjust the slat at the other end so it's 2" from the end *(Fig. 14b)*.

BACK REST. The back rest uses ten slats. The slat at the end of the rail toward the pivot dowel hole is 2" from the end.

At the other end, the slat is not inset at all. Instead, I positioned it so it projects $1/2$" from the ends of the rails. Then the exposed corners are rounded over *(Figs. 14 and 14c)*.

PILOT HOLES. When the slats in each assembly are clamped to final position, drill the pilot holes for the screws. Try to center the bit in each of the shank holes when you drill (Step 2 in *Fig. 15*). Then screw a brass woodscrew in each hole.

JOIN LEG REST AND SEAT. When the leg rest and seat are assembled, they are hinged together with a 3" strap hinge *(Fig. 16)*. (On this hinge, each leaf is 3" long for a total of 6" when open.)

I mounted this hinge "upside down" on the bottom edges of the two rails *(Fig. 16a)*. This puts the countersinks on the wrong side, so I used panhead screws to mount the hinges.

After the platforms were assembled, I mounted them to the frame. The first step here is installing the pivot pins for the back rest and seat.

PIVOT PINS. The pivot pins (J) are just dowels that pass through the side rails and into the stopped holes in the platform rails *(Fig. 17)*.

After inserting these pins, I secured them with brass woodscrews *(Fig. 18)*.

ADJUSTMENT PINS. Next, I installed the adjustment pins (K) that fit into the

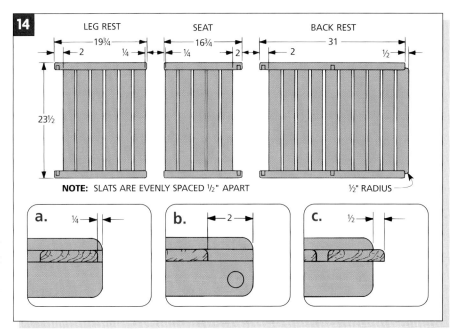

14

LEG REST   SEAT   BACK REST

19¾   16¾   31

2   ¼   ¼   2   2   ½

23½

NOTE: SLATS ARE EVENLY SPACED ½" APART   ½" RADIUS

a. ¼   **b.** 2   **c.** ½

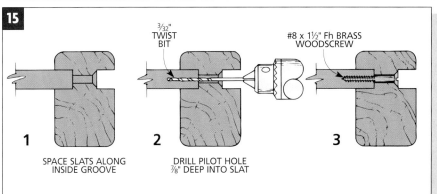

15

3/32" TWIST BIT   #8 x 1½" Fh BRASS WOODSCREW

1 SPACE SLATS ALONG INSIDE GROOVE   **2** DRILL PILOT HOLE ⅞" DEEP INTO SLAT   **3**

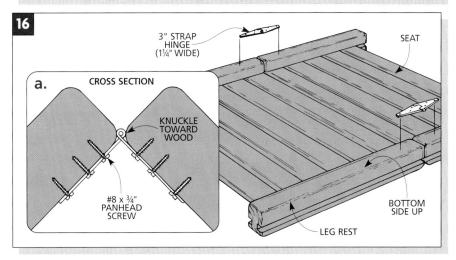

16

3" STRAP HINGE (1¼" WIDE)   SEAT

a. CROSS SECTION

KNUCKLE TOWARD WOOD

#8 x ¾" PANHEAD SCREW

BOTTOM SIDE UP

LEG REST

two position notches ("f", "g") to control the angle of the leg rest *(Fig. 19)*.

FRAME SLATS. The two remaining slats are fastened with brass woodscrews directly to the side rails between the seat rest and back rest *(Fig. 20)*.

Begin by trimming the slats to a length equal to the distance between

the outside edges of the side rails. (Mine were $20^5/8$".) Next, drill and countersink $3/16$" shank holes centered $3/4$" from the ends of the slats.

Note: When mounting these slats, there should be $1/2$" of space between them and the slats in the seat and leg rest *(Fig. 20a)*. Then screw the slats in place.

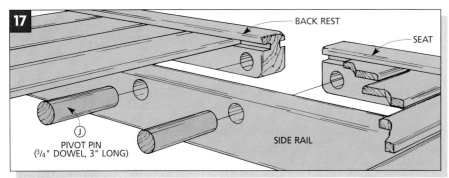

17
BACK REST
SEAT
PIVOT PIN
(³/₄" DOWEL, 3" LONG)
SIDE RAIL

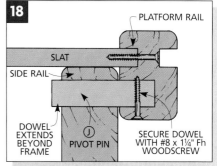

18
PLATFORM RAIL
SLAT
SIDE RAIL
DOWEL EXTENDS BEYOND FRAME
PIVOT PIN
SECURE DOWEL WITH #8 x 1¼" Fh WOODSCREW

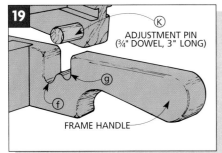

19
ADJUSTMENT PIN (³/₄" DOWEL, 3" LONG)
g
f
FRAME HANDLE

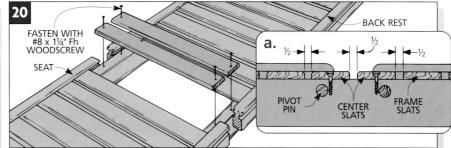

20
FASTEN WITH #8 x 1¼" Fh WOODSCREW
SEAT
BACK REST
a.
½ ½ ½
PIVOT PIN
CENTER SLATS
FRAME SLATS

BACK REST SUPPORT

After the seat and leg platforms were mounted, I made the assembly that supports the back rest. This assembly is a simple frame that also pivots on ³/₄"-dia. dowels *(Fig. 21).*

CUT STOCK. Begin by ripping "two-by" stock to 1¹/₂" square. Then cut the two support uprights (M) for the back rest support to a length of 14" *(Fig. 21).*

CUT DADOES. These two uprights are joined by two back support rails (N) that fit into ¹/₂"-deep dadoes cut on the inside edges of the uprights *(Figs. 21 and 21a).* Locate these dadoes 2¹/₂" from each end of the uprights.

PIVOT PIN HOLES. To complete the uprights, drill a ³/₄"-dia. hole at each end. To locate these holes, first drill holes ³/₄" from the top ends *(Fig. 21).*

Then, to get the location of the bottom holes, insert a pin in the top hole and place the upright alongside the side rails (A) (refer to *Fig. 22* on page 36). With the pin in notch "c", mark the position of the other hole in line with notch "a."

Finally, to secure the support rail (N) to the support upright (M), drill and countersink for flathead brass screws and ¹/₂"-dia. plugs *(Fig. 21a).*

RAILS. When the uprights have been completed, cut the rails (N) to final length so the support frame fits between the main side rails (A) of the chaise (refer to *Fig. 23* on page 36). Then glue and screw the back rest support frame together.

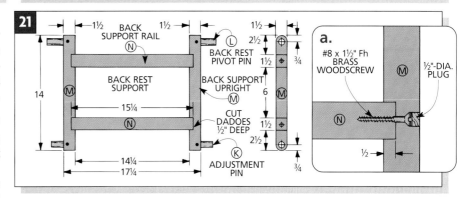

21
1½ BACK SUPPORT RAIL 1½
N
1½
2½
L
BACK REST PIVOT PIN
1½
¾
14
BACK REST SUPPORT
15¼
BACK SUPPORT UPRIGHT
M
6
M
CUT DADOES ½" DEEP
1½
2½
14¼
17¼
ADJUSTMENT PIN
K
¾

a.
#8 x 1½" Fh BRASS WOODSCREW
M
½"-DIA. PLUG
N
½

SHOP INFO ..... Redwood Grades

Redwood is an ideal choice for a project that is going to sit outside. It's durable and has a natural resistance to both insects and decay. But, it's important to realize that there are different grades of redwood, which affect its ability to fend off these damaging factors.

Each grade falls into one of two main groups: heartwood and sapwood. For outdoor projects it's best to choose heartwood (identified by its red-

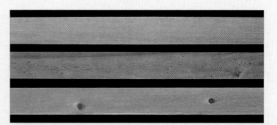

dish-brown color). The heartwood is cut from the inner part of a redwood log — the part that makes it so resistant to rot and insects.

The two best grades are Clear All Heart — with straight grain and no knots and Heart 'B' — with some irregular

grain and a few small, tight knots (top two boards in photo above).

A less expensive grade of redwood would be Construction Heart/Deck Heart (bottom board in photo). This grade will have larger knots and mostly irregular grain.

INSTALL PINS. The support frame is mounted to the chaise with two pairs of pins. The back rest pivot pins (L) let the frame assembly pivot on the back rest rails *(Fig. 23)*. The lower pair of pins (K) fits into the height adjustment notches.

To install the pins into the support frame, press them into the lower holes until the ends are flush with the inside of the frame. Then secure them with screws. Next, insert the back rest pivot pins (L) through the holes in the upper part of the support assembly (securing these pins with screws) and also into the holes in the back rest rails *(Fig. 23)*.

INSTALL THE WHEELS

All that's left is installing the wheels. You can purchase wheels to fit this chaise, but I decided to make my own (see Technique on the following page).

After the wheels (O) are made, they're mounted to the chaise with an axle assembly. It consists of a 1" dowel for an axle (Q) and an axle pin (R) to hold the wheel in place. The axle extends about $^3/_4$" beyond the outside edge of the wheel on both sides *(Fig. 25)*. Drill a hole for each axle pin near each end of the axle *(Fig. 24)*. To keep the wheel from rubbing on the head-end legs, make spacer washers (P) from hardboard. (For more on making them, see the Shop Tip below.)

AXLE PINS. Next, mount the washers and the wheels to the axle and hold them on with axle pins made out of $^1/_4$" dowels *(Fig. 24)*. (Taper the axle pins to fit.)

FINISH. Finally, to get a smooth, satin finish that adds protection for outdoor use, I applied my own mixture of tung oil and spar varnish.

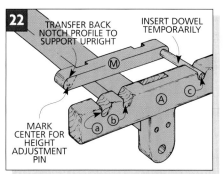

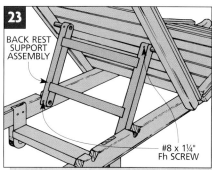

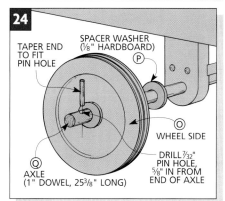

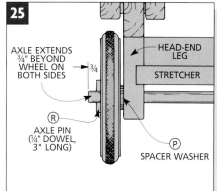

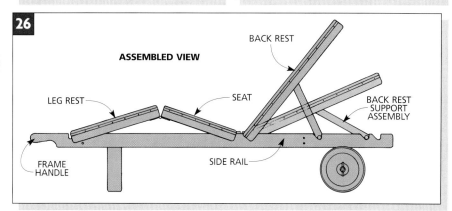

ASSEMBLED VIEW. Once construction of the chaise lounge is complete, the back rest will be adjustable in three positions and the leg rest and seat assembly will be adjustable in two positions, as shown in *Fig. 26*. ■

SHOP TIP .... *Spacer Washers*

To make the spacer washers, you need a scrap piece of plywood to support the hardboard.

First, tack the hardboard to the plywood scrap. Then drill four axle holes using a 1" Forstner bit *(Fig. 1)*.

Now, to cut the washers to size, center a 2" hole saw over the axle holes and cut the washers *(Fig. 2)*.

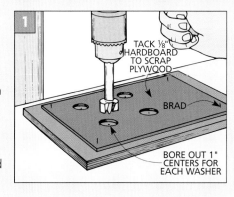

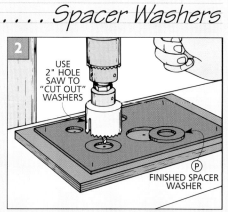

Although you can buy metal (or even plastic) wheels at most hardware stores that will work on the chaise, they're usually pretty small. Besides, I wanted mine to match the redwood I used for the rest of the chaise lounge. So I made my own. The wheel consists of two wheel sides (O) with rabbets on the inner perimeters. When the two sides are screwed together, the facing rabbets form a groove that holds a V-belt "tire."

I used a router with a trammel point attachment to rout the rabbet for the tire and also the decorative profiles on the outside face of the wheel.

MAKE JIGS. To hold the square workpieces securely, make four holding jigs. (They're needed so duplicate cuts can be made on all four disks without changing the router setting.) Each holding jig is a scrap of ³/₄" plywood that's fastened to a 2x4 so it can be held in a vise *(Fig. 1)*.

The workpieces are made from "one-by" redwood *(Fig. 1)*. Drill a ⁹/₆₄" centered hole in each for the trammel point.

To position the workpiece, drive a finish nail with the head cut off into the center of the jig. Then place the workpiece over this pin *(Fig. 4)*.

To keep the square from moving, I also drove four 1" brads through the bottom of the jig so that they projected about ¹/₄" into the workpiece.

ROUTING. Now the squares can be routed into disks. I used a trammel attachment and a ¹/₄"-dia. straight bit to rout these circles *(Fig. 2)*. Set the trammel attachment to rout a 9¹/₂" diameter circle (4³/₄" radius) on each disk and rout successively deeper grooves in

a counter-clockwise direction until the circle (wheel) is complete.

Next, switch to a ¹/₂"-dia. straight bit to cut a ⁵/₁₆"-deep rabbet around the perimeter of each disk *(Fig. 3)*. Begin by cutting this rabbet to width so it's a little larger than the inner diameter of the V-belt "tire", decreasing the diameter until the V-belt fits tightly around the disk in the rabbet.

After the rabbet has been cut on all four disks, pry them up, flip them over, and press them back on the brads. Then cut the perimeter contour on all four disks using a ¹/₄"-dia. roundover bit *(Fig. 4)*.

Finally, a recess is routed just a little deeper than ¹/₄" on only two disks to make the outside face of the wheels. This requires using two bits: a ¹/₂"-dia. core box bit and a ¹/₂"-dia. straight bit *(Fig. 4)*.

ASSEMBLY. Now put the V-belt over the rabbet on one inside disk *(Fig. 5)*. Make sure the grain in the facing disks is at right angles and fasten them together with glue and screws. Finally, drill a centered 1"-dia. hole for the axle.

WHEEL SIDE (INSIDE FACE)
RABBET FOR V-BELT
#8 x 1¼" Fh BRASS WOODSCREW
30" x ⅝" V-BELT
WHEEL SIDE (OUTSIDE FACE)

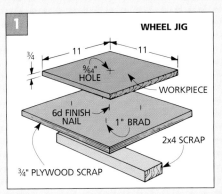

1 **WHEEL JIG**
¾
11 — 11
⁹/₆₄" HOLE
WORKPIECE
6d FINISH NAIL
1" BRAD
2x4 SCRAP
¾" PLYWOOD SCRAP

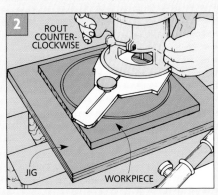

2 ROUT COUNTER-CLOCKWISE
JIG
WORKPIECE

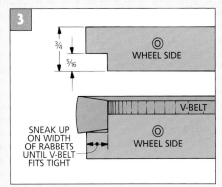

3
¾
⁵/₁₆
WHEEL SIDE
V-BELT
SNEAK UP ON WIDTH OF RABBETS UNTIL V-BELT FITS TIGHT
WHEEL SIDE

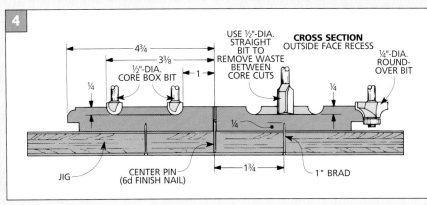

4
4¾
3⅜
½"-DIA. CORE BOX BIT
1
¼
¼
USE ½"-DIA. STRAIGHT BIT TO REMOVE WASTE BETWEEN CORE CUTS
CROSS SECTION OUTSIDE FACE RECESS
¼"-DIA. ROUND-OVER BIT
¼
¼
JIG
CENTER PIN (6d FINISH NAIL)
1¾
1" BRAD

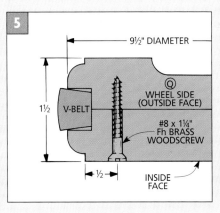

5
9½" DIAMETER
1½
V-BELT
WHEEL SIDE (OUTSIDE FACE)
#8 x 1¼" Fh BRASS WOODSCREW
½
INSIDE FACE

Redwood Bench

Each slat in the back of this bench is locked into a pair of mortises. There's a quick way to make these mortises line up perfectly from top to bottom, and it's done without any drilling or chopping.

The classic design of this English bench makes it a beautiful piece to accent your garden or deck. And this bench is as strong as it is attractive. Legs that are 2½" thick, pinned mortise and tenon joints, and a custom-mixed outdoor finish mean it will last for years.

ANGLES. Even if you're an old hand at mortises and tenons, you'll find the bench offers a few twists on this joint.

To make it comfortable to sit in, the back of the bench angles backwards. Of course, any time you introduce an angle, you also introduce some complexity. But laying out the angle on the legs is as easy as using a tape measure.

Then you'll need to cut angled tenons on the arms to fit mortises in the legs. A simple jig using a cut-off scrap makes quick work of this.

As for the mortises for the back slats, there's an easy way to make these that doesn't involve drilling or chiseling.

DURABILITY. Any project that sits outdoors has to withstand the elements. This bench was built from redwood, which resists decay over the years.

Instead of the usual yellow glue, a plastic resin glue was used. It's designed to stand up to the weather as well as (and maybe even better than) the redwood.

Rust-proof brass screws fasten down the seat slats and a few other pieces. The screws are hidden from sight beneath redwood plugs.

FINISH. The finish used on the bench in the photo is a shop-mixed combination of spar varnish and a tung oil sealer. This combination offers the penetrating protection of an oil and the slight sheen provided by a varnish.

MATCHING CHAIR. With just a few modifications to the bench, you can build a matching Redwood Armchair and put together a set of furniture for your garden. See the Designer's Notebook on page 47 for details.

EXPLODED VIEW

OVERALL DIMENSIONS:
33³⁄₈H x 23¹⁄₄D x 59L

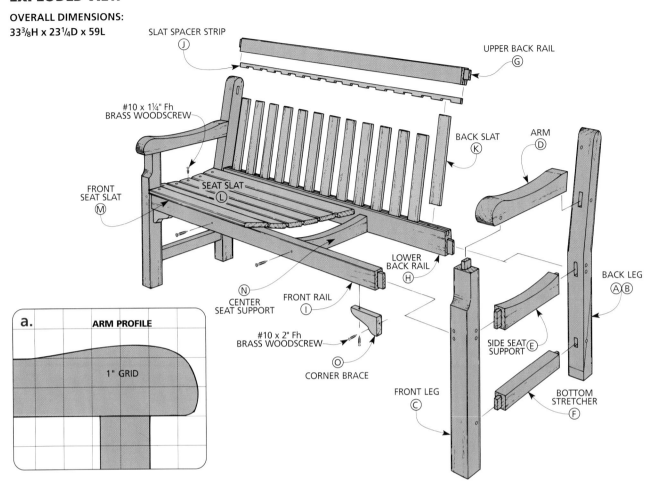

SLAT SPACER STRIP
Ⓙ

UPPER BACK RAIL
Ⓖ

#10 x 1¼" Fh
BRASS WOODSCREW

BACK SLAT
Ⓚ

ARM
Ⓓ

FRONT
SEAT SLAT
Ⓜ

SEAT SLAT
Ⓛ

BACK LEG
Ⓐ Ⓑ

LOWER
BACK RAIL
Ⓗ

Ⓝ

FRONT RAIL
Ⓘ

CENTER
SEAT SUPPORT

SIDE SEAT
SUPPORT Ⓔ

#10 x 2" Fh
BRASS WOODSCREW

CORNER BRACE

Ⓞ

FRONT LEG
Ⓒ

BOTTOM
STRETCHER
Ⓕ

a. **ARM PROFILE**

1" GRID

CUTTING DIAGRAM

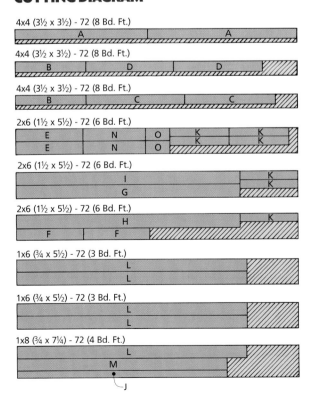

4x4 (3½ x 3½) - 72 (8 Bd. Ft.)
A | A

4x4 (3½ x 3½) - 72 (8 Bd. Ft.)
B | D | D

4x4 (3½ x 3½) - 72 (8 Bd. Ft.)
B | C | C

2x6 (1½ x 5½) - 72 (6 Bd. Ft.)
E | N | O | K | K
E | N | O | K | K

2x6 (1½ x 5½) - 72 (6 Bd. Ft.)
I | K
G | K

2x6 (1½ x 5½) - 72 (6 Bd. Ft.)
H | K
F | F

1x6 (¾ x 5½) - 72 (3 Bd. Ft.)
L
L

1x6 (¾ x 5½) - 72 (3 Bd. Ft.)
L
L

1x8 (¾ x 7¼) - 72 (4 Bd. Ft.)
L
M
J

MATERIALS LIST

WOOD

A	Long Bk. Leg Pc. (2)	2½ x 3¼ - 35
B	Short Bk. Leg Pc. (2)	2½ x 3¼ - 18
C	Front Leg Blanks (2)	2½ x 2½ - 25
D	Arm Blanks (2)	2½ x 2½ - 22
E	Side Seat Spprt. (2)	1½ x 2½ - 16
F	Btm. Stretchers (2)	1½ x 1¾ - 16
G	Upper Back Rail (1)	1½ x 2½ - 56
H	Lower Back Rail (1)	1½ x 3½ - 56
I	Front Rail (1)	1½ x 2½ - 56
J	Slat Spacer Strip (1)	¾ x 1½ - 54
K	Back Slats (13)	½ x 2 - 14 rough
L	Seat Slats (5)	¾ x 2½ - 59
M	Front Seat Slat (1)	¾ x 2½ - 54
N	Ctr. Seat Spprt. (2)	1½ x 2½ - 15
O	Corner Braces (2)	1 x 2½ - 5

HARDWARE

(24) No. 10 x 1¼" Fh brass woodscrews
(8) No. 10 x 2" Fh brass woodscrews
(28) ½"-dia. wood plugs
(26) ⅜"-dia. wood plugs
(26) ⅜" x 1½" dowel pins (or one ⅜"-dia.
dowel x 48")

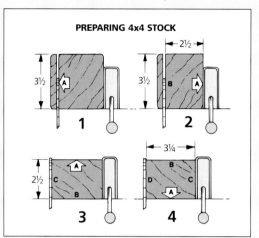

SHOP TIP .... Squaring up Stock

To get a flat side with square edges, trim off one side of the post (Side A in *Step 1*). Then with Side A against the fence, resaw the post to 2½" thick (*Step 2*).

Next, turn the workpiece 90° counterclockwise and trim ⅛" off one edge (*Step 3*). Then flip the piece 180° and trim the piece to final width (*Step 4*).

PREPARING 4x4 STOCK

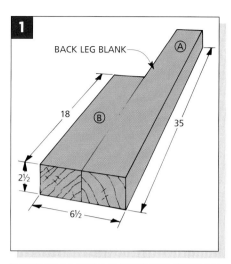

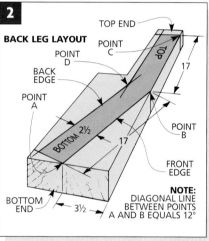

LEGS

I started on the bench by working on the trickiest part — the angled back legs. They're cut from step-shaped blanks.

BACK LEGS. To make the blanks, start by cutting two long back leg pieces (A) and two short back leg pieces (B) from 4x4 stock (*Fig. 1*). These pieces are squared up and trimmed to size before being glued together. The Shop Tip above shows how to do this.

GLUE UP BLANK. Once the back leg pieces are cut to size, glue a long piece (A) to a short piece (B) to form a blank for each leg (*Fig. 1*). Mark the top and bottom of each blank to help you keep

them straight as you lay out the angles and cut the legs to shape (*Fig. 2*).

LAYOUT. When the blanks are dry, lay out the legs. To do this, start by measuring over from the bottom front corner 3½" to mark Point A (*Fig. 2*).

Then from Point A, measure 17" to the front edge of the leg and mark Point B. Connect these two points to establish a 12° angle.

To mark the overall length of the leg, start at Point B and measure 17" along the front edge of the leg to the top front corner and mark Point C.

Complete the leg layout by marking the back edges of the leg parallel to and 2½" from the front edges. Label the

point where these two lines intersect (the back of the knee) as Point D.

CUT TO SHAPE. To end up with straight, clean edges, I decided to use the table saw to cut the legs to shape. However, this presents a couple of problems. The first is cutting the front edge on the bottom of the leg. Since you can't run the opposite face against the rip fence, a simple jig is used to carry the leg as shown in the Shop Jig at left.

Note: Save the triangular cutoff from the bottom of one blank to use later when setting up other cuts.

INSIDE ANGLE. The second problem is cutting the "inside bend" at Point D. Making this cut takes two passes. The first pass stops just short of the back of the knee. The second pass also stops short of the back of the knee, but from the other end. But first, you need to determine where to stop.

The best way to do this is to lay out a reference line from Point D, across the short board, and down the side (*Fig. 3*).

Next, raise the blade 2¾" high and place a pencil mark on the saw table

SHOP JIG .... Carrier

The front legs can be cut on the table saw by tacking a ¼"-thick plywood carrier (about 10" x 36") to the leg blank so one edge of the jig lines up on the angled pencil line

connecting Points A and B (*Fig. 1*). (Make sure the nail heads are set below the surface of the plywood.) Then make a cut right on the edge of the plywood to trim the leg (*Fig. 2*).

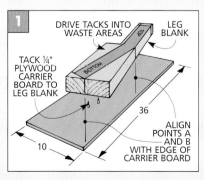

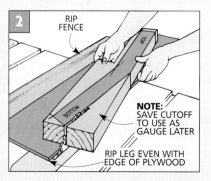

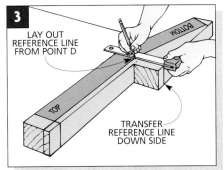

3 LAY OUT REFERENCE LINE FROM POINT D

TRANSFER REFERENCE LINE DOWN SIDE

TOP

BOTTOM

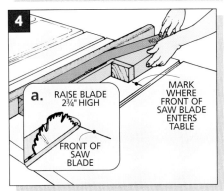

4

a. RAISE BLADE 2¾" HIGH

FRONT OF SAW BLADE

MARK WHERE FRONT OF SAW BLADE ENTERS TABLE

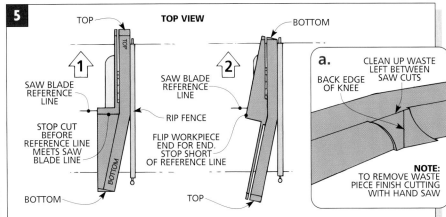

5 TOP VIEW

TOP   BOTTOM

①   **②**

SAW BLADE REFERENCE LINE

STOP CUT BEFORE REFERENCE LINE MEETS SAW BLADE LINE

BOTTOM

SAW BLADE REFERENCE LINE

RIP FENCE

FLIP WORKPIECE END FOR END. STOP SHORT OF REFERENCE LINE

TOP

a. CLEAN UP WASTE LEFT BETWEEN SAW CUTS

BACK EDGE OF KNEE

NOTE: TO REMOVE WASTE PIECE FINISH CUTTING WITH HAND SAW

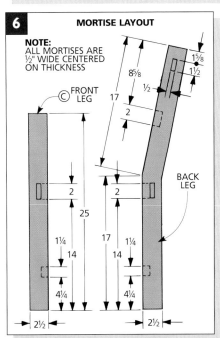

6 MORTISE LAYOUT

NOTE: ALL MORTISES ARE ½" WIDE CENTERED ON THICKNESS

ⓒ FRONT LEG

BACK LEG

$1^{5}/_{8}$
$1^{1}/_{2}$
½
2
$8^{5}/_{8}$
17

2   2
25
$1^{1}/_{4}$ 17 $1^{1}/_{4}$
14   14
$4^{1}/_{4}$ $4^{1}/_{4}$
2½   2½

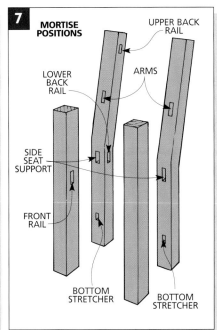

7 MORTISE POSITIONS

UPPER BACK RAIL

LOWER BACK RAIL

ARMS

SIDE SEAT SUPPORT

FRONT RAIL

BOTTOM STRETCHER

BOTTOM STRETCHER

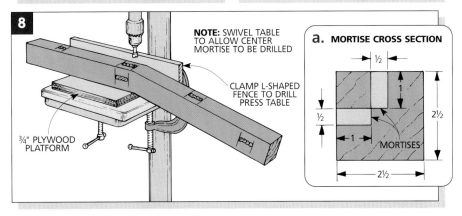

8

NOTE: SWIVEL TABLE TO ALLOW CENTER MORTISE TO BE DRILLED

CLAMP L-SHAPED FENCE TO DRILL PRESS TABLE

¾" PLYWOOD PLATFORM

a. MORTISE CROSS SECTION

½   1   ½   2½
1   MORTISES
2½

exactly at the point where the front of the blade enters the opening in the table *(Fig. 4)*. Extend a reference line from this mark about 5" out from the blade.

Now set the rip fence to make a 2½"-wide cut and saw the top of the leg to width, stopping before the reference mark on the workpiece lines up with the mark on the saw table (Step 1 in *Fig. 5*). Turn off the saw and wait for the blade to stop before removing the leg.

To cut the bottom of the leg, flip the leg over and turn it end for end. Once again, stop short of where the two reference lines intersect (Step 2 in *Fig. 5*).

Use a hand saw or band saw to complete the cut. Then clean up the back of the knee with a sharp chisel *(Fig. 5a)*.

After the backs of the legs are cleaned up, cut both ends to final length (17" from Point B) *(Fig. 2)*.

FRONT LEGS. Next cut two front legs (C) to a rough length of 25" *(Fig. 6)*. Follow Steps 1 and 2 in the Shop Tip to resaw the front legs to 2½" thick and then rip them 2½" wide.

MORTISES

Once all four legs are cut to size, I laid out the positions of the mortises.

Note: I found it was easiest to keep everything straight and get mirrored sets by standing all four legs in position *(Fig. 7)*. Then pencil in rough reference marks where the mortises are located.

All the mortises are centered on the thickness of the stock and are ½" wide. It's the lengths and locations that vary.

I started on the top inside faces of the back legs laying out the mortises for the upper back rail *(Figs. 6 and 7)*.

Then I worked my way down the legs, laying out the mortises for the arms, the

front and back rails, the seat supports, and the stretchers.

I then roughed out the mortises on a drill press and cleaned up the cheeks with a chisel *(Fig. 8)*.

Note: Since the back leg won't sit flat on the drill press table, I built a temporary platform to support it *(Fig. 8)*.

COMPLETE LEGS. There are still a couple of items to complete on the legs. First, the top end of each back leg is rounded to a 1¼" radius *(Fig. 9a)*. Then use a band saw to cut a ¾"-deep decorative scoop on the front face of the front legs *(Fig. 9)*.

Finally, to keep the bottoms from chipping, rout ⅜" roundovers on the bottom edges of the legs *(Fig. 9b)*.

ARMS, SUPPORTS, & STRETCHERS

Next, work can begin on the arms, seat supports, and bottom stretchers which fit between the front and back legs.

CUT TO SIZE. Start by cutting two arm blanks (D) to 2½" square (follow the same procedure as the front legs) and to a rough length of 22" *(Fig. 10)*.

Now cut two seat support blanks (E) and the two bottom stretcher blanks (F) to width from "two-by" lumber *(Fig. 10)*. Trim the supports and stretchers to a finished length of 16".

TENONS. After these six pieces were cut to size, I began work on the tenons. The tenons on the back of the arms are angled, but the tenons on the seat supports and bottom stretchers are straight. I like to do the easy ones first, so I started on the straight tenons.

The tenons on both ends of the seat supports are ½" thick, 1" long, and cut to width (height) to fit the mortises in the legs *(Fig. 10)*.

The tenons on the bottom stretchers are the same, except that they're only 1¼" wide *(Fig. 10)*.

ANGLED TENON. Now comes the fun part — cutting the angled tenon on the arm so it matches the 12° bend in the leg *(Fig. 10)*. To do this, use the cutoff saved from the back leg to set the miter gauge to 78° (12° on some gauges) *(Fig. 11)*. Then raise the table saw blade to a height of 1" and set the rip fence 1¾" from the *outside* edge of the blade to act as a stop *(Fig. 12)*.

Note: Before making any cuts on the arm, I cut a test tenon on a piece of scrap the same thickness as the arm.

Once the saw is set up, make the angled shoulder cut on the arm. Then make repeated passes over the blade until one side of the tenon is cut.

Now flip the workpiece over and switch the miter gauge so it's set at the opposite 78° (12°) setting *(Fig. 13)*. Leave the rip fence at the same setting

and cut the other side to form the tenon.

To cut the tenon to length, move the rip fence out of the way and raise the blade. Use the same miter gauge setting and trim the tenon to 1" long *(Fig. 14)*.

Finally, I laid out the width of tenon using the end of a ruler as a square *(Fig. 15)*. After it was laid out, I trimmed the shoulders down with a hand saw.

DRY-ASSEMBLE. There's one more mortise and tenon joint to cut — the one needed to attach the arm to the front

leg. To determine the location of this joint, dry-assemble the back leg, arm, seat support, and stretcher *(Fig. 16)*.

Then to locate the position of the mortise on the bottom of the arm, place a straightedge against the shoulders of the tenons on the seat support and stretcher. Run the straightedge up to the bottom of the arm and mark a line at this position *(Fig. 16)*. Then lay out a 1¼"-long mortise spaced ¼" in front of this line and bore it out.

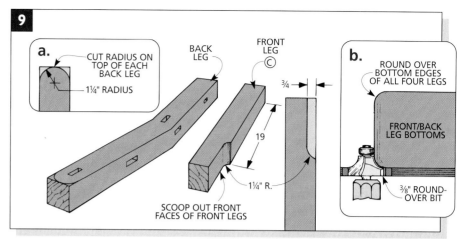

9

a. CUT RADIUS ON TOP OF EACH BACK LEG — 1¼" RADIUS

BACK LEG
FRONT LEG C
¾

19

1¼" R.

SCOOP OUT FRONT FACES OF FRONT LEGS

b. ROUND OVER BOTTOM EDGES OF ALL FOUR LEGS

FRONT/BACK LEG BOTTOMS

⅜" ROUND-OVER BIT

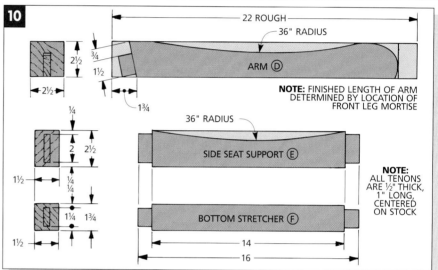

10

22 ROUGH
36" RADIUS
2½
¾
1½
2½
1¾
ARM D

NOTE: FINISHED LENGTH OF ARM DETERMINED BY LOCATION OF FRONT LEG MORTISE

¼
2 2½
1½
¼
¼

36" RADIUS
SIDE SEAT SUPPORT E

NOTE: ALL TENONS ARE ½" THICK, 1" LONG, CENTERED ON STOCK

1½
1¼ 1¾

BOTTOM STRETCHER F

14
16

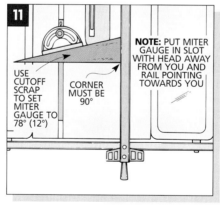

11

USE CUTOFF SCRAP TO SET MITER GAUGE TO 78° (12°)

CORNER MUST BE 90°

NOTE: PUT MITER GAUGE IN SLOT WITH HEAD AWAY FROM YOU AND RAIL POINTING TOWARDS YOU

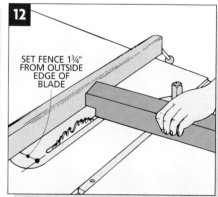

12

SET FENCE 1¾" FROM OUTSIDE EDGE OF BLADE

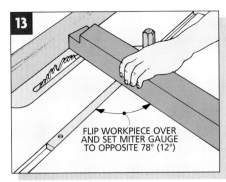

13
FLIP WORKPIECE OVER AND SET MITER GAUGE TO OPPOSITE 78° (12°)

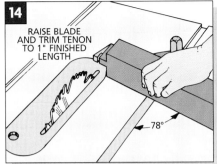

14
RAISE BLADE AND TRIM TENON TO 1" FINISHED LENGTH

78°

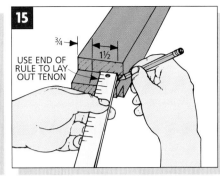

15
USE END OF RULE TO LAY OUT TENON

¾

1½

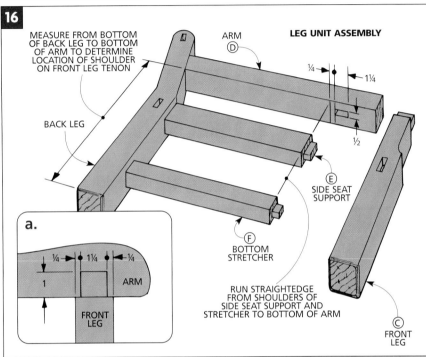

16
MEASURE FROM BOTTOM OF BACK LEG TO BOTTOM OF ARM TO DETERMINE LOCATION OF SHOULDER ON FRONT LEG TENON

ARM ⒟

LEG UNIT ASSEMBLY

BACK LEG

¼   1¼

½

Ⓔ
SIDE SEAT SUPPORT

Ⓕ
BOTTOM STRETCHER

RUN STRAIGHTEDGE FROM SHOULDERS OF SIDE SEAT SUPPORT AND STRETCHER TO BOTTOM OF ARM

Ⓒ
FRONT LEG

a.
¼   1¼   ¼
1
ARM
FRONT LEG

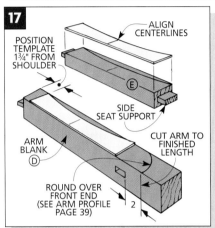

17
ALIGN CENTERLINES

POSITION TEMPLATE 1¾" FROM SHOULDER

Ⓔ

SIDE SEAT SUPPORT

CUT ARM TO FINISHED LENGTH

ARM BLANK ⒟

ROUND OVER FRONT END (SEE ARM PROFILE PAGE 39)

2

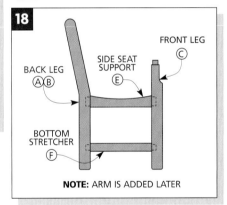

18
FRONT LEG Ⓒ

SIDE SEAT SUPPORT Ⓔ

BACK LEG Ⓐ Ⓑ

BOTTOM STRETCHER Ⓕ

NOTE: ARM IS ADDED LATER

TENON. The next step is to cut the mating tenon on the top of the front leg. To determine the location of the tenon's shoulder, measure from the bottom of the back leg to the bottom of the arm *(Fig. 16)*. Transfer this measurement to the front leg, then cut the tenon to fit the mortise *(Fig. 16a)*.

RADIUS. The tops of the seat supports and the center seat supports (added later) are curved to make a comfortable seat. To make the curve the same on each piece, I made a template (see the Shop Tip at right).

Start by aligning the centerline of the pattern with the centerline of each seat support and mark the curve *(Fig. 17)*.

Then use the template to mark the curve on the top edge of the arm, except this time the template is placed 1¾" from the shoulder of the tenon *(Fig. 17)*. Now you can cut the curves.

Finally, cut the arm to finished length, then lay out and round over the front end *(Fig. 16a* and refer to detail 'a' on page 39).

ASSEMBLY. Now the leg units can be glued and clamped together *(Fig. 18)*.

SHOP TIP *.... Making a Template*

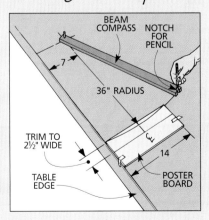

To lay out identical curves on several pieces, I use a template.

I made mine by attaching a piece of posterboard to the edge of a table. Then, using a strip of wood as a simple beam compass, strike a 36" radius on the posterboard *(see drawing)*.

To help align the template on the workpiece, mark the centerline at the low point of the arc. Finally, cut the template 2½" wide to match the thickness of the workpieces.

BEAM COMPASS   NOTCH FOR PENCIL

7

36" RADIUS

TRIM TO 2½" WIDE

TABLE EDGE

14

POSTER BOARD

Now work can begin on the three rails that connect the two leg units.

CUT TO SIZE. Start by ripping the upper back rail (G), lower back rail (H), and front rail (I) to width, then cut them to finished length *(Fig. 19)*.

TENONS. After the rails are cut to size, 1"-long tenons are cut on the ends of each rail. Notice that the tenons on the upper and lower back rails (G, H) are offset on the width of the rails *(Fig. 20)*. This allows clearance for the grooves that are cut next.

GROOVES. The back slats would typically be mounted in the rails by cutting a series of individual mortises. But there's an easier way. I used a notched spacer strip that's set into a groove on the edge of the rails (refer to *Fig. 22*).

I cut the grooves with a dado blade. The groove in the upper back rail is simple enough. It's centered on the thickness of the rail *(Fig. 20)*. But to match the angle of the back rest on the back leg, the groove in the lower back rail is cut at a 12° angle *(Fig. 20)*. Here again, you can use the triangular cutoff from the back leg, this time to set the tilt of your table saw blade.

SPACER STRIPS. Once the grooves are cut in the rails, I cut the notched spacer strips (J) to hold the slats. I cut the notches in a wide blank and then ripped two spacer strips from it. This way, the mortises in the upper rail will line up with the mortises in the lower rail.

Start with a piece of "one-by" stock 1½" wide and trimmed to length to match the shoulder-to-shoulder length of the rails *(Fig. 21)*. Now lay out and cut the notches (dadoes) for the back slats along the spacer strip *(Fig. 21)*.

Note: The strip starts and stops with a space, not a dado.

When all the dadoes are cut, this piece is ripped to form the two spacer strips. But before doing that, I marked a line across one end of the blank to help position the strips later *(Fig. 21)*. Then rip each strip to width so it fits snugly in the grooves in the rails.

Once the strips fit the grooves, glue them in place making sure that the ends of the strips are flush with the shoulders of the tenons and that the reference mark is at the same end of each rail *(Fig. 22)*. When the glue is dry, trim the spacers flush with the edge of the rails *(Fig. 23)*.

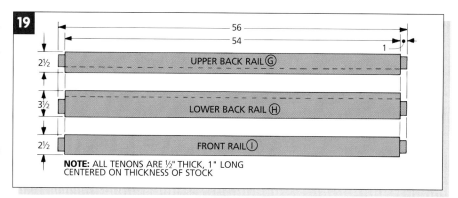

NOTE: ALL TENONS ARE ½" THICK, 1" LONG CENTERED ON THICKNESS OF STOCK

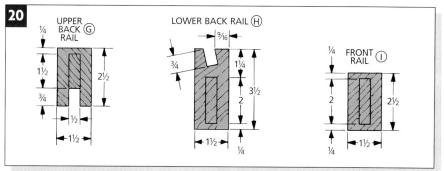

BACK SLATS

Before joining the rails to the leg units, the back slats (K) have to be cut and placed between the rails.

CUT TO SIZE. To make the back slats, start with seven pieces of "two-by" stock cut 2" wide and to a rough length of 15". Now resaw these pieces to final thickness to match the "mortises."

To determine their final length, dry-assemble the leg units and the rails and measure between the grooves in the upper and lower rails *(Fig. 24)*.

ASSEMBLY. After the slats are cut to length, mount them between the rails, but don't use any glue. The slats "float" in the mortises. Once all the slats are in place, clamp the back assembly together. Now you can glue and clamp the back assembly, the leg units and the front rail together *(Fig. 24)*.

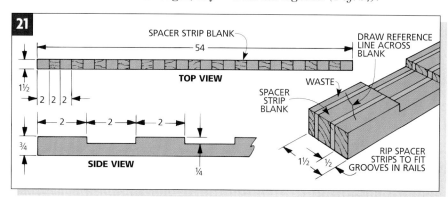

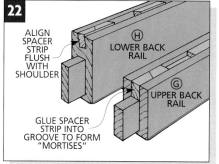

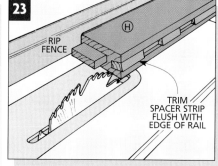

SEAT SLATS

Next, work can begin on the seat slats. There are five long seat slats (L) and one shorter slat (M). The short slat fits on the front of the bench between the legs (refer to *Fig. 26*).

CUT TO SIZE. The slats are cut from "one-by" stock. Start by cutting the blanks to a width of $2^{1}/_{2}$" *(Fig. 25)*.

The long seat slats (L) will be positioned flush with the outside edges of the legs *(Fig. 26)*. So to determine the finished length of these slats, measure the distance from the outside of one front leg to the outside of the other front leg. (In my case this was 59".) Cut five slats to this length. The finished length of the front slat (M) is the distance *between* the front legs. (In my case this was 54".)

CENTER SEAT SUPPORTS

Before attaching the seat slats, two center seat supports (N) are added.

These are cut from "two-by" stock to a width of $2^{1}/_{2}$" *(Fig. 26)*. To determine their length, measure the distance between the front rail (I) and the lower back rail (H). (In my case this was 15".) Then cut the pieces to length and use the template from the side seat supports to lay out the curve on the top edge.

MOUNT SUPPORTS. When the center seat supports have been cut to shape, position them between the rails so each one is centered 17" from the inside edges of the legs *(Fig. 26)*. Then to mount them, drill counterbored screw holes $1^{1}/_{4}$" from the bottom edge of the front and back rails and centered on the thickness of each support *(Fig. 27)*.

SCREW HOLES. After the center seat supports are attached, drill four counterbored holes in each slat *(Fig. 25)*. The holes at each end should line up with the centers of the seat supports (E). The other two holes are each centered over a center seat support (N).

Once the counterbores are drilled, rout $1/8$" chamfers on all the edges and ends of each slat (except the ends of the front slat) *(Fig. 25)*.

ASSEMBLY. Now screw down each seat slat (L) to the side seat supports (E) at each end *(Fig. 27)*. Then drill pilot holes into the center seat supports and screw the slats down in the center. Finally, fill all of the counterbored holes by gluing in $1/2$"-dia. wood plugs.

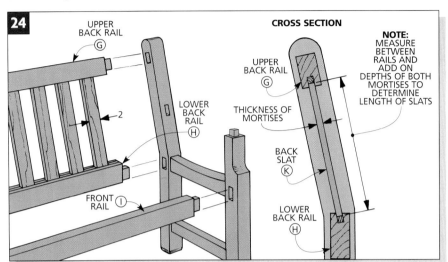

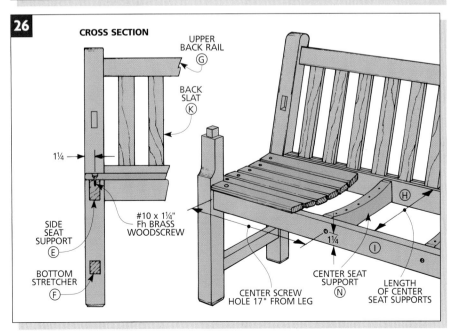

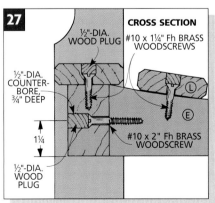

ARMS & CORNER BRACES

Once all the plugs were sanded flush, I glued the arms in place. This is just a matter of sliding the tenon into the mortise in the back leg, then lowering the arm onto the front leg *(Fig. 28)*.

After the arms are glued in place, corner braces (O) are added under the front rail where it meets the front legs *(Fig. 30)*. Cut these braces to shape from a piece of "two-by" stock resawn to 1" thick *(Fig. 29)*. Then screw the corner braces in place *(Fig. 30)*.

Note: Since these holes face down, there is no need to use plugs in them.

PINNING TENONS

There's only one more step in building the bench — pinning the mortise and tenon joints. Since the bench is going to sit outside, the wood will expand and contract, possibly weakening the joints. So I put dowel pins through each joint to hold it tight *(Fig. 31)*.

HOLE LOCATIONS. The holes for the pins that secure the upper back rail *(Fig. 32a)*, the two bottom stretchers *(Fig. 32c)*, and both arms *(Figs. 32d and 32e)* are centered on the width of these pieces. There are two pins in each of the joints that attach the front rail, side seat supports, and lower back rail *(Fig. 32b)* to the legs.

All the holes are $1/2$" from the shoulder line of the tenon. When all the holes are located, fasten a depth stop to a $3/8$" drill bit (or wrap a piece of masking tape around the bit as an indicator) and drill each hole $1^7/8$" deep.

DOWELING PINS. For the pins, I used $3/8$" x $1^1/2$" doweling pins (sometimes called gluing dowels). These pins (with spiral or fluted grooves and tapered ends) slide into the holes a little easier. After applying glue and driving all the pins to the bottom of the holes, I glued a $3/8$"-dia. redwood plug into each hole and cut the plugs off flush.

FINISHING

Before applying the finish, I slightly rounded all the exposed edges with 150-grit sandpaper to prevent splinters. Then I applied a shop-blended finish that was a 50/50 mix of spar varnish and a tung oil sealer. Three coats of this gave me the protection of a varnish with the light sheen of an oil finish. ■

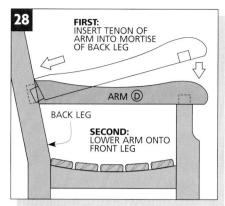

28 FIRST: INSERT TENON OF ARM INTO MORTISE OF BACK LEG
ARM (D)
BACK LEG
SECOND: LOWER ARM ONTO FRONT LEG

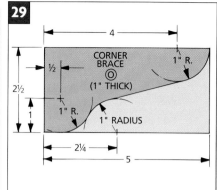

29 CORNER BRACE (O) (1" THICK)
4
1/2
2 1/2
1
1" R.
1" R.
1" RADIUS
2 1/4
5

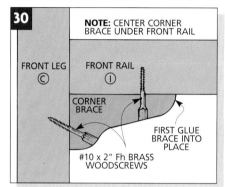

30 NOTE: CENTER CORNER BRACE UNDER FRONT RAIL
FRONT LEG (C)
FRONT RAIL (I)
CORNER BRACE
FIRST GLUE BRACE INTO PLACE
#10 x 2" Fh BRASS WOODSCREWS

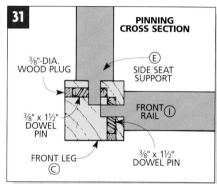

31 PINNING CROSS SECTION
$3/8$"-DIA. WOOD PLUG
(E) SIDE SEAT SUPPORT
$3/8$" x $1^1/2$" DOWEL PIN
FRONT RAIL (I)
FRONT LEG (C)
$3/8$" x $1^1/2$" DOWEL PIN

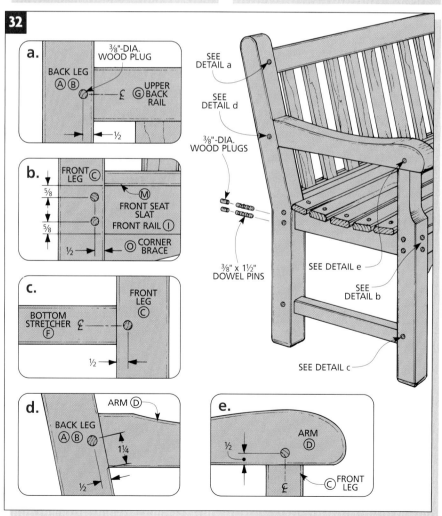

32

a. BACK LEG (A)(B)
$3/8$"-DIA. WOOD PLUG
(G) UPPER BACK RAIL
1/2

b. FRONT LEG (C)
5/8
5/8
(M) FRONT SEAT SLAT
FRONT RAIL (I)
(O) CORNER BRACE
1/2

c. FRONT LEG (C)
BOTTOM STRETCHER (F)
1/2

d. ARM (D)
BACK LEG (A)(B)
1 1/4
1/2

e. ARM (D)
1/2
(C) FRONT LEG

SEE DETAIL a
SEE DETAIL d
$3/8$"-DIA. WOOD PLUGS
$3/8$" x $1^1/2$" DOWEL PINS
SEE DETAIL e
SEE DETAIL b
SEE DETAIL c

DESIGNER'S NOTEBOOK

This armchair will fit nicely into a smaller space in your garden. It's also a perfect companion piece for the bench. They're built the same way — you just make a few pieces shorter.

CONSTRUCTION NOTES:

■ Most of the pieces for the armchair are identical to the Redwood Bench. Several pieces are simply cut to shorter lengths. The upper back rail (G), lower back rail (H), and front rail (I) are each cut 24" long (see drawing below).

■ The tenons on each of these pieces are the same as for the bench (refer to *Figs. 19 and 20* on page 44). The grooves in the upper and lower back rails (G, H) are also cut the same as for the bench (refer to *Fig. 21* on page 44).

■ The blank for the slat spacer strip (J) is cut to a length of 22" (see drawing below). Since there are only five back slats (K), five dadoes are cut in the spacer strip before ripping the strips from the blank.

■ The seat slats (L) are cut 27" long (see drawing below). The front seat slat (M) is cut to fit between the front legs (22").

■ The chair assembly is the same as for the bench. However, you won't need either of the center seat supports (N).

REDWOOD ARMCHAIR

MATERIALS LIST

CHANGED PARTS
G	Upper Back Rail (1)	$1\frac{1}{2} \times 2\frac{1}{2}$ - 24
H	Lower Back Rail (1)	$1\frac{1}{2} \times 3\frac{1}{2}$ - 24
I	Front Rail (1)	$1\frac{1}{2} \times 2\frac{1}{2}$ - 24
J	Slat Spacer Strip (1)	$\frac{3}{4} \times 1\frac{1}{2}$ - 22
K	Back Slats (5)	$\frac{1}{2} \times 2$ - 14 rough
L	Seat Slats (5)	$\frac{3}{4} \times 2\frac{1}{2}$ - 27
M	Front Seat Slat (1)	$\frac{3}{4} \times 2\frac{1}{2}$ - 22

Note: Do not need part N.

HARDWARE SUPPLIES
(12) No. 10 x 1¼" Fh brass woodscrews
(4) No. 10 x 2" Fh brass woodscrews
(12) ½"-dia. wood plugs
(26) ⅜"-dia. wood plugs
(26) ⅜" x 1½" dowel pins (or one ⅜"-dia. dowel x 48")

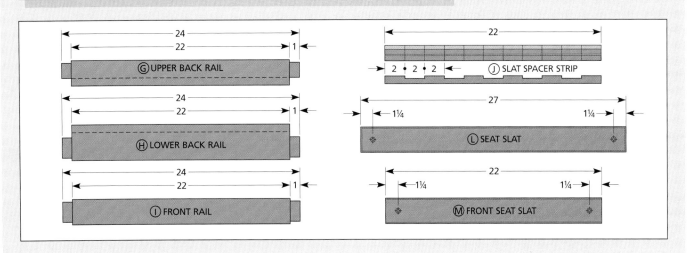

Even in the most temperate climates, projects that spend time outdoors need to be able to withstand moisture, sunlight, and changes in temperature and humidity. Any one of these elements is tough on joinery, wood, and the finish. Together, they can turn a new project into kindling.

The good news is that you can do quite a bit to make a project more durable. By selecting the best types of wood, glue, fasteners and finish, you can make sure it's ready to stand up to whatever Mother Nature has in store.

Note: For information on outdoor screws, refer to Shop Info on page 79.

WOOD

There are several types of wood that are suitable for outdoor projects.

REDWOOD. Probably the most common wood associated with outdoor furniture is redwood. It's soft and easy to work, although it tends to splinter. For details about different types of redwood, see the Shop Info box on page 35.

CEDAR. Another wood that stands up well outdoors is cedar. There are several species, but the two best suited for outdoor projects are incense cedar and Western red cedar. They're both soft and easy to work, but are fairly weak in strength and shock resistance. They have a strong resistance to decay.

TEAK. The Redwood Bench is similar to English benches traditionally made of teak. Teak is decay resistant, straight grained, very stable, and feels waxy. Because of it's natural resistance to moisture, it's the preferred wood for boat decks and hulls.

The biggest drawback to using teak is the price. Teak also contains silica, a very fine sand that dulls tools quickly. You should expect to spend some additional time sharpening blades and honing edges when working with teak.

MAHOGANY. Boatbuilders also use three types of mahogany: African (khaya), Phillipine (luaun), and genuine (Honduran). Genuine mahogany is the strongest and most decay resistant (and most expensive), but all three are acceptable for outdoor use.

African and genuine mahogany are close in appearance. Both vary from a pale to a dark reddish-brown and have similar textures. Phillipine mahogany is coarser and is not as dimensionally stable as the other two.

OAK. White oak was used by coopers to make barrels, casks and tubs. That's because it's more water resistant than red oak. However, one of the properties that made it perfect for barrels also works against it in outdoor furniture. The cooper wanted his barrels to swell shut when filled with liquid. And white

oak does just that. If you choose white oak, you should probably paint the project or use a spar varnish to keep it from absorbing moisture.

PRESSURE-TREATED. This type of lumber is readily available at most lumberyards. Its name comes from the process of saturating the wood with water-borne copper salts under extreme pressure.

Pressure-treated wood is likely to be the most affordable lumber for outdoor use, but one drawback is its color — usually light green or light brown. However, it can be easily painted or stained a darker color.

GLUES

Just as there are a number of types of lumber that work well outdoors, there are several outdoor adhesives you can choose from.

YELLOW AND WHITE. First, let's talk about glues that won't work well outside. These include traditional white, yellow, and hide glues. They simply aren't designed to stand up to moisture.

However, there are yellow glues that *are* formulated for exterior use. The label will tell you if it is.

PLASTIC RESIN. Readily available and reasonably priced, plastic resin is a very water resistant adhesive.

Ironically, it comes in a powder form that you'll have to mix with water before using (see photo at left). Once mixed to the consistency of frosting, the glue sets up quickly (from five to fifteen minutes). So for large assemblies with lots of parts, you'll need to work quickly.

EPOXY. Another glue that needs to be mixed before being used is epoxy (see photo below). It offers a very strong bond, is waterproof and won't shrink.

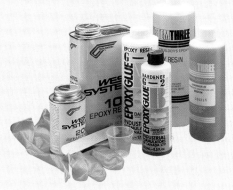

Epoxy works by mixing together two parts: a resin and a hardener. With epoxy systems, you can vary the curing time from ten minutes to an hour by using different hardeners.

You'll want to clean up any squeeze-out quickly. Once it dries, it's next to impossible to remove from the project without taking a chunk of wood with it.

POLYURETHANE. This type of glue is ready to use right out of the bottle. But there is an extra step in preparing the surfaces you want to join.

Since polyurethane glues cure by reacting with moisture in the wood, I

lightly mist one surface with a spray bottle, then apply the glue to the mating surface (see photo below left). The glue will also react with the moisture in your skin, so wear rubber gloves.

Another feature of this glue is that it expands as it cures (see photo below). This makes it great for filling less than perfect joints. But for this same reason, you don't want to apply too much glue. A plastic scraper helps spread the glue thinly and evenly. (The squeeze-out can be removed easily with a chisel.)

Poly glues also provide a long working time (20-30 minutes). That's

one reason I used it when assembling the large pieces of the Garden Arbor (pages 74-85).

CONSTRUCTION ADHESIVE. For outdoor durability (and price), construction adhesive is tough to beat. Although it's not a typical choice for furniture construction, I used it on the Adirondack Chair (pages 16-23) and the Adirondack Table (pages 24-28). It comes in tubes, can be found at most hardware stores, and is easy to apply with a caulking gun (see photo above). Just keep the adhesive well away from the joint line. As the parts are pressed together, the adhesive will spread out. If any squeezes out, let it dry overnight, then cut it off with a sharp chisel or utility knife.

FINISHES

When selecting an outdoor finish, you have to consider the level of protection it provides, the maintenance required to preserve the finish, and of course, the appearance of the finish.

OIL. The easiest finish to apply is a penetrating oil specially formulated for outdoor use. The oil penetrates the wood to provide protection.

Since the oil doesn't build up on the surface, it won't crack or peel. And it preserves the natural look and feel of the wood (see photo below).

Oil is a higher maintenance finish,

though. It will lose its sheen and ability to repel moisture after only a few months. Wiping on a fresh coat will renew the finish.

Note: Refer to the Finishing Tip on page 83 for details on using a stain, then applying an oil for a top coat.

SPAR VARNISH. For a more durable finish that preserves the natural beauty of the wood, spar varnish is a good choice (see photo below). Look for one that has ultra-violet (UV) filters. These filters absorb UV rays from the sun that would break down the finish.

While more durable than oil, you'll still need to refresh the finish with a fresh coat about once a year.

PAINT. By preventing moisture and sunlight from reaching the wood, paint is the best choice for preserving a piece (see photo below). Since it also hides the wood, you may not want to choose paint for a project made from an expensive species. Paint is also the most durable finish. If it's applied carefully, paint will protect the wood for several years. And of course, you have thousands of color choices.

Penetrating Oil. Even though it darkens the wood, the most natural-looking outdoor finish is an oil.

Spar Varnish. This finish is more durable than oil and also glossier. It will probably need an annual touch-up.

Paint. It hides the natural beauty of the wood, but also offers the best protection against the weather.

GARDEN ACCENTS

There's nothing quite like natural wood to complement a yard or garden. This section features projects that add the beauty of wood to your outdoor space, along with options to make each project uniquely yours.

The bird feeder and birdhouse are easy to customize to suit both you and the birds in your area. Redwood planters sitting on your deck or mounted below a window add greenery, even when garden space is limited. The arbor can serve as a grand garden entrance or, if built with a bench, a quiet retreat where you can enjoy a private moment.

Bird Feeder

The copper roof and cedar shingles may make this look like a difficult project. But a store-bought bag of shingles and a simple technique for wrapping the roof in copper make the Bird Feeder easy to build.

Several years ago, I helped a friend side his house with cedar shingles. The job took time, but it sure looked great when we were done.

SMALL SHINGLES. I remembered that look as I was browsing through a local hobby store. Hanging on a display rack were bags of scaled-down cedar shingles. (The package said they're meant for dollhouses.) It occurred to me that they would make an attractive siding for a bird feeder I'd been planning.

Fortunately, the cedar shingles I used on this bird feeder didn't take nearly as long to apply as the full-size versions on my friend's house.

COPPER ROOF. Another eye-catching feature of the bird feeder is the real copper roof. After spending some time

outdoors, the roof will take on the attractive green patina that's typical of aged copper.

Making the copper roof doesn't require any special metalworking equipment. The roof is actually made of plywood wrapped with a thin copper foil. The foil can be found at many hobby stores. Or you can order a hardware kit from *Woodsmith Project Supplies* that includes the shingles and the copper foil. See page 126 for more details about this.

OPTIONS. If you'd like a different look for the feeder, you can put square shingles on the roof instead of copper and make clapboard siding for the ends. Details for this version are found in the Designer's Notebook on page 59.

EASY FILLING. With most feeders, you lift the top to fill it with seed. But since I wanted to mount mine on a pole, that method wouldn't work very well. Instead, the roof stays attached to the top of the pole while the bottom drops down to allow you to pour in more seed (see inset photo). A pin through the pole holds the feeder at the proper height for filling. Once the feeder is full, a second hole higher on the pole accepts the pin to hold the feeder in place under the roof.

CEDAR. I used cedar for all of the solid wood portions of the feeder. Since the ends are covered with shingles, I used exterior-grade plywood there.

EXPLODED VIEW

OVERALL DIMENSIONS:
12W x 12D x 12½H

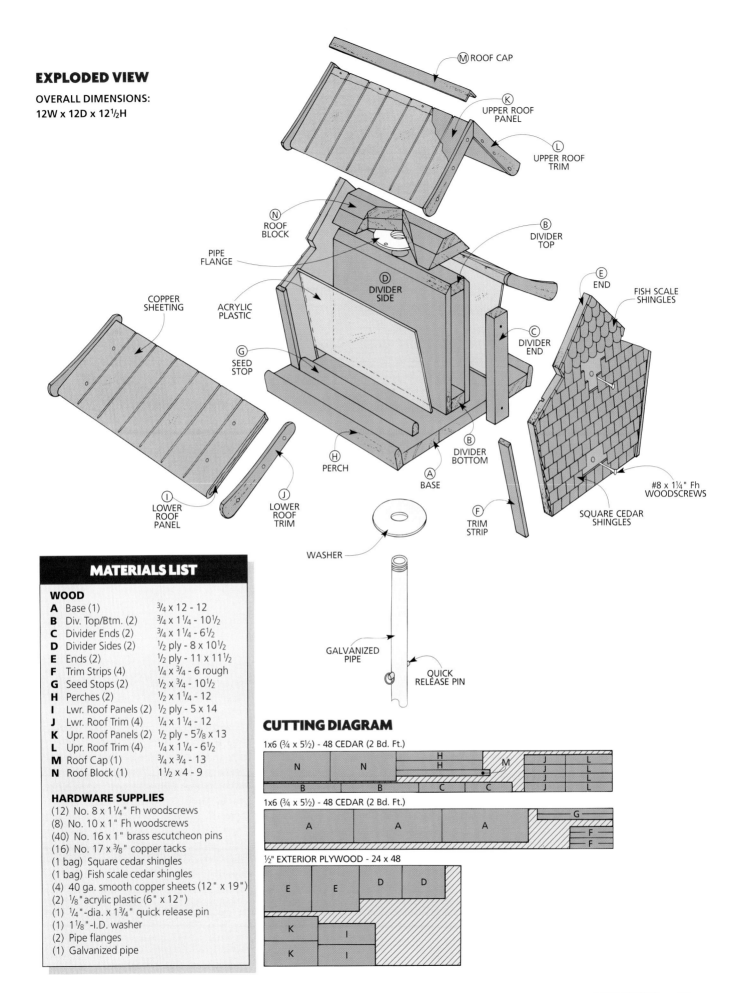

M ROOF CAP

K UPPER ROOF PANEL

L UPPER ROOF TRIM

N ROOF BLOCK

PIPE FLANGE

B DIVIDER TOP

E END

FISH SCALE SHINGLES

COPPER SHEETING

ACRYLIC PLASTIC

D DIVIDER SIDE

C DIVIDER END

G SEED STOP

B DIVIDER BOTTOM

H PERCH

A BASE

F TRIM STRIP

#8 x 1¼" Fh WOODSCREWS

SQUARE CEDAR SHINGLES

I LOWER ROOF PANEL

J LOWER ROOF TRIM

WASHER

GALVANIZED PIPE

QUICK RELEASE PIN

MATERIALS LIST

WOOD

A	Base (1)	¾ x 12 - 12
B	Div. Top/Btm. (2)	¾ x 1¼ - 10½
C	Divider Ends (2)	¾ x 1¼ - 6½
D	Divider Sides (2)	½ ply - 8 x 10½
E	Ends (2)	½ ply - 11 x 11½
F	Trim Strips (4)	¼ x ¾ - 6 rough
G	Seed Stops (2)	½ x ¾ - 10½
H	Perches (2)	½ x 1¼ - 12
I	Lwr. Roof Panels (2)	½ ply - 5 x 14
J	Lwr. Roof Trim (4)	¼ x 1¼ - 12
K	Upr. Roof Panels (2)	½ ply - 5⅞ x 13
L	Upr. Roof Trim (4)	¼ x 1¼ - 6½
M	Roof Cap (1)	¾ x ¾ - 13
N	Roof Block (1)	1½ x 4 - 9

HARDWARE SUPPLIES

(12) No. 8 x 1¼" Fh woodscrews
(8) No. 10 x 1" Fh woodscrews
(40) No. 16 x 1" brass escutcheon pins
(16) No. 17 x ⅜" copper tacks
(1 bag) Square cedar shingles
(1 bag) Fish scale cedar shingles
(4) 40 ga. smooth copper sheets (12" x 19")
(2) ⅛" acrylic plastic (6" x 12")
(1) ¼"-dia. x 1¾" quick release pin
(1) 1⅛"-I.D. washer
(2) Pipe flanges
(1) Galvanized pipe

CUTTING DIAGRAM

1x6 (¾ x 5½) - 48 CEDAR (2 Bd. Ft.)

1x6 (¾ x 5½) - 48 CEDAR (2 Bd. Ft.)

½" EXTERIOR PLYWOOD - 24 x 48

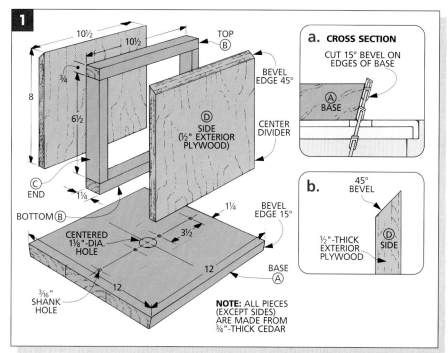

1

10½
10½
TOP
Ⓑ

¾

8

6½

SIDE
Ⓓ
(½" EXTERIOR
PLYWOOD)

BEVEL
EDGE 45°

CENTER
DIVIDER

Ⓒ
END

1¼

BOTTOM Ⓑ

1¼

BEVEL
EDGE 15°

CENTERED
1⅛"-DIA.
HOLE

3½

12

12

BASE
Ⓐ

³⁄₁₆"
SHANK
HOLE

NOTE: ALL PIECES
(EXCEPT SIDES)
ARE MADE FROM
¾"-THICK CEDAR

a. CROSS SECTION

CUT 15° BEVEL ON
EDGES OF BASE

Ⓐ
BASE

b.

45°
BEVEL

½"-THICK
EXTERIOR
PLYWOOD

Ⓓ
SIDE

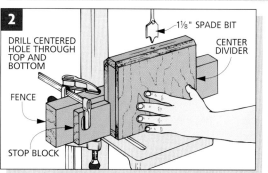

2

1⅛" SPADE BIT

DRILL CENTERED
HOLE THROUGH
TOP AND
BOTTOM

CENTER
DIVIDER

FENCE

STOP BLOCK

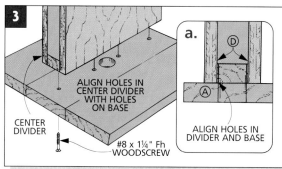

3

ALIGN HOLES IN
CENTER DIVIDER
WITH HOLES
ON BASE

CENTER
DIVIDER

#8 x 1¼" Fh
WOODSCREW

a.

Ⓓ

Ⓐ

ALIGN HOLES IN
DIVIDER AND BASE

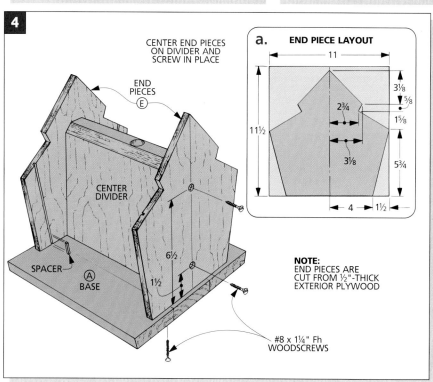

4

CENTER END PIECES
ON DIVIDER AND
SCREW IN PLACE

END
PIECES
Ⓔ

CENTER
DIVIDER

SPACER

Ⓐ
BASE

6½

1½

#8 x 1¼" Fh
WOODSCREWS

a. END PIECE LAYOUT

11

3⅛

⅝

2¾

1⅝

11½

3⅛

5¾

4

1½

NOTE:
END PIECES ARE
CUT FROM ½"-THICK
EXTERIOR PLYWOOD

BASE

I began work on the bird feeder by making a ¾"-thick base (A). This is just a glued-up 12"-square blank of cedar with beveled edges *(Figs. 1 and 1a)*.

Note: Since the feeder is going to be exposed to the weather, I used two types of water-resistant glue for assembly. For most of the bird feeder, I used an exterior-grade yellow glue. Epoxy will be used later when the shingles are attached.

After cutting the base to size, the next step is to drill a 1⅛"-dia. hole in the center for a support pipe. While I was at it, I also drilled the shank holes for attaching the center divider which is added next.

Note: Cedar splinters easily, so make sure you back up the base with a piece of scrap before drilling the holes.

CENTER DIVIDER. The center divider separates the feeder into two sections. (This lets me put different types of seed in each half.) It also provides a way to attach the sides of the feeder later. The divider consists of a top/bottom (B) and two ends (C) that are sandwiched between two sides (D).

Here again I used cedar, but only for the top, bottom, and ends. For the sides I used ½" exterior-grade plywood. And to make the opening wider so it's easier to fill the feeder, I beveled the top edges at a 45° angle *(Fig. 1b)*.

After gluing the center divider together, the next step is to drill centered holes for the support pipe to pass through *(Fig. 2)*. The only problem is the drill bit is shorter than the divider. So the holes have to be drilled from both the top and the bottom. To do this, I set up a fence and stop block on the drill press. After drilling through the top, flip the divider over and drill through the bottom. Keep the same end against the stop block or the holes may not align with each other.

DIVIDER INSTALLATION. After the holes have been drilled, the divider can be screwed to the base. Just be sure the divider is positioned square on the base and the holes in the divider and base align *(Figs. 3 and 3a)*. (An easy way to align the holes is to run a length of pipe through them.)

END PIECES. After attaching the divider to the base, work can begin on the end pieces. I started by cutting a blank for each end piece (E) from ¹⁄₂"-thick exterior-grade plywood *(Fig. 4a)*. After laying out the shape on one blank, I fastened both blanks together with carpet tape. Then I cut both pieces at once on the band saw (or you could use a jig saw). This ensured that both pieces were identical.

Before the end pieces can be attached to the divider, there are a couple of things to do. First, two shallow grooves are cut on the inside face of each end piece. These grooves will be used to hold the ¹⁄₈"-thick acrylic plastic panels that create each food compartment. It's easy to cut them on the table saw *(Figs. 5 and 5a)*.

Second, to hold the panels at the correct height for the seed to flow out I glued 1"-long spacers at the bottom of each groove *(Fig. 5b)*.

Once the spacers are in, center the end pieces (E) on the base (A) and clamp them in place. After drilling shank and pilot holes, secure the ends to the divider with screws *(Fig. 4)*.

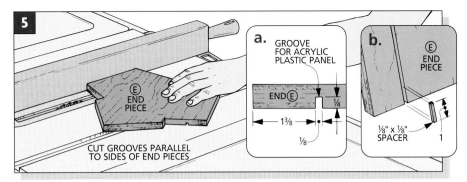

CUT GROOVES PARALLEL TO SIDES OF END PIECES

a. GROOVE FOR ACRYLIC PLASTIC PANEL

b. ⅛" x ⅛" SPACER

SHINGLES & TRIM

After attaching the end pieces, I added the shingles. I used two different styles of cedar dollhouse shingles for this project. The lower section has typical square-cut shingles. But I wanted something different for the gable area, so here I used fish scale (half-round) shingles *(Fig. 6)*. I found both types at a local hobby shop. They are also included in the hardware kit offered by *Woodsmith Project Supplies*. See page 126 for information. There are a few tricks that will help you align the shingles properly. The Shop Tip below shows you how.

TRIM STRIPS. Finally, to cover the exposed edges of the sides and shingles, I attached ¹⁄₄"-thick trim strips (F), using a water-resistant glue *(Fig. 6)*.

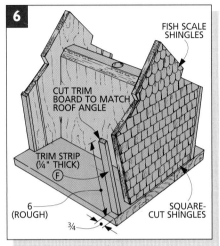

FISH SCALE SHINGLES

CUT TRIM BOARD TO MATCH ROOF ANGLE

TRIM STRIP (¼" THICK)

SQUARE-CUT SHINGLES

Since the angles make it tough to secure these pieces with clamps, I just held the strips in place with my hands until the glue became tacky.

SHOP TIP . . . . *Attaching Shingles*

The angled sides of the feeder posed a challenge when it came time to install the shingles. I couldn't use the slanted edges as vertical reference points. So I decided to lay the shingles by working outward from a vertical centerline *(see drawing)*.

I also marked layout lines to help maintain a ³⁄₄" spacing from the bottom of one course (row) to the bottom of the next *(see drawing)*. Once the lines are drawn, the bottom row of shingles can be glued in place.

Note: Because of its strength and gap-filling abilities, I used quick-set (5-minute) epoxy to attach the shingles.

With the first course complete, you can lay an overlapping second course. Work your

way up the side, one course at a time, overlapping each course as you go.

There are just a few tips to keep in mind. First, I found it easiest to let the end shingles hang over the edge, and then come back and trim them flush with a utility knife (see photo).

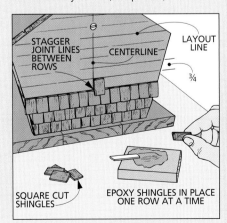

STAGGER JOINT LINES BETWEEN ROWS

CENTERLINE

LAYOUT LINE

SQUARE CUT SHINGLES

EPOXY SHINGLES IN PLACE ONE ROW AT A TIME

Second, the shingles look best if they're staggered between courses (just like real shingle siding). To do this, it's simply a matter of shifting each alternating course half a shingle's width from the course immediately below it.

Before starting work on the copper roofs of the feeder, there are a few things that need to be done.

First, to create the outer walls of the food compartments, I cut two pieces of acrylic plastic to fit in the grooves in the end pieces *(Figs. 7 and 7b)*.

SEED STOP. Next, to prevent bird seed from spilling out, I added a seed stop (G) to each side. To make these stops, I rounded over one edge of an oversize blank of $1/2$"-thick cedar. Then I ripped the blank to a finished width (height) of $3/4$" *(Fig. 7b)*. Finally, cut the seed stops to fit between the ends (F) of the feeder and glue them in place *(Figs. 7 and 7b)*.

PERCHES. The last pieces to add to the base are the perches (H). These $1^1/4$"-wide pieces are made the same way as the seed stops. Then they're trimmed to match the length of the base (12") and glued and nailed in place with brass escutcheon pins *(Figs. 7 and 7b)*.

LOWER ROOF

Now you can move on to one of the most eye-catching features of this feeder: the copper-covered roof panels. (For some tips on working with copper, see the Woodworker's Notebook on page 57.)

LOWER ROOF PANELS. I started with the lower roof panels (I) *(Fig. 7)*. These are $1/2$" plywood cut to a finished size of 5" x 14" with a roundover routed on one

edge *(Fig. 7a)*. Then, to create the look of "seams" in the roof, I cut six evenly-spaced kerfs in the top side of each piece *(Figs. 8 and 8a)*.

The copper foil that covers the roof is trimmed $1/4$" longer ($14^1/4$") than the roof panels. Then, after applying spray adhesive, I wrapped the copper around

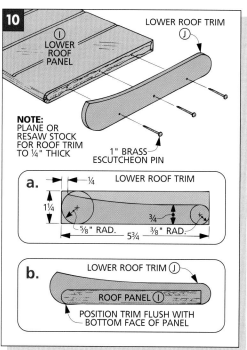

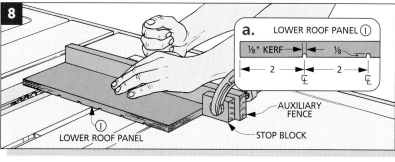

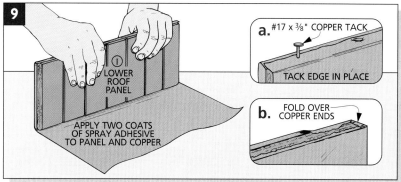

the roof starting at the top edge and tacked the foil in place with copper tacks *(Figs. 9 and 9a)*. Next, trim any excess and fold over the ends *(Fig. 9b)*. After the copper is fastened to the roof, lightly press the copper into the kerfs with a dowel to make the "seams" (see the photo below).

LOWER ROOF TRIM. To complete the panels, I added lower roof trim (J) to each end *(Fig. 10)*. These pieces are $1/4$"-thick cedar attached with epoxy and escutcheon pins flush to the bottom edge of each panel *(Fig. 10b)*.

Once the lower panels are complete, they're centered over the ends of the feeder and nailed in place.

UPPER ROOF

Like the lower roof, the upper roof is made up of two plywood panels. But this time, these pieces are glued together to form an L-shaped assembly. To do this, I started by cutting the upper roof panels (K) to finished size ($5^7/8$" x 13") with a 45° bevel on each top edge *(Figs. 11 and 11a)*. Then I routed a roundover along the other edge.

Since the upper roof panels are narrower than the lower roof panels, the outer kerfs are spaced a bit differently than those on the lower roof *(Fig. 11b)*. This is so the kerfs will line up between the upper and lower roof. Once these kerfs are cut, the two upper roof panels can be glued together.

COPPER. As with the lower roof, trim the copper $1/4$" longer ($13^1/4$") than the upper roof panels. After applying spray adhesive, I wrapped the upper roof,

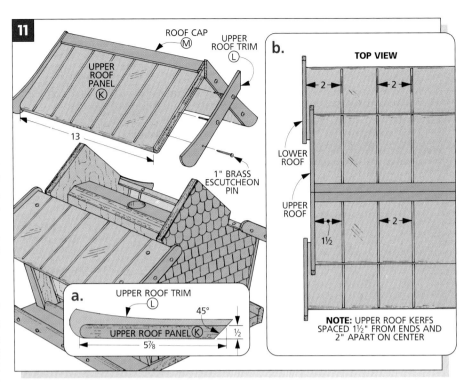

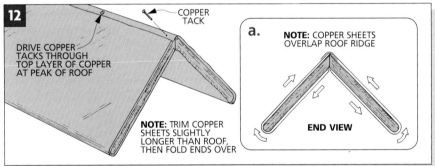

starting at the underside of the peak *(Fig. 12a)*. Wrap the first sheet of copper around one side until it overlaps the peak. Then, use a second piece to wrap the opposite side of the roof. Now tack the edge of the copper in place *(Fig. 12)*. Finally, create the decorative "seams" (see the photo below).

WOODWORKER'S NOTEBOOK

COPPER FOIL

The 40-gauge copper foil used on the bird feeder roof is about the same thickness as the heavy-duty aluminum foil you'd use in the kitchen. This makes it easy to bend, shape and cut it without specialized tools.

You can trim copper foil easily with a pair of scissors. And since it's so pliable, it can be fastened to a surface using just a spray adhesive. (I used two coats on each surface when attaching the copper to the bird

feeder roof.) Since the feeder would be out in the elements, I also used tacks to hold the copper in place.

Note: One thing to be aware of is that you shouldn't use steel brads or nails to secure any type of copper. The contact between the copper and steel forms a small electric current. This isn't dangerous to you (or to the birds), but it will eat away at the nail until it dissolves. Instead, use only copper or brass fasteners.

The grooves in the roof simulate the seams between copper panels on full-sized buildings. On the bird feeder, the "seams" are created by using a dowel to press the copper foil into the kerfs cut earlier in the roof panel.

UPPER ROOF TRIM. The next step is to attach the upper roof trim (L) *(Fig. 13)*. These pieces are constructed the same as those on the lower roofs except one end of each is mitered *(Fig. 13a)*. Then they're nailed and epoxied to the ends of the roof.

ROOF CAP. To cover the seam and tacks, I made a roof cap (M). It's a 3/4"-thick piece cut in an L-shape *(Fig. 13)*.

To do this, first use a table saw and dado blade to make a 5/8"-wide by 5/8"-deep rabbet on one edge of an oversized blank *(Fig. 13b)*. Then rip the roof cap free *(Fig. 13c)*. Now cut it to match the length of the roof ridge (13") and epoxy it in place.

MOUNTING

To refill this bird feeder, you don't remove the roof, as you might expect. Instead, the upper roof is mounted to the top of a support pipe that passes through the hole in the base of the feeder. When it's time to add more birdseed, all you have to do is drop the base of the feeder.

ROOF BLOCK. To attach the upper roof to the end of the pole, I made a roof block (N). This is just two 3/4"-thick pieces of cedar glued together and beveled on the edges to fit under the roof *(Fig. 14)*.

Then I screwed a pipe flange to the bottom of the roof block. This flange allows the roof to be screwed to the threaded end of the support pole.

Before attaching the roof block underneath the roof, I removed a portion of the copper foil with a utility knife *(Fig. 14b)*. Then I glued the block to the roof with epoxy, making sure that the block was centered.

SUPPORT POLE. To assemble the feeder, simply slip a piece of pipe through the hole in the base of the feeder. (I used a 6'-long, 3/4"-I.D. galvanized pipe.) Then screw the pipe into the flange on the upper roof.

Note: Ask to have the pipe threaded at both ends when you purchase it.

The feeder itself is held up with a washer and removable locking pin inserted through a hole drilled in the pipe. To locate the position for drilling the hole, hold the feeder up against the roof *(Fig. 14)*. A second hole drilled below the first allows you to reposition the pin and drop the feeder down to refill it with birdseed.

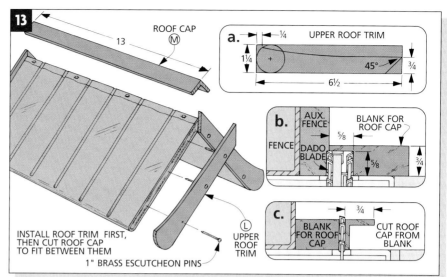

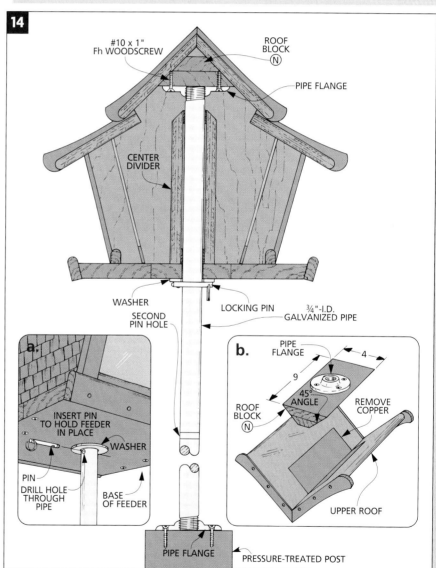

To mount the pole, I screwed a second pipe flange onto the end of a short, pressure-treated post. I mounted the post in a hole with ready-mix concrete, and then screwed the pole into the flange *(Fig. 14)*.

DESIGNER'S NOTEBOOK

Just a few cosmetic changes give this version of the Bird Feeder a different look. It's built the same as the original, except that strips of siding are used on the ends and square shingles are used on the roof.

CONSTRUCTION NOTES:

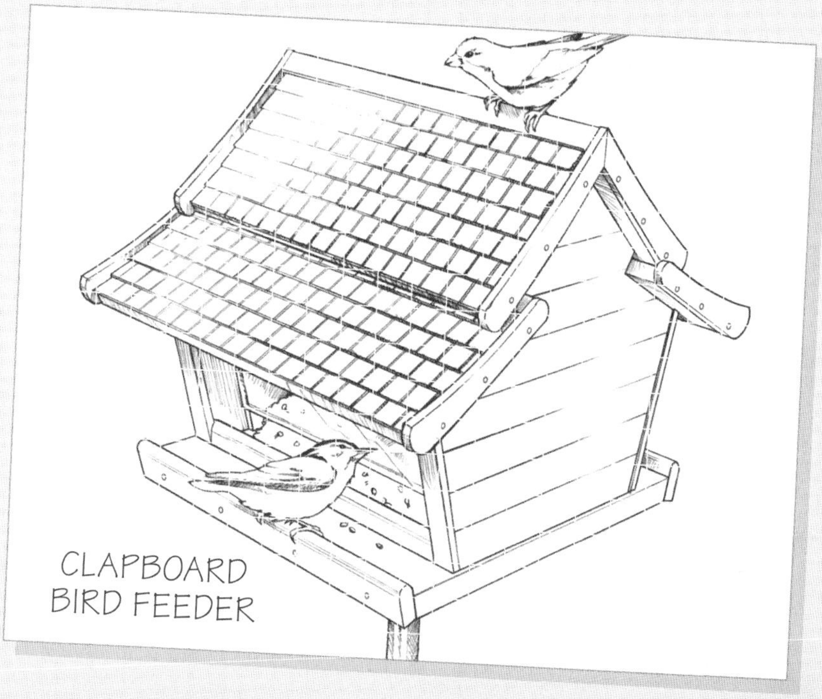

CLAPBOARD
BIRD FEEDER

- For this variation of the Bird Feeder, construction is the same until it's time to apply the siding on the ends.
- After the end pieces (E) have been fastened to the divider, cut the siding strips (O) *(Fig. 1)*.
- The clapboard siding is butted edge to edge *(Fig. 1)*. Start by gluing the bottom strip in place, leaving an overhang on each end. Then butt the next strip in place. As you work up to the narrower top portion, cut one long strip to make two shorter siding strips.
- Once the glue has dried on the siding, trim them flush with the edge of the end pieces. Then attach the trim strips (F).
- The roof panels (I, K) are cut slightly narrower to allow for a fascia strip added later and the overhang of the shingles *(Fig. 2)*. You won't need to cut the decorative kerfs.
- A fascia strip (P, Q) is attached to each roof panel to hide the plywood edge *(Fig. 2)*. These 1/4"-thick strips are wider than the thickness of the plywood and have a 5° bevel cut on one edge *(Fig. 2a)*. This raises the bottom row of shingles slightly.
- Glue the fascia flush with the bottom edge of the roof panels *(Fig. 2)*.
- Lay out and fasten the shingles to the roof the same way you would have for the siding on the regular Bird Feeder. The bottom row should begin 7/8" from the outside face of the fascia *(Fig. 3)*. Space the remaining courses 3/4" apart.
- Now cut the upper roof trim (L) to length (6 1/4") and glue it in place *(Fig. 2)*.

1

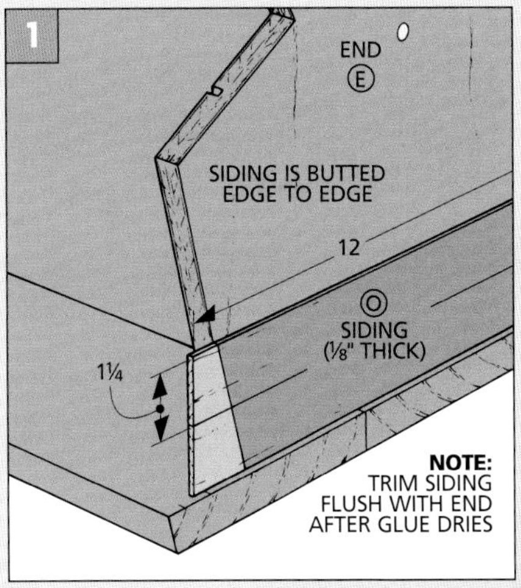

END
E
SIDING IS BUTTED EDGE TO EDGE
12
O
SIDING (1/8" THICK)
1 1/4
NOTE: TRIM SIDING FLUSH WITH END AFTER GLUE DRIES

MATERIALS LIST

CHANGED PARTS

I	Lower Roof Panels (2)	1/2 ply - 4 1/2 x 14
K	Upper Roof Panels (2)	1/2 ply - 5 1/8 x 13
L	Upper Roof Trim (4)	1/4 x 5/8 - 6 1/4

NEW PARTS

O	Siding (14)	1/8 x 1 1/4 - 12
P	Lower Fascia (2)	1/4 x 9/16 - 14
Q	Upper Fascia (2)	1/4 x 9/16 - 13

HARDWARE SUPPLIES

(1) additional bag of square cedar shingles. Do not need copper sheets, copper tacks, or fish scale cedar shingles

2

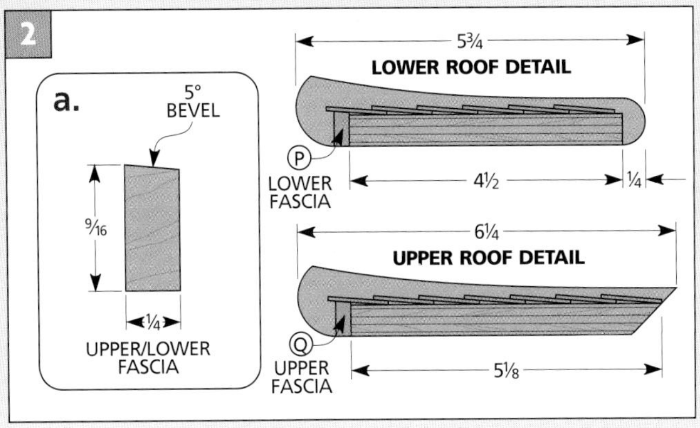

a.
5° BEVEL
9/16
1/4
UPPER/LOWER FASCIA
5 3/4
LOWER ROOF DETAIL
P
LOWER FASCIA
4 1/2
1/4
6 1/4
UPPER ROOF DETAIL
Q
UPPER FASCIA
5 1/8

3

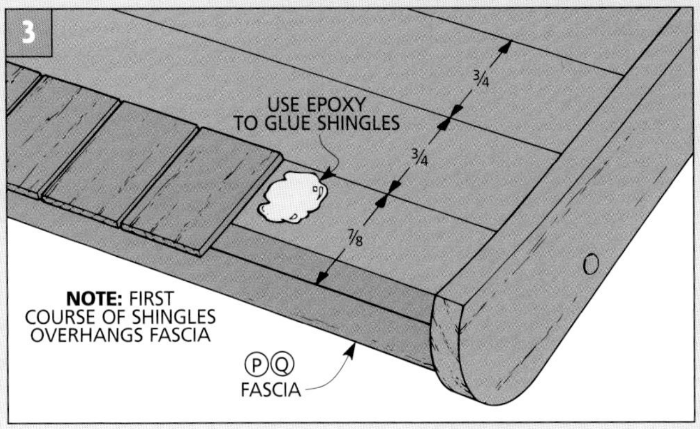

3/4
USE EPOXY TO GLUE SHINGLES
3/4
7/8
NOTE: FIRST COURSE OF SHINGLES OVERHANGS FASCIA
P Q
FASCIA

Redwood Planter

It's easy to customize the size of this planter to fit wherever you want it. And the decorative, extended box joints — pinned together, not glued — are simple to make with the help of a shop-made jig.

Around the first of the year, a flood of garden and flower catalogs begins to fill my mailbox. Just like the woodworking catalogs I receive, I enjoy looking through them to get ideas. But this time, the idea that came to mind got me into the shop, not the garden. What better way to display my newly planted flowers than in an attractive wooden planter box?

LINER. The problem with most planters is that the bottom rots out from the moisture in the soil. To solve this, I made a redwood box that fits around a plastic liner. This box holds the liner securely and hides it at the same time.

Plastic liners can be found in a variety of sizes in home centers and discount stores, so you can build a planter to fit just about any location. When you're choosing a liner, make sure that it has a sturdy lip along the edge because the lip supports the weight of the soil and plants as it rests on the top edge of the planter.

FEATURES. Instead of building a plain box, I dressed up the corners by using box joints with extended pins. Making the pins a little longer draws attention to them. The pins are chamfered, too. A simple jig makes it easy to cut the box joints and the chamfers.

I also built a small base for the planter. This lifts it enough to allow you to get your fingers under the planter if you need to move it.

PINNED JOINT. One detail you can't see is how the box joints are held together. Instead of gluing them, I drilled holes and pinned them with short lengths of dowel from the top and bottom of each corner.

OPTIONS. This planter works two ways. It can sit on a deck as shown above or, supported by a pair of brackets, it can hang on a wall. Details for a wall-mounted box are in the Designer's Notebook on page 63.

EXPLODED VIEW

OVERALL DIMENSIONS:
$30^5/_8$W x 8D x $6^7/_8$H

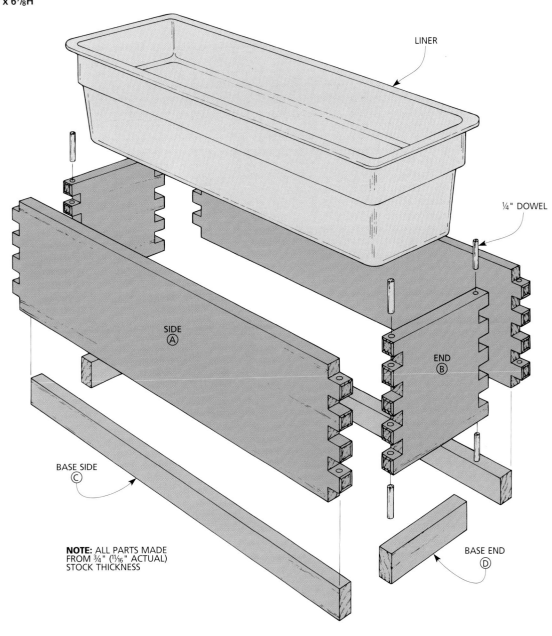

LINER

¼" DOWEL

SIDE
Ⓐ

END
Ⓑ

BASE SIDE
©

BASE END
Ⓓ

NOTE: ALL PARTS MADE
FROM ¾" (¹¹⁄₁₆" ACTUAL)
STOCK THICKNESS

MATERIALS LIST

WOOD
A	Sides (2)	¾ x 7¼ - 30⅝*
B	Ends (2)	¾ x 7¼ - 8*
C	Base Sides (2)	¾ x 1½ - 29⅛**
D	Base Ends (2)	¾ x 1½ - 5**

*Cut to fit your liner.
**Cut to fit inside dimensions of planter.

HARDWARE SUPPLIES
(1) ¼" dowel, 24" long

CUTTING DIAGRAM

1x8 (¾ x 7¼) - 84 (4.7 Bd. Ft.)

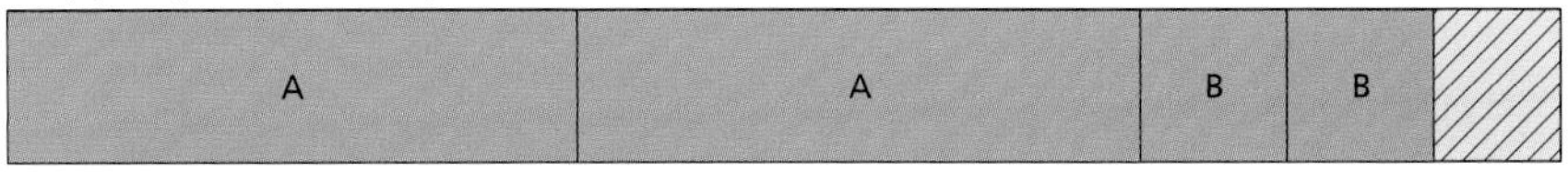

A	A	B	B	

1x4 (¾ x 3½) - 36 (1.3 Bd. Ft.)

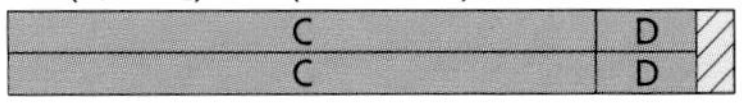

C	D
C	D

To build this planter, you simply make a bottomless box to fit around a plastic liner. But since liners come in various sizes, it's a good idea to have the liner before you start to build.

SIDES AND ENDS. With the liner in hand you'll need to take a few measurements to determine the dimensions of the sides (A) and ends (B). First, they have to be tall enough to cover the liner. (My liner was $5\frac{1}{2}$" deep. So my pieces were cut from a 1x8 piece of redwood.) They are trimmed to final width after the box joints are cut.

But determining the length of the pieces isn't quite as easy. You have to work from the inside out. First, measure the length of the liner just underneath the lip (refer to *Fig. 4*). Then add in a little extra for clearance (about $\frac{1}{8}$") so you can lift the liner in and out.

Next add the length of the box joint at each end ($\frac{13}{16}$"). For the $28\frac{7}{8}$"-long liner I used, my sides were $30\frac{5}{8}$" and the ends were 8" long.

Now the box joints can be cut. (For an easy-to-make box joint jig and instructions on cutting the joint, refer to page 64.) The goal is to end up with either a full slot or pin along each edge of the workpiece. To do that, I cut all my workpieces extra-wide, then used the table saw to trim the waste from the sides and ends *(Fig. 1)*. My pieces ended up $6\frac{3}{16}$" high (wide).

CHAMFER PINS. Then, to complete the box joints, I added a decorative $\frac{1}{16}$" chamfer to the ends of the pins. What's a little unusual is how you cut the chamfer on the inside of the pins. I used the box joint jig.

All you need to do is tilt the saw blade to 45° and reposition the jig so the blade just trims the edge of the pin *(Figs. 2 and 2a)*. Then lower the blade so it doesn't cut into the socket of the joint.

Now, trim one side of each pin, then flip the workpiece around to chamfer the opposite side. To chamfer the outside edges, remove the box joint jig and use the rip fence to guide the workpiece past the blade *(Figs. 3 and 3a)*.

ASSEMBLY. With the pins chamfered, the box can be assembled. But rather than glue the joints and have to clean up squeeze-out around the protruding pins, I secured the joints with $\frac{1}{4}$" dowel pins (refer to the Exploded View on page 61 and the Shop Tip at right).

You have a couple of options for displaying the planter. It can hang on brackets under a window (at rear in photo) or it can sit on a surface such as a porch or a wide railing (in the foreground). In fact, it's easy to build a set. Once you're set up to cut the box joints, it doesn't take much more time to cut the pieces needed to build one or two additional planters.

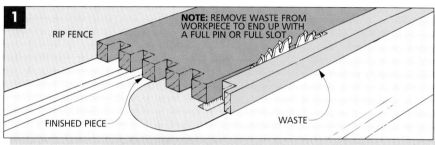

1   RIP FENCE   **NOTE:** REMOVE WASTE FROM WORKPIECE TO END UP WITH A FULL PIN OR FULL SLOT   FINISHED PIECE   WASTE

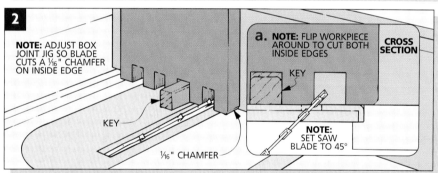

2   **NOTE:** ADJUST BOX JOINT JIG SO BLADE CUTS A $\frac{1}{16}$" CHAMFER ON INSIDE EDGE   KEY $\frac{1}{16}$" CHAMFER   **a. NOTE:** FLIP WORKPIECE AROUND TO CUT BOTH INSIDE EDGES   **CROSS SECTION**   KEY   **NOTE:** SET SAW BLADE TO 45°

SHOP TIP . . . . *Pinning Box Joints*

Instead of gluing box joints, you can secure them with a dowel pin through each corner.

To do this, simply drill a hole from the top and bottom at all four corners and insert a length of dowel. You don't need to drill all the way through the joint, just deep enough to allow each dowel to capture a pin from the mating side (see drawing).

Cut each dowel a little longer than the depth of the hole. Once the dowels are tapped in, trim them with a chisel, and sand them flush.

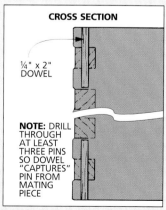

CROSS SECTION

$\frac{1}{4}$" x 2" DOWEL

NOTE: DRILL THROUGH AT LEAST THREE PINS SO DOWEL "CAPTURES" PIN FROM MATING PIECE

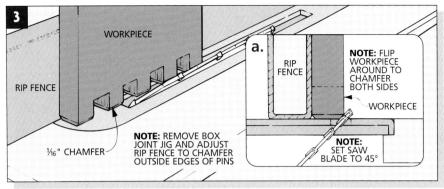

NOTE: REMOVE BOX JOINT JIG AND ADJUST RIP FENCE TO CHAMFER OUTSIDE EDGES OF PINS

1/16" CHAMFER

WORKPIECE

RIP FENCE

a.

RIP FENCE

NOTE: FLIP WORKPIECE AROUND TO CHAMFER BOTH SIDES

WORKPIECE

NOTE: SET SAW BLADE TO 45°

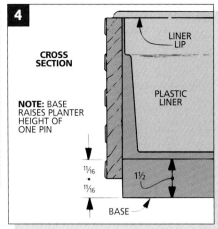

CROSS SECTION

NOTE: BASE RAISES PLANTER HEIGHT OF ONE PIN

LINER LIP

PLASTIC LINER

11/16

11/16

1 1/2

BASE

BASE

At this point the "box" of the planter is complete, but the project isn't. If you want the planter to sit on a deck, you need to add a base. It raises the planter up and makes it easier to grasp.

Note: If you intend to hang the planter on a wall or railing, you won't need the base. See the Designer's Notebook below for instructions on building brackets to hang the planter.

BASE. The base is just four pieces of redwood — two base sides (C) and two base ends (D) — cut to fit inside the box *(Fig. 4)*. I cut the sides to fit the inside length of the box. Then the ends are cut to fit between the base sides.

Once the pieces were cut to size, I turned the planter upside down to make it easier to clamp and glue the base pieces in place.

Note: Allow about ¹¹/₁₆" of the base to extend below the box *(Fig. 4)*. This matches the pin width. To help position the base pieces, I cut an ¹¹/₁₆"-wide spacer from scrap. ∎

DESIGNER'S NOTEBOOK

Turn your planter into a window box by mounting it to a wall with a pair of these simple brackets.

CONSTRUCTION NOTES:

∎ Each bracket consists of two pieces: a mounting board and a support. Two brackets will be needed to attach the planter to a wall. (If your planter is over 24" long, you may want to consider using a third bracket.)

∎ The mounting board (E) is a 1½" x 12¼" piece of redwood with four holes drilled in it (see drawing). The top two holes are countersunk from the front. The bottom two holes are countersunk from the back.

∎ Attached to each mounting board is an arch shaped support (F). A notch is cut on each top corner to keep the box from sliding off (see detail 'a'). The distance between the notches should match the inside width of your box. (Mine was 6³⁄₈".)

∎ Once the notches are cut, draw the arch onto the support (detail 'a' in drawing). Use the band saw or a jig saw to cut the arch, staying ¹/₁₆" outside the line. Then sand up to the line.

∎ To complete the bracket, rout ¹/₈" chamfers on the outside edges of the arched support and the mounting board. Then glue and screw the support to the mounting board (see drawing).

∎ When screwing the brackets to a wall, position them so they will sit in from each end of the box. To support the weight of the dirt, planter, and plants, screw the brackets into studs and make sure they are level with each other. Then set the planter in place.

HANGING BRACKETS

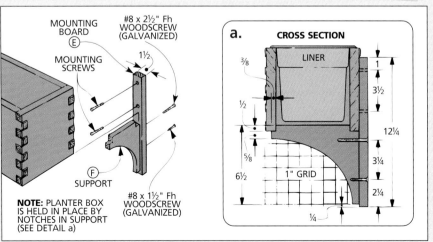

MOUNTING BOARD
(E)

MOUNTING SCREWS

#8 x 2½" Fh WOODSCREW (GALVANIZED)

1½

(F) SUPPORT

NOTE: PLANTER BOX IS HELD IN PLACE BY NOTCHES IN SUPPORT (SEE DETAIL a)

#8 x 1½" Fh WOODSCREW (GALVANIZED)

a.

CROSS SECTION

LINER

3/8

1/2

5/8

6½

1

3½

12¼

3¼

2¼

1" GRID

1/4

The box joint is often thought of as the poor cousin of the dovetail. That's unfortunate because it's really quite handsome as well as being strong.

Once this joint is cut (if it's cut well) it takes only a little glue to make an extremely strong bond. That makes it particularly nice for boxes like the Redwood Planter on pages 60-63. It's also a good choice for drawers.

WHAT YOU NEED

There are just two things needed to cut a box joint. The first is a simple jig that attaches to the miter gauge of your table saw. It's a piece of ³/₄" plywood (or MDF) with a notch for a hardwood key *(Steps 1 and 4)*. The jig is easy to make, but you do have to be precise when you attach it to the miter gauge. I'll explain all this a bit later.

The second requirement is a dado blade that cuts flat-bottomed dadoes. (Wobble blades, for example, don't.) This will give you a tight fit between the pins and the bottom of the slots.

LAYING OUT THE JOINT

Before making the jig, some thought must be given to the final appearance of the joint. The pins and slots can be any width your dado blade will cut. The joint of the Redwood Planter shown in the photo has "square" pins. This means the width of each pin and slot is the same as the thickness of the stock. (The pin looks square when viewed from the end of the board.)

WIDTH. The width of the workpieces must also be determined. The ideal situation is a workpiece that's an odd multiple of the height of each pin, plus some extra for trim. (For example, 9 x ¹¹/₁₆", plus ¹/₄" extra.) This odd multiple gives a joint with a pin at the top and bottom. If it's an even multiple, there'll be a pin on top and a slot on the bottom, and the joint will look unbalanced.

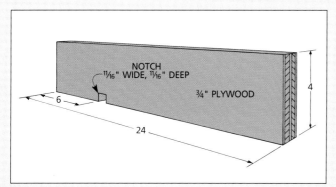

1 To make a simple box joint jig, cut a piece of ³/₄"-thick ply-wood or MDF to size. Then clamp it to your miter gauge and cut a notch about 6" from one end. The notch should be exactly as wide as the box joint pins (¹¹/₁₆" for the planter), but can be about ¹/₈" shorter in height.

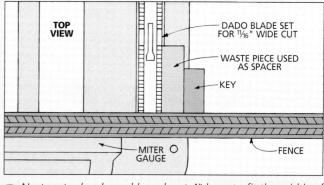

2 Next, cut a hardwood key about 4" long to fit the width of the notch. Cut a length of waste from the key to use as a spacer. Then glue the key into the notch. To position the jig, place the waste piece between the key and the dado blade. Clamp the fence to the miter gauge.

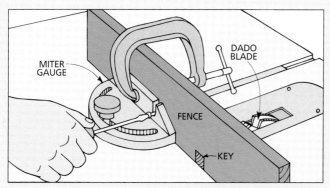

3 The miter gauge should have slots or holes for attaching the fence. If not, bore ¹/₄"-dia. holes. (These oversize holes allow adjustments later.) Then mark the positions for pilot holes on the back of the fence. Remove the fence, drill the pilot holes, then attach the fence to the miter gauge with roundhead screws.

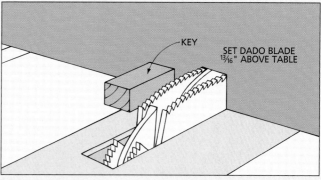

4 To check alignment of the fence, just barely nick the front edge of the fence. The width of the key, width of the nick and the distance between the two should all be exactly the same. Since the workpieces are ¹¹/₁₆" thick, I made the cut ¹³/₁₆" high so that the pins extend past the mating piece.

The "little extra" allows for some "fudge factor" when cutting the joint. For example, if you're cutting a joint with five pins (and four slots), and each slot and pin is just $1/64$" too wide, the cumulative error is over $1/8$". With some extra width, you can trim the workpiece after the joint is cut so the last pin or slot matches the width of the others.

MAKING THE JIG

The jig is easy to make. I used $3/4$" plywood for the fence *(Step 1)*. A small piece of hardwood is needed for the key.

DADO BLADE. Once the fence is cut to size, I set up my dado blade to match the width of the pin I need. (For the planter, this is $11/16$".) Next, cut a notch to hold the key about 6" from the end of the fence. This notch is a little shallower than the length of the pins. (I cut an $11/16$"-deep notch for the $13/16$"-long pins on the planter.) This way, the notches won't "bottom out" when they're placed over the key (refer to *Step 6*).

KEY. Now a hardwood key is cut to fit this notch. Accuracy here is essential. The key must be *exactly* as wide as the notch. It may take several attempts to get it right, but this will save many headaches later.

The key is about $1\frac{1}{2}$" long, but make it a couple of inches longer so you can cut off a small waste piece to use later when aligning the jig. Then glue the key into the notch.

MOUNTING. Now, mount the jig to the miter gauge. First, position the jig as shown in *Step 2*, using the waste section of the key as a spacer. Clamp the jig to the miter gauge, and mark the locations of pilot holes for the screws. Remove the jig, drill the holes, and then screw it to the miter gauge *(Step 3)*.

To double-check the jig alignment, just nick the bottom edge of the jig. Carefully check the spacing. The space between the key and the nick should be exactly the same as the width of the key, and the width of the nick. If not, adjust the jig left or right as needed.

Making the pins slightly long (as shown in the photo) is easy. Use a workpiece as a gauge by laying it next to the dado blade. Then adjust the blade $1/8$" higher than the thickness of the stock. Now you're ready to cut the joint.

FIRST BOARD. To start, position one board against the key *(Step 5)*. This board will have a full pin on the top edge. Make the first cut, then place the notch you just cut over the key. Now make a series of cuts the same way, leaving the last pin a little wide *(Step 6)*.

SECOND BOARD. The first cut on the second board will be a notch. I've found the best way to align this cut is to use the first board as a spacer.

Simply flip the first board around so the first pin is between the key and the second board. Push the second board against it and make the cut *(Step 7)*. Now cut notches across the board. When you're finished, trim both boards to final width *(Step 8)*.

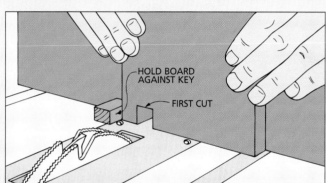

5 Before making cuts on your workpieces, you should cut a test joint with two scraps the same thickness as your workpieces. To make the first cut, slide the board up against the key. Hold the workpiece firmly against the jig, then push the jig through the dado blade.

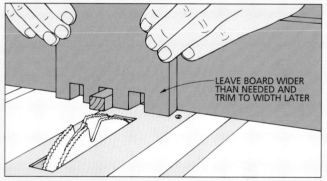

6 After the first cut, lift the board and place the notch over the key. Then just keep cutting and moving the new notch over the key. The board should be cut wider than needed (exaggerated in drawing). Leave the last pin a little wide. The boards will be trimmed to final width later.

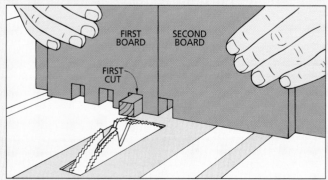

7 Now you can start cutting the joint on the mating piece. Use the first pin in the first board to align the second board. Hold the second board firmly against the first, then make a cut. Then set the first board aside, slide the notch in the second board over the key and cut a series of notches across the end.

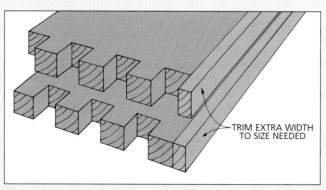

8 All that remains is to trim the waste off both boards. The two boards should now have perfectly matched box joints. If the fingers are too wide (joint won't slide together), adjust the jig so the key is closer to the blade. If the joint is loose, move the key away from the blade slightly.

Birdhouse

A simple, yet ingenious rolling technique makes this cylindrical birdhouse easy to build — even without a lathe. And whether you want to attract birds or just attention, there are lots of ways to customize it.

When you first look at this birdhouse, you might think it's a turning project. How else but on a lathe could you make a cylinder? Well believe it or not, you don't need a lathe to build this project. Instead, the cylinder is assembled from a number of narrow vertical strips. Each strip is beveled on both sides. Then the strips are laid side-by-side and "rolled" into a circle. Don't worry though — it's not a complicated process. I'll take you through it a little later.

There are also circular pieces at the top and bottom of the birdhouse. Cutting these pieces is easy with the help of a simple jig for the band saw.

OPTIONS. Aside from the shape of the birdhouse, one of the neat things about this project is all of the customizing options that are available. Whether you're building a birdhouse to actually shelter the birds or simply for display, choose the features you prefer.

Take the roof, for example. I built one birdhouse with a galvanized sheet metal roof (see main photo) and another with a copper roof (see inset photo). Either way, you'll get to try something a little bit different — working with sheet metal. And you won't need any special equipment other than a pair of tin snips and some gloves.

But the roof isn't the only option. You can build the birdhouse to hang from a tree (main photo) or to mount on a pole (inset photo). Selecting different stain combinations is another way to give your house a custom look. And if the birdhouse is meant more for display than use, you might even want to add a decorative perch (inset photo).

WOOD SELECTION. When it comes to choosing a wood, pick something that is decay-resistant, like redwood or cedar. But don't use pressure-treated lumber. It contains arsenic, which is poisonous to birds, just as it is to humans. Also be sure to use an exterior glue. (Refer to the Shop Info article on page 48.)

FOR THE BIRDS. Before you start building your birdhouse, it's helpful to consider the type of birds that you want to attract. Different birds prefer different housing arrangements. The Woodworker's Notebook on page 69 should help you.

EXPLODED VIEW

OVERALL DIMENSIONS:
$8^3/_8$D x 14H

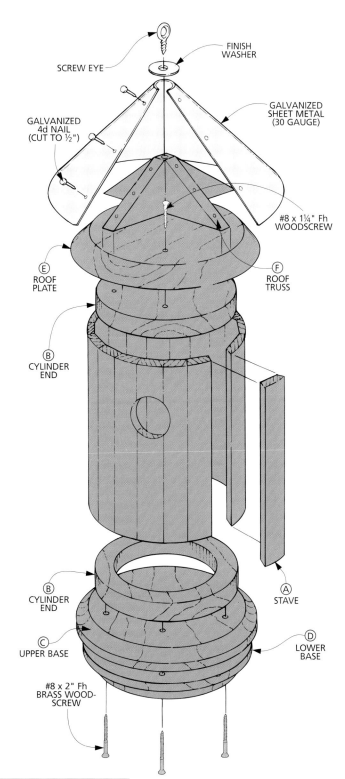

SCREW EYE

FINISH
WASHER

GALVANIZED
SHEET METAL
(30 GAUGE)

GALVANIZED
4d NAIL
(CUT TO ½")

#8 x 1¼" Fh
WOODSCREW

Ⓔ
ROOF
PLATE

Ⓕ
ROOF
TRUSS

Ⓑ
CYLINDER
END

Ⓐ
STAVE

Ⓑ
CYLINDER
END

Ⓒ
UPPER BASE

Ⓓ
LOWER
BASE

#8 x 2" Fh
BRASS WOOD-
SCREW

MATERIALS LIST

WOOD

A	Staves (20)	¼ x ⅞ - 7
B	Cylinder Ends (2)	¾ x 5 dia. rough
C	Upper Base (1)	¾ x 6½ dia.
D	Lower Base (1)	¾ x 5¾ dia.
E	Roof Plate (1)	¾ x 8 dia.
F	Roof Trusses (2)	½ x 3 - 6½

HARDWARE SUPPLIES

(4) No. 8 x 1¼" Fh woodscrews
(4) No. 8 x 2" Fh brass woodscrews
(1) 12" x 12" sheet metal (30-gauge
   galvanized or 26-gauge copper)
(14) 4d (1½") copper or galv. box nails
(1) 2½" stainless steel screw eye
(1) ¼" x 1" stainless steel finish washer

CUTTING DIAGRAM

¼ x 4 - 36 (1 Sq. Ft.)

¾ x 7½ - 48 (2.7 Bd. Ft.)

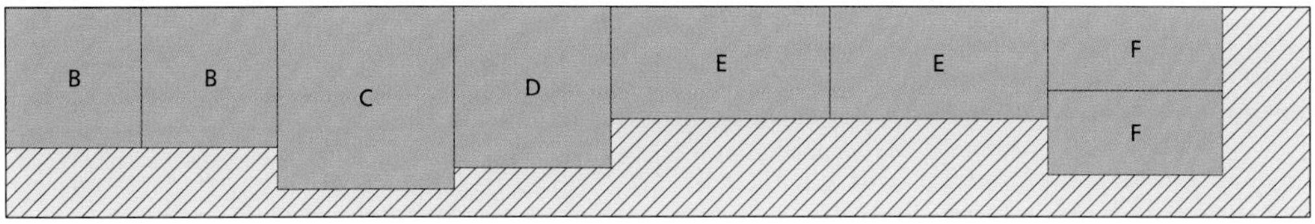

The construction of this birdhouse is pretty straightforward. The first step is to create a cylinder that will be the main portion of the house. This cylinder is probably the most challenging (and rewarding) part of this project. It's built using a technique known as stave construction. A number of staves, or slats, are beveled along their edges and glued together to create a cylinder.

STAVES. The staves (A) are only $1/4''$ thick. To build the birdhouse, you'll need twenty staves. I cut mine to final length but made them a bit wide ($1 1/4''$). This makes it easier to bevel the edges.

The trick with any stave construction project is determining the angle of the bevel and making sure all the bevels are consistent. For the birdhouse, there are twenty staves, each with two beveled sides. If you divide 40 into 360° you wind up with a 9° bevel. So all you have to do is tilt your saw blade 9° and rip both sides of each stave *(Fig. 1)*.

Once all the staves are cut to size and beveled, the next step is to assemble them into a cylinder. Because there are so many pieces, gluing them all together poses a bit of a problem. But there's a little trick to this. Start by laying the staves edge-to-edge on top of your bench (with the bevels facing down) *(Fig. 2)*. Then place two or three strips of masking tape across the staves to hold them together.

After turning the entire assembly over and applying glue to all the beveled edges, you can "roll" the staves into a cylinder, almost the same way you would roll up a sleeping bag.

The tape holds the staves together, but you still need a way to clamp them.

Fortunately, there's a simple solution (see the Shop Tip at right).

At this point, the thin-walled cylinder is a bit fragile and vulnerable. So to strengthen and support the walls, I made a couple of cylinder ends (B) that fit inside the cylinder. These pieces are simply round disks that will be glued into each end of the cylinder *(Fig. 5)*.

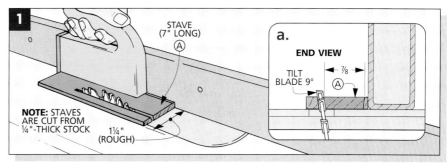

1 STAVE (7" LONG) Ⓐ

NOTE: STAVES ARE CUT FROM $1/4''$-THICK STOCK
$1 1/4''$ (ROUGH)

a. END VIEW
TILT BLADE 9° Ⓐ — $7/8$

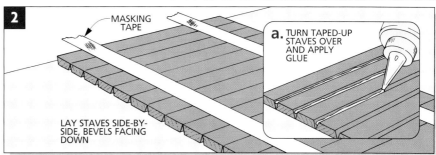

2 MASKING TAPE

LAY STAVES SIDE-BY-SIDE, BEVELS FACING DOWN

a. TURN TAPED-UP STAVES OVER AND APPLY GLUE

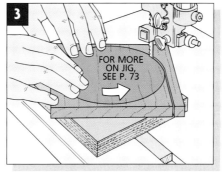

3 FOR MORE ON JIG, SEE P. 73

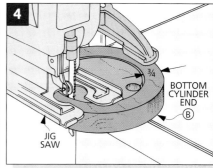

4 $3/4$ BOTTOM CYLINDER END Ⓑ
JIG SAW

FOR MORE ON JIG, SEE P. 73

5 NOTE: SEE CHART ON PAGE 69 FOR OPENING SIZE AND PLACEMENT

Ⓑ TOP CYLINDER END

NOTE: CYLINDER ENDS ARE $3/4''$ THICK

CENTER HOLE ON STAVE

VARIES

BOTTOM CYLINDER END Ⓑ

a. CROSS SECTION
Ⓑ
SIZE ENDS TO FIT IN CYLINDER
$3/4$
Ⓑ

SEE CHART ON PAGE 69 FOR OPENING SIZE AND PLACEMENT

SHOP TIP

Rubber Band Clamps

Regular band clamps are much too large and cumbersome to clamp up a small cylinder like the birdhouse. A good alternative is to secure the cylinder with a few rubber bands.

Note: The bottom cylinder end has a large hole to allow you to clean out the birdhouse after the birds leave.

CIRCLE-CUTTING JIG. To cut the round disks for the cylinder end, I made a special circle-cutting jig for the band saw. It's easy to make and will be used later to make other parts of this birdhouse. To find out how the jig is made and used, turn to page 73.

The disks are cut to rough shape using the jig (*Fig. 3*). After this, they're sanded on a disc sander until they just fit inside the opening of the cylinder. Then a jig saw or coping saw can be used to cut out the center of the bottom cylinder end (*Fig. 4*). The cylinder ends are simply glued in place inside the cylinder, flush with the ends (*Fig. 5a*).

OPENING. The next step is to drill the hole that will serve as the entrance for the birds. After selecting an opening size from the chart below, you can drill the hole using a hole saw and a drill press. I clamped a piece of scrap to my drill press table to serve as a stop block and to help hold the cylinder in place during this procedure (*Fig. 6*).

SMOOTH OUT THE CYLINDER. With the hole drilled, you can smooth out the sides of the cylinder. I did this by using a block plane to knock down the peaks of the staves (*Fig. 7*). Then all it takes is a little sanding to make the cylinder smooth and round.

BASE

The base of the birdhouse is made up of two pieces — an upper base (C) and a lower base (D). These are just two round pieces of stock with a cove routed around one edge of each piece (*Figs. 8a and 8b*). Here again, the circle-cutting jig makes quick work of cutting out these pieces.

Before screwing the base pieces to the birdhouse, you'll need to decide how you want to mount the birdhouse. If you're going to mount it on a post, you'll need to drill a hole in the lower base (D) to accept the post. (See the Designer's Notebook on page 72 for more on this.) Then the two base pieces can be glued together and screwed to the birdhouse. It's important that you don't glue the base to the birdhouse, however. Each year, after the birds fly south for the winter, you want to be able to remove the base in order to clean out the old nesting material.

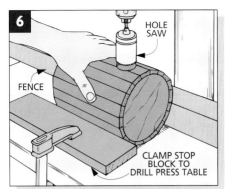

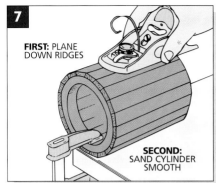

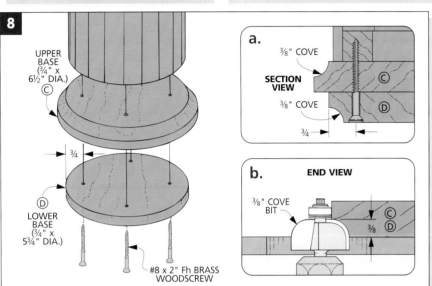

WOODWORKER'S NOTEBOOK
OPENINGS FOR BIRDS

If you want to attract a certain type of bird and keep out the "riff-raff," you'll do well to pay attention to the size of the entry hole and its height above the floor. Make the hole too small, and the birds you want to attract will have a difficult time getting into the house. If you make the hole too large, the young birds inside can fall prey to predators.

To help you out, the chart below lists some common birds and the recommended hole size and height to use with each one.

SPECIES OF BIRD	DIA. OF ENTRANCE	HEIGHT OF ENTRANCE FROM FLOOR
Bluebird	1½"	6"
Chickadee	1⅛"	8"
Tufted Titmouse	1¼"	8"
White-Breasted Nuthatch	1¼"	8"
House Wren	⅞"	1 to 6"
Tree Swallow	1½"	1 to 6"
Downy Woodpecker	1¼"	8"
House Finch	2"	4"

All that remains to complete the birdhouse is to add the roof. You have another choice to make here. You can use galvanized sheet metal or copper. I found 30-gauge sheet metal at a local home center. The copper may be more difficult to find. Mine came from a nearby sheet metal supplier. For mail-order sources, see page 126.

Whichever material you choose, the construction of the roof is the same. (If you decide on copper, refer to the Woodworker's Notebook on page 57 for information about selecting nails.)

The roof consists of three parts. A round base, or plate, sits on top of the birdhouse and overhangs the cylinder wall. Then a couple of roof trusses are added to support the sheet metal and to provide a nailing surface *(Fig. 9)*.

ROOF PLATE. I started by gluing up a blank for the roof plate. Like many of the other parts of the birdhouse, the roof plate (E) is a round disk that's cut on the band saw using the same circle-cutting jig. But this time there's a little twist. Since the sheet metal extends

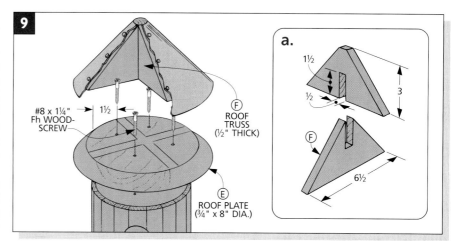

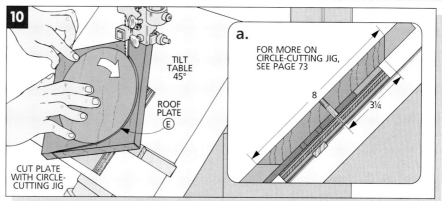

DESIGNER'S NOTEBOOK

Perches are dangerous for birds that live in the house, but they dress up a house that's built for display.

CONSTRUCTION NOTES:

■ Bird experts tell me that a perch should only be added to a house that will be used for display. It isn't needed by the birds that live in the house, since they'll fly right on inside. In fact, a perch poses a threat since it provides a place for predators to sit.

■ I made a simple two-piece perch out of ¼"-thick stock. The parts are cut out on a scroll saw (or band saw) according to

the pattern *(Fig. 3)* and sizes shown in *Fig. 1*. Then they're glued together.

■ To create a hollow along the back edge of the perch assembly, I placed a piece of adhesive-backed sandpaper on the outside of the birdhouse. Then I sanded the back of the perch *(Fig. 2)*.

■ Once the back edges were contoured, I glued the perch to the front of the house, just below the opening *(Fig. 1)*.

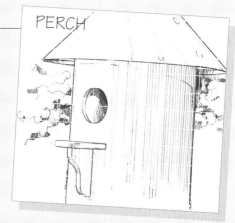

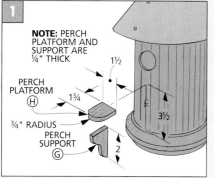

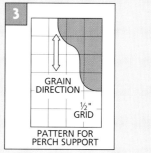

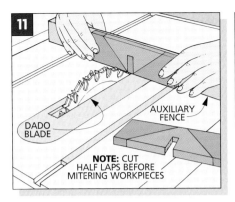

11

DADO BLADE

AUXILIARY FENCE

NOTE: CUT HALF LAPS BEFORE MITERING WORKPIECES

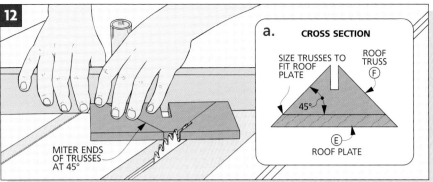

12

MITER ENDS OF TRUSSES AT 45°

a. **CROSS SECTION**

SIZE TRUSSES TO FIT ROOF PLATE

ROOF TRUSS (F)

45°

(E)

ROOF PLATE

below the roof plate, the edge of the plate is beveled at a 45° angle to line up with the trusses (refer to *Fig. 12a*). To cut this piece, you'll have to tilt the table of your band saw *(Figs. 10 and 10a)*. Keep firm pressure on the workpiece and the jig as you make the cut.

After the roof plate is cut to size, it can be glued and screwed to the top of the birdhouse. Just make sure to center the roof plate on the cylinder.

ROOF TRUSSES. The second part of the roof is the truss system. This consists of a couple of triangular-shaped pieces that fit together with a half lap joint to form a "cross" that supports the sheet metal *(Fig. 9a)*.

To make the roof trusses (F), start by cutting two blanks from $1/2$"-thick stock. (My blanks were each 3" wide and 9" rough length.)

After laying out a truss on each blank, I set up a dado blade in the table saw to cut the half laps *(Fig. 11)*. (I found it easier to cut the joint before mitering the pieces.) The blade should be set to cut a slot the same width as the thickness of the blank.

Once the half lap is cut in both pieces, each end can be mitered at a 45°

angle *(Fig. 12)*. As you're mitering the trusses, check to make sure that their finished length will match the small diameter of the roof plate *(Fig. 12a)*. The trusses should be flush with the edge of the roof plate. If you need to trim the length of a truss, make a small cut from each side so that the half lap joint stays centered.

When the trusses are cut to size, they are glued together and then glued to the roof plate. Once this is done, you're ready to start working on the sheet metal roof.

SHEET METAL. To cut the roofing material, start by laying out the pattern on your sheet metal. I did this by making a template out of paper, then tracing it onto the sheet metal with a permanent marker *(Fig. 13)*.

To cut the sheet metal, I used a pair of tin snips. Wearing a pair of leather

gloves to protect your hands, start by cutting a 12"-dia. circle. To make the circle as uniform as possible, take your time and make long, even cuts.

Then to allow you to "roll" the metal into a cone, remove a section of the circle *(Fig. 14)*. To cut out the small opening in the center of the circle, I had to "nibble" away at the metal with the very tips of the tin snips *(Fig. 15)*.

Once you have the sheet metal cut, the next step is to bend it into a cone to fit on the roof of the birdhouse. The trick here is to pre-bend the metal by gradually working the flat sheet into a cone before placing it on the birdhouse. The thing you want to avoid is kinking the metal by bending it too sharply. I found it helpful to use a large-diameter dowel as a forming tool to back up the sheet metal while "rolling" it into a cone (see the photo below).

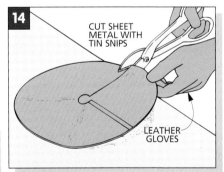

14

CUT SHEET METAL WITH TIN SNIPS

LEATHER GLOVES

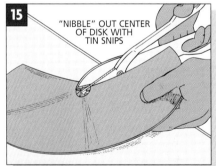

15

"NIBBLE" OUT CENTER OF DISK WITH TIN SNIPS

13

PATTERN FOR METAL ROOF

WASTE

12"-DIA. CIRCLE

12

12

1" DIA.

6

12

$1/2$

$9^{1}/4$

NOTE: TRANSFER PATTERN TO 12" x 12" SHEET OF COPPER OR GALVANIZED STEEL

Using a large-diameter dowel provides support as you form the sheet metal into a cone. This helps prevent kinking. Be careful when you work with the metal. The edges are sharp. A pair of leather gloves will allow you to handle it safely and a leather apron will provide additional protection.

NAILING DOWN THE METAL. The sheet metal is attached to the roof with small nails. But even with the metal preformed, nailing it down can be tricky. Here's how I tackled it.

First, I nailed the "flap" of the sheet metal down to one edge of the trusses with a couple of nails. This anchors the sheet metal in place. Then I shaped the metal around the roof and held the ends together with a couple strips of masking tape *(Fig. 16)*. Now it's a simple matter to nail the sheet metal to the trusses.

FINISHING TOUCHES. The last step to complete the construction of the birdhouse is to top it off. If you want to hang the birdhouse, you'll need to add a screw eye and washer *(Fig. 17a)*. Another option is to mount the house on a pole (see the Designer's Notebook below). In this case, you can add a finial *(Fig. 17b)*. And finally, apply a stain. ■

SHOP TIP . . . . Aging Copper

If you don't want your new birdhouse to look too new, try aging the copper before mounting the roof.

Heating the copper burns off oily fingerprints and gives the metal a brown, weathered look, like an old penny. This is optional, but if you want to try it, be sure to heat the copper and allow it to cool *before* placing it on the birdhouse.

16

4d NAIL (CUT TO ½")

USE TAPE TO HOLD ENDS OF "CONE" TOGETHER

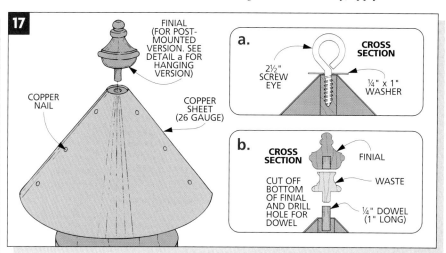

17

FINIAL (FOR POST-MOUNTED VERSION. SEE DETAIL a FOR HANGING VERSION)

COPPER NAIL

COPPER SHEET (26 GAUGE)

a. CROSS SECTION

2½" SCREW EYE

¼" x 1" WASHER

b. CROSS SECTION

FINIAL

CUT OFF BOTTOM OF FINIAL AND DRILL HOLE FOR DOWEL

WASTE

¼" DOWEL (1" LONG)

DESIGNER'S NOTEBOOK

If you don't have a place where you can hang the birdhouse, mount it on top of a pole.

CONSTRUCTION NOTES:

■ I used a 1¼"-dia. copper pipe as the post. You can have the pipe cut to whatever length you need.

■ To mount the birdhouse to the post, I drilled a 1½"-dia. hole through the center of the lower base piece (see drawing).

■ Then I used epoxy to secure a 1¼"-dia. copper end cap into the hole (detail 'a'). (You'll find copper end caps in the plumbing section of your local hardware store.)

■ The end cap allows you to fit the birdhouse over the end of the pipe. Don't fasten the end cap to the post or you won't be able to remove the birdhouse.

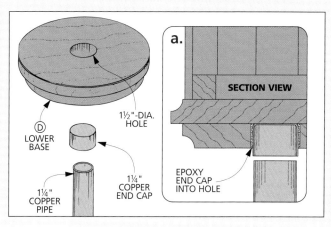

1½"-DIA. HOLE

LOWER BASE

1¼" COPPER END CAP

1¼" COPPER PIPE

a. SECTION VIEW

EPOXY END CAP INTO HOLE

POLE MOUNT

SHOP JIG .... *Circle-Cutting Jig*

To make it easier to cut the various sizes of disks for the birdhouse, I came up with a simple circle-cutting jig. It has a pivot pin set in a sliding arm that can be adjusted to the diameter of the circle you want to cut.

JIG BASE. The base for the jig is a square piece of 3/4" plywood (*Fig. 1*). I used a router table with a straight bit to cut a smooth-bottomed groove centered in the base. This groove is for the sliding arm to ride in.

To keep the sliding arm from moving around, add a pair of screws with washers to hold it in place. To do this, drill two shallow counterbores in the base on each side of the groove (*Figs. 1 and 1a.*) They should be deep enough for the flat washer to sit just below the surface of the base.

Note: Drill a countersink in the washer for the woodscrew.

SLIDING ARM. The washers pinch the sliding arm to hold it in place. So after ripping the hardboard to the correct width (it should fit in the groove and slide easily without any slop), rout a rabbet on each top edge. They should end up slightly shallower than the counterbores for the washers (*Fig. 1a*).

To hold a 1/4" dowel for the pivot pin, drill three offset holes in the sliding arm (*Fig. 1*). This makes it easy to flip the arm to cut larger circles, and the screws and washers will still hold it securely.

RUNNER. Finally, a hardwood runner is cut to fit the band saw's miter gauge slot, and a stop is attached to one end. This runner is the key to aligning the sliding arm with the band saw blade. You want the pin in the arm to stay parallel to the cutting edge of the blade.

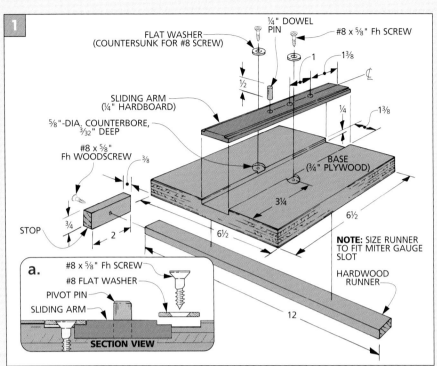

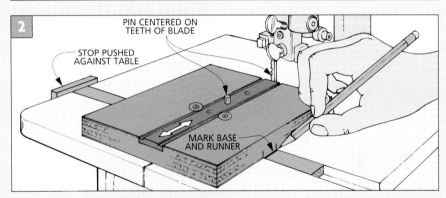

To do this, place the base on the runner, lining it up so that the pin is centered near the front of the saw blade (*Fig. 2*). Then carefully align the pieces of the jig and mark the position of the base on the runner and the runner on each side of the base. Finally, glue the base and runner together.

USING THE JIG

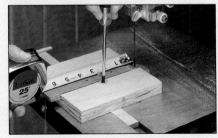

1 *Adjust the pin on the sliding arm to match the radius of the circle you want to cut. Measure from the blade to the center of the pin.*

2 *Drill a centered hole on the blank and set the blank on the pin. Start the saw, then push the jig and piece into the blade until the stop hits the edge of the table.*

3 *Keeping the stop pressed against the table, rotate the workpiece on the pivot pin until the circle is completely cut from the blank.*

Garden Arbor

Building a large outdoor project doesn't have to be complicated. This arbor is designed to be built in sections with very basic joinery. Then the pieces are taken outside and assembled later.

Ask me what's different about building an outdoor project, and I'd probably rattle off a quick list: the different kinds of woods you might use, the need for exterior grade hardware and glue, as well as the different finishing options.

But this outdoor project is different for another reason — its size. Standing almost 8-feet tall, this garden arbor is easily the biggest woodworking project I've ever tackled.

And even though there was plenty of woodworking involved in building the arbor, it also allowed me to get out of my usual woodworking "routine." After all, when building a project of this scale, you just can't always approach things the same way.

For instance, cutting a tenon is usually a simple matter on the table saw — unless the piece happens to be an 8-foot-long 4x4 post. But in this case, I got in a little practice with a tool I don't often get to use: a hand saw.

And if it's been a while since you've used a hand saw, don't worry. The pieces don't have to fit like a glove. In fact, having a little "play" in the fit is what you're after. It'll allow the arbor to go together more easily later on.

OUTDOOR MATERIALS. I built my arbor out of redwood. But there are a number of other woods that could be used with great results, including cedar, white oak, and Douglas fir.

And an outdoor project also has to withstand extremes in weather. This means using screws that won't rust and glue that's going to hold. So I chose silicon bronze screws. (There's more about these screws on page 79.) And I used a strong, "weatherproof" adhesive: polyurethane glue.

ADD A BENCH. The arbor shown here can serve as an entry point to your garden. If you'd rather have a place where you can sit and relax, it's easy to add a bench between the sides of the arbor. The Designer's Notebook on page 84 shows how to do this.

OUTDOOR INSTALLATION. Finally, you won't need a large crew to put the project in place. It's designed to be built and assembled in smaller sections, so you and a helper can break it down and reassemble it easily.

When it's time to install the arbor, you get to be a construction worker for a day. (I was the foreman, of course.) My arbor is set on concrete pads and secured with L-brackets.

EXPLODED VIEW

OVERALL DIMENSIONS:
75W x 47D x 91¾H

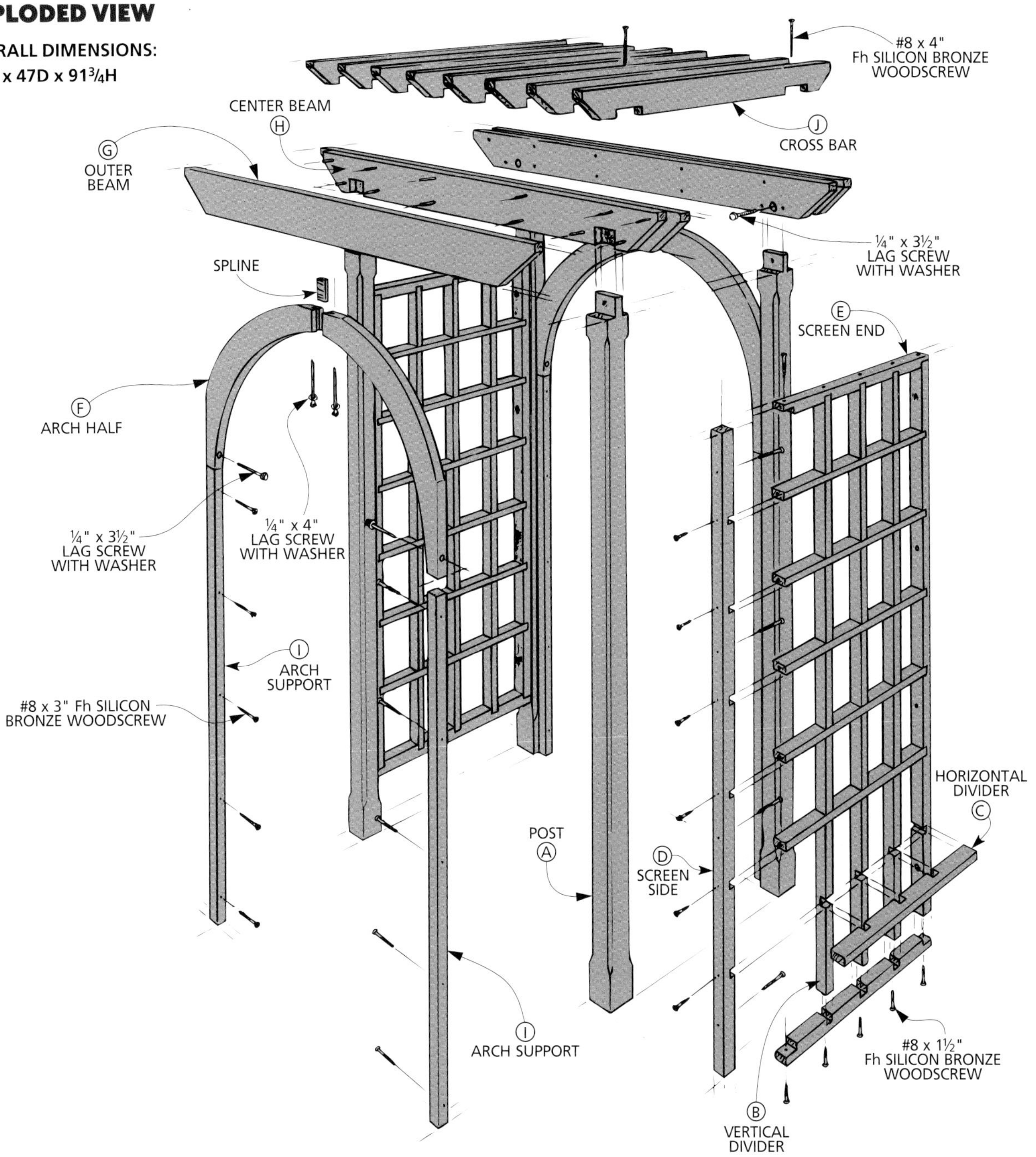

#8 x 4"
Fh SILICON BRONZE
WOODSCREW
CENTER BEAM
H
J
CROSS BAR
G
OUTER
BEAM
¼" x 3½"
LAG SCREW
WITH WASHER
SPLINE
E
SCREEN END
F
ARCH HALF
¼" x 3½"
LAG SCREW
WITH WASHER
¼" x 4"
LAG SCREW
WITH WASHER
I
ARCH
SUPPORT
#8 x 3" Fh SILICON
BRONZE WOODSCREW
HORIZONTAL
DIVIDER
C
POST
A
D
SCREEN
SIDE
I
ARCH SUPPORT
#8 x 1½"
Fh SILICON BRONZE
WOODSCREW
B
VERTICAL
DIVIDER

MATERIALS LIST

WOOD

A	Posts (4)	3½ x 3½ - 86¾
B	Vertical Dividers (6)	1½ x ¾ - 69
C	Horiz. Dividers (12)	1½ x ¾ - 27¾
D	Screen Sides (4)	1½ x 1½ - 69
E	Screen Ends (4)	1½ x 1½ - 29¼
F	Arch Halves (4)	1½ x 11¼ - 36 rgh.
G	Outer Beams (4)	1½ x 5¼ - 75
H	Center Beams (2)	1½ x 5¼ - 71
I	Arch Supports (4)	1½ x 1½ - 58
J	Cross Bars (8)	1½ x 3½ - 47

HARDWARE SUPPLIES

- (44) No. 8 x 1½" Fh woodscrews
- (48) No. 8 x 2½" Fh woodscrews
- (36) No. 8 x 3" Fh woodscrews
- (16) No. 8 x 4" Fh woodscrews
- (8) ¼" x 2" lag screws
- (8) ¼" x 3½" lag screws
- (4) ¼" x 4" lag screws
- (12) ¼" washers
- (4) Concrete forms and concrete
- (4) Concrete anchors
- (4) 3" L-brackets

Note: Use exterior-grade hardware. All woodscrews are silicon bronze.

CUTTING DIAGRAM

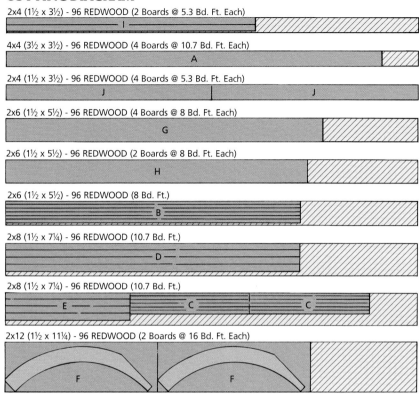

2x4 (1½ x 3½) - 96 REDWOOD (2 Boards @ 5.3 Bd. Ft. Each)

I

4x4 (3½ x 3½) - 96 REDWOOD (4 Boards @ 10.7 Bd. Ft. Each)

A

2x4 (1½ x 3½) - 96 REDWOOD (4 Boards @ 5.3 Bd. Ft. Each)

J   J

2x6 (1½ x 5½) - 96 REDWOOD (4 Boards @ 8 Bd. Ft. Each)

G

2x6 (1½ x 5½) - 96 REDWOOD (2 Boards @ 8 Bd. Ft. Each)

H

2x6 (1½ x 5½) - 96 REDWOOD (8 Bd. Ft.)

B

2x8 (1½ x 7¼) - 96 REDWOOD (10.7 Bd. Ft.)

D

2x8 (1½ x 7¼) - 96 REDWOOD (10.7 Bd. Ft.)

E   C   C

2x12 (1½ x 11¼) - 96 REDWOOD (2 Boards @ 16 Bd. Ft. Each)

F   F

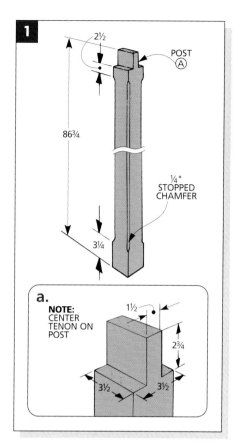

1

2½

POST Ⓐ

86¾

¼" STOPPED CHAMFER

3¼

a.

NOTE: CENTER TENON ON POST

1½

2¾

3½   3½

SIDE ASSEMBLIES

To build the arbor, I started with the side assemblies. This includes the four posts for the corners and the lattice screens that connect the posts at the sides of the arbor (refer to the Exploded View on page 75).

POSTS. I began with the posts (A) *(Fig. 1)*. These are designed to be cut from 8-foot-long 4x4s (3½" x 3½"). But it's more important that the posts are straight. So if you have a hard time finding straight 4x4s at the lumber yard, you can glue up the posts from three pieces (refer to the Shop Tip below).

Note: If you glue up the posts, be sure to use a "weatherproof" glue. For

SHOP TIP .... Laminated Posts

Depending on where you live, you may have a tough time finding nice, straight 4x4 redwood posts for the Garden Arbor. (I had to search three different lumberyards.)

Fortunately, there's an easy alternative. You can "make" your own posts by gluing up straight pieces of thinner stock.

In order to get the necessary thickness and width, just sandwich a 1x6 between a couple of 2x6s *(Fig. 1)*. But before gluing the pieces together, rip the edges to remove the "factory" roundovers.

To keep the pieces flush during glue-up, use some scrap blocks when you clamp them *(Fig. 2)*.

Once the glue dries, the posts can be trimmed down to final size on a jointer or a planer *(Fig. 3)*.

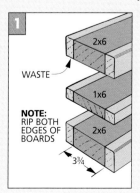

1

2x6

WASTE

1x6

NOTE: RIP BOTH EDGES OF BOARDS

2x6

3¾

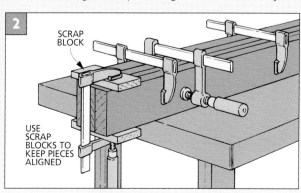

2

SCRAP BLOCK

USE SCRAP BLOCKS TO KEEP PIECES ALIGNED

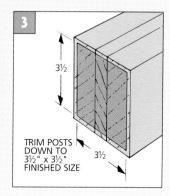

3

3½

TRIM POSTS DOWN TO 3½" x 3½" FINISHED SIZE

3½

this project, I used polyurethane glue (refer to Shop Info on page 48).

The first thing to do is to cut the posts to length $(86^3/_4")$ *(Fig. 1)*. My initial instinct was to use the table saw. But then I realized that these pieces were too long to handle on the table saw safely. So I used a hand saw. (A circular saw will also work, but you'll have to make two cuts from opposite sides of the post.)

With the posts cut to length, the next step is to cut the tenon on the top end of each *(Fig. 1a)*. These tenons will fit into the beam assemblies later. And since the mortises in the beams will equal the thickness of "two-by" material, I cut these tenons $1^1/_2$" thick.

Once more, the posts are too long to cut their tenons easily on the table saw. So again, I reached for my hand saw (although you could use a circular saw instead). Refer to the Technique box below for details on doing this.

All that's left to complete the posts is to rout a stopped chamfer on each edge, *(Fig. 1)*. Using a hand-held router, rout a $1/_4$" chamfer on each edge of the posts. Each chamfer starts $3^1/_4$" from the bottom of the post and stops $2^1/_2$" from the shoulder of the tenon. I marked lines around both ends of the posts to indicate the start and stop points.

TECHNIQUE .... *Cutting Large Tenons*

When it comes to making tenons, I typically cut them on the table saw. But because the posts of the Garden Arbor are so long (nearly 8 feet), I decided to use a tool I don't get to work with all that often.

HAND SAW. To cut these tenons, I found it quickest and easiest to use a hand saw. (Although you could also use a circular saw as shown below.) To do this, start by laying out the tenon with a knife and a straightedge *(Fig. 1)*. (Scoring with a knife will help you get clean edges on the cuts.)

Next, use a sharp hand saw to make the cheek cuts *(Fig. 2)*. Try to stay just to the waste side of your layout lines. As you approach the shoulder, square up the saw *(Fig. 3)*.

GUIDE BLOCK. To help ensure a straight cut when making the shoulders of the tenon, clamp a guide block to the post right along the layout line. Then use the block to guide your saw during the cut *(Fig. 4)*.

Finally, if necessary, clean up the faces of the tenons with a sharp chisel.

Lay out tenon. *Score the layout lines with a utility knife to prevent splintering.*

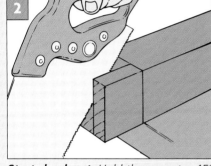

Start cheek cut. *Hold the saw at a 45° angle to the end of the workpiece.*

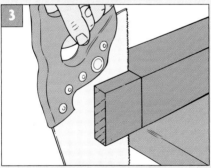

Complete cuts. *As you reach the bottom of the cut, square up the saw.*

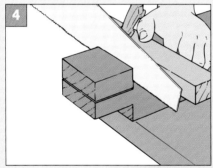

Cut shoulders. *A guide block clamped along the layout line guides the saw.*

CIRCULAR SAW METHOD

Another option is to cut the tenons with a circular saw.

All you have to do is set the depth of cut to match the shoulder depth of the tenon. Then cut a series of closely spaced kerfs until you reach the shoulder line of the tenon *(Fig. 1)*.

Note: Start cutting the kerfs at the end of the post and work in so that the saw will always be firmly supported.

To finish the tenon, just knock the waste off with a hammer. Then clean up the tenon with a wide chisel *(Fig. 2)*.

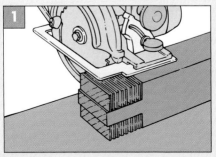

Cut kerfs. *Start at the end of the post and cut a series of kerfs across the tenon.*

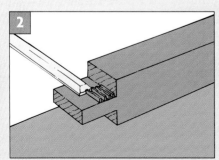

Remove waste. *Knock off the waste with a hammer. Then chisel sides clean.*

The secret to making the lattice screens align is to cut all the notches at once in a wide blank, then rip the individual slats from the blank.

Start by cutting a 2x8 blank to final length and then lay out the positions of the notches along one edge *(Fig. 1).*

Next, cut a series of dadoes across the blank. Fasten an auxiliary fence to your miter gauge to help support the piece and to prevent tearout on the back edge *(Fig. 2).*

Once all the dadoes are cut, set the rip fence and rip the pieces to final width. Make sure you mark one end of the blank so that you can orient the strips the same way when you assemble the screens *(Fig. 3).*

This same procedure can be used when cutting the frame pieces that surround the screens (refer to *Fig. 3* on page 79).

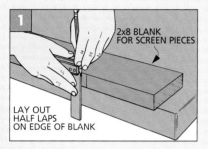

2x8 BLANK FOR SCREEN PIECES

LAY OUT HALF LAPS ON EDGE OF BLANK

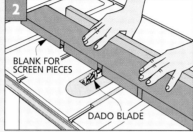

BLANK FOR SCREEN PIECES

DADO BLADE

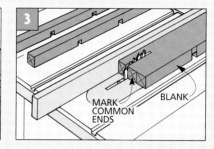

MARK COMMON ENDS

BLANK

LATTICE SCREENS. The next step is to make the lattice screens that join the posts (refer to *Fig. 3*). These screens are built in two steps. First, I made the dividers that go inside. Then I added the frame that surrounds them *(Fig. 3).*

SCREEN DIVIDERS. To make the screens, I started with the vertical (B) and horizontal dividers (C) *(Fig. 2).* And to join these dividers, I used simple half lap joints.

You might think that cutting all those half laps (and getting them to line up) would be a hassle. But it's really not. The secret is to lay out and cut a series of notches in 2x8 blanks and then rip the strips from the blanks. This way, all the half laps line up perfectly. (See the Shop Tip above for more about this.)

After the notches were cut on the blanks for these pieces, I ripped them

$3/4$" wide (thick). Then I assembled the dividers, putting a tiny spot of glue on each half lap to hold the pieces together. (I used polyurethane glue here, too.)

SCREEN SIDES AND ENDS. With the dividers assembled, the sides (D) and ends (E) of the screen can be added as a frame around the dividers *(Fig. 3).* This frame allows you to attach the screens to the posts later.

The frame pieces are notched just like the dividers, but these aren't true half laps — the notches simply fit over the ends of the dividers.

I built the sides first, again starting with an oversize blank. But this time, I laid out the notches by setting them against the divider assembly and marking them from the horizontal pieces. Then after the notches are cut in the blank, rip the screen sides to width

so they match the thickness of the divider pieces ($1^{1}/2$").

The screen ends (E) are a little different from the other screen pieces. In addition to the $3/4$"-wide notches that hold the vertical dividers, the ends also have $1^{1}/2$"-wide rabbets to hold the screen sides *(Figs. 3a and 3c).*

Now before screwing the frames to the dividers, drill a series of countersunk shank holes in the sides (D) *(Figs. 3b and 3c).*

Note: The holes for attaching the sides to the dividers are countersunk on the outside face (the face that will go against the post). The holes for securing the frame to the post are countersunk on the inside face.

ASSEMBLY. Once these holes are drilled, the sides and ends can be glued and screwed to the dividers *(Fig. 3c).*

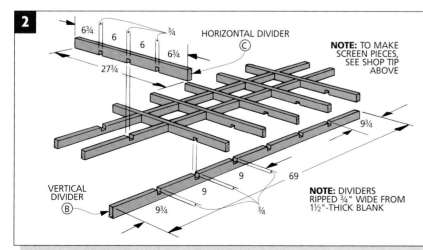

2

$6^{3}/4$ 6   6 $3/4$

HORIZONTAL DIVIDER Ⓒ

$6^{3}/4$

$27^{3}/4$

NOTE: TO MAKE SCREEN PIECES, SEE SHOP TIP ABOVE

$9^{3}/4$

9   69

VERTICAL DIVIDER Ⓑ

9

$9^{3}/4$ $3/4$

NOTE: DIVIDERS RIPPED $3/4$" WIDE FROM $1^{1}/2$"-THICK BLANK

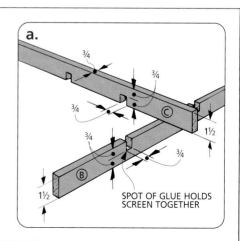

a.

$3/4$ $3/4$

$3/4$ Ⓒ $1^{1}/2$

$3/4$

$3/4$

$1^{1}/2$ Ⓑ

SPOT OF GLUE HOLDS SCREEN TOGETHER

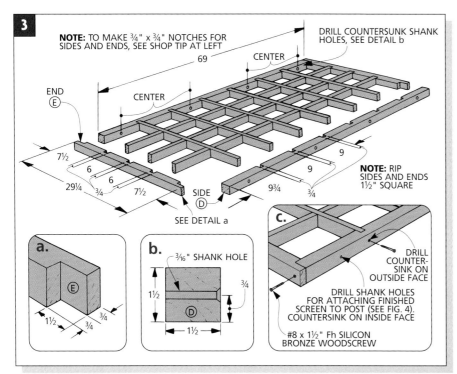

3

NOTE: TO MAKE ¾" x ¾" NOTCHES FOR SIDES AND ENDS, SEE SHOP TIP AT LEFT

DRILL COUNTERSUNK SHANK HOLES, SEE DETAIL b

69

CENTER

CENTER

END
Ⓔ

7½

6

6

29¼   ¾   7½

SIDE
Ⓓ

SEE DETAIL a

9

9

9¾   ¾

NOTE: RIP SIDES AND ENDS 1½" SQUARE

a.

Ⓔ

1½   ¾

¾
¾

b.

³⁄₁₆" SHANK HOLE

1½

¾

Ⓓ

1½

C.

DRILL COUNTER-SINK ON OUTSIDE FACE

DRILL SHANK HOLES FOR ATTACHING FINISHED SCREEN TO POST (SEE FIG. 4). COUNTERSINK ON INSIDE FACE

#8 x 1½" Fh SILICON BRONZE WOODSCREW

SHOP TIP
Tight-Space Screwdriver

You can still drive screws even when there's no room for a regular screwdriver. Just put a Phillips head driver bit into a ¼" socket and turn it with a ratchet.

Then the completed screens can be screwed to the posts *(Fig. 4)*. To do this, I set the screens on spacers to center them on the posts *(Fig. 4a)*. Then position the bottom ends of the legs 7½" from the bottom of the screen and screw the screens in place. The only problem is there's not enough room for a screwdriver. So I improvised and used a ratchet with a driver bit (see the Shop Tip above right).

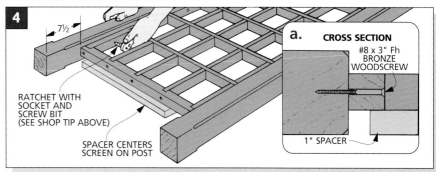

4

7½

RATCHET WITH SOCKET AND SCREW BIT (SEE SHOP TIP ABOVE)

SPACER CENTERS SCREEN ON POST

a.   CROSS SECTION

#8 x 3" Fh BRONZE WOODSCREW

1" SPACER

SHOP INFO . . . . *Outdoor Screws*

Regular zinc-plated steel woodscrews ("A" in photo) are the type used for most indoor projects. They're made from iron-based metal. This makes them strong and inexpensive, but they can rust quickly when exposed to moisture. Even though they're coated to resist rust, the coating isn't meant to stand up outdoors. Fortunately, there are several alternatives.

SOLID BRASS. For years, woodworkers have relied on brass screws for exterior projects ("B" in photo). They don't rust and are readily available. The big disadvantage is that they're soft. So if you twist them too hard, you may strip the head, or even break it off. (To prevent this, drive a regular zinc-plated screw first to pre-thread the pilot hole.)

STAINLESS STEEL. Another choice that won't rust is stainless steel screws ("C" in photo). They aren't as strong as regular steel screws, but they are stronger than brass.

They're a good choice for outdoor projects, but I didn't use them on the arbor because the shiny heads wouldn't blend well with the redwood.

SILICON BRONZE. I chose this type of screw ("D" in photo) for a couple of reasons. First, they're the preferred fasteners for boatbuilders, so you know they resist rust. They're made from a copper alloy with silicon included for additional corrosion resistance. Plus, the brown color blends better with the redwood.

However, they can cost three to four times as much as regular screws.

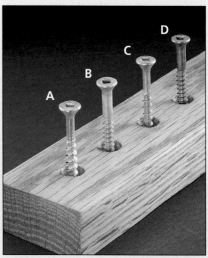

A. Zinc-plated steel   C. Stainless steel
B. Solid brass   D. Silicon bronze

Now that the side assemblies of the arbor are complete, it's time to connect them at the front and back with arches and cross beams *(Fig. 5)*.

ARCHES. To keep things simple, I made each arch out of two pieces. There are a number of ways to do this, but to make all the pieces identical, I made a template.

ARCH TEMPLATE. The arch template starts out as a square hardboard blank (26" x 24") *(Fig. 6)*. This will create a 26"-tall arch that will be 48" wide after the halves are glued up.

To lay out the arch template, I made a simple compass from a thin piece of scrap. A hole for the centerpoint and two holes for the pencil determine the final size of the curves (26$\frac{1}{8}$" for the top curve, 22$\frac{1}{2}$" for the bottom) *(Fig. 6)*. I used a nail for the centerpoint, holding it against the outside corner while drawing the curves *(Fig. 6a)*.

Note that the size of the top curve creates a flat spot at the top of the arch. This is intentional — it lets the arch fit tight against the cross beam later (refer to *Fig. 11a* on page 81).

ARCH HALVES. After the template has been cut out and sanded smooth, it can be used to lay out the arch pieces. Each of the four arch halves (F) starts out as a 36"-long 2x12 blank *(Fig. 7)*. Then after using the template to lay out the pieces, they can be cut out on the band saw and sanded smooth.

Next, to keep the halves of each arch aligned during glue-up, I added a spline. To do this, I cut a centered groove in the top end of each arch half, cutting it in two passes *(Fig. 8)*.

Note: To prevent the workpiece from tipping as the groove is cut I attached a tall auxiliary fence to the rip fence and clamped a scrap piece to the arch to act as a runner.

After cutting the grooves on the arch halves, I cut splines to fit. To prevent the spline from splitting, make sure the grain runs across the joint line *(Fig. 9a)*.

ARCH ASSEMBLY. Now the arches are ready to be glued together *(Fig. 9)*. To

5

OUTER BEAM (G) CENTER BEAM (H) 71

5$\frac{1}{4}$ 75   5$\frac{1}{4}$

SPLINE

ARCH HALF (F)

ARCH SUPPORT (I)

58

TEMPORARY BRACE

a.
CROSS SECTION
$\frac{1}{8}$" ROUND-OVER
$\frac{1}{4}$" x 3$\frac{1}{2}$" LAG SCREW WITH WASHER
$\frac{3}{4}$"-DIA. COUNTER-BORE, $\frac{1}{2}$" DEEP
1$\frac{3}{8}$

b.
$\frac{3}{4}$"-DIA. COUNTERBORE, $\frac{1}{2}$" DEEP
(F)
$\frac{1}{4}$" x 3$\frac{1}{2}$" LAG SCREW WITH WASHER
(I)
CROSS SECTION
3
#8 x 3" Fh WOODSCREW
3

NOTE: ARCH SUPPORTS CUT TO FIT BETWEEN BOTTOM OF ARCHES AND BOTTOM OF POSTS

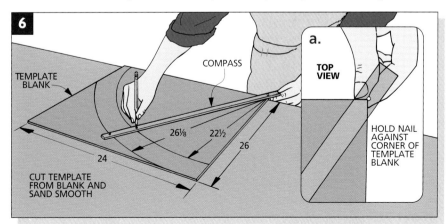

6
TEMPLATE BLANK
COMPASS
a. TOP VIEW
HOLD NAIL AGAINST CORNER OF TEMPLATE BLANK
26$\frac{1}{8}$ 22$\frac{1}{2}$ 26
24
CUT TEMPLATE FROM BLANK AND SAND SMOOTH

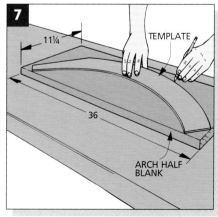

7
11$\frac{1}{4}$ TEMPLATE
36
ARCH HALF BLANK

hold the joint in place, I clamped a pair of cleats to each piece and then clamped the cleats together.

Since the arches will be "framed in" by the posts and cross beams, it's important that they end up square. So before the glue has a chance to set up, measure across the arch assembly at the top and bottom of the flat edges to make sure the dimensions are the same (*Fig. 9*). (Mine were 48".)

All that's left to complete the arches is to rout $\frac{1}{8}$" roundovers along the curved edges (*Fig. 9a*).

CROSS BEAMS

Now, work can begin on the cross beams (refer to *Fig. 5*). Each beam is a lamination of three nearly identical 2x6s: two outer beams (G) and a shorter center beam (H) (*Fig. 10*).

MORTISES. Before laminating the pieces, I created the mortises for the tenons on the posts. To do this, just cut two notches in the center beams — the outer beams will form the cheeks of the mortise (*Figs. 10 and 10a*).

Note: The distance between these notches should equal the final width of the arches (48").

ASSEMBLY. When the notches are complete and the bevels on the ends of the beams are cut, I began gluing and screwing the beams together. But work from the outside in so the screws end up on the inside faces (*Fig. 10b*). (And be sure to offset the screws.)

When the glue is dry, all that's left to do is to rout $\frac{1}{8}$" roundovers on the edges and drill counterbored shank holes so you can "pin" the tenons with lag screws (*Fig. 5a*). Then drill counterbored shank holes in the arch assemblies (*Figs. 5b and 11a*). The trick to adding the arches and beams to the posts is standing the posts upright. An easy solution is to temporarily clamp braces across the posts (*Fig. 5*).

ARCH SUPPORTS. With the beams and arches screwed in place, I added arch supports (I) to the inside faces of the posts (*Figs. 5 and 11*). These extend from the arches to the bottoms of the posts. (Mine were 58" long.) And they match the bottom ends of the arches ($1\frac{1}{2}$" x $1\frac{1}{2}$" with $\frac{1}{8}$" roundovers on their outside faces).

When the arch supports are complete, they're simply screwed to the posts (*Fig. 5b*).

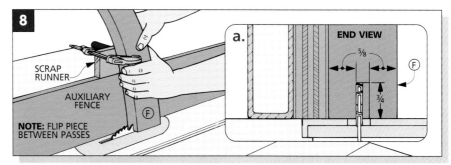

8

SCRAP RUNNER
AUXILIARY FENCE
F
NOTE: FLIP PIECE BETWEEN PASSES

a. **END VIEW**
$\frac{5}{8}$
F
$\frac{3}{4}$

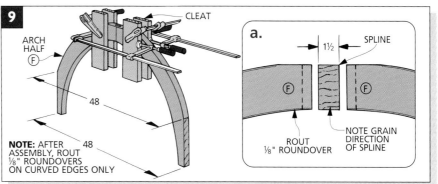

9

CLEAT
ARCH HALF
F
48
NOTE: AFTER ASSEMBLY, ROUT $\frac{1}{8}$" ROUNDOVERS ON CURVED EDGES ONLY
48

a.
$1\frac{1}{2}$
SPLINE
F
F
ROUT $\frac{1}{8}$" ROUNDOVER
NOTE GRAIN DIRECTION OF SPLINE

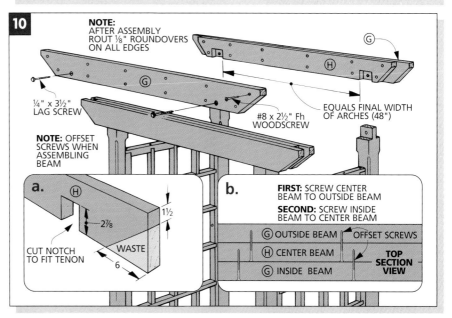

10

NOTE: AFTER ASSEMBLY ROUT $\frac{1}{8}$" ROUNDOVERS ON ALL EDGES
G
G
H
EQUALS FINAL WIDTH OF ARCHES (48")
$\frac{1}{4}$" x $3\frac{1}{2}$" LAG SCREW
#8 x $2\frac{1}{2}$" Fh WOODSCREW
NOTE: OFFSET SCREWS WHEN ASSEMBLING BEAM

a.
H
$1\frac{1}{2}$
$2\frac{7}{8}$
CUT NOTCH TO FIT TENON
WASTE
6

b.
FIRST: SCREW CENTER BEAM TO OUTSIDE BEAM
SECOND: SCREW INSIDE BEAM TO CENTER BEAM
G OUTSIDE BEAM
H CENTER BEAM
G INSIDE BEAM
OFFSET SCREWS
TOP SECTION VIEW

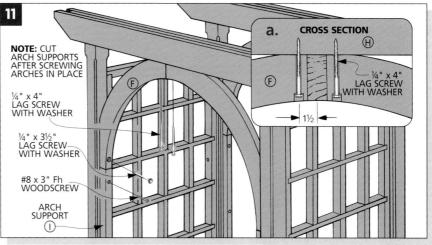

11

NOTE: CUT ARCH SUPPORTS AFTER SCREWING ARCHES IN PLACE
F
$\frac{1}{4}$" x 4" LAG SCREW WITH WASHER
$\frac{1}{4}$" x $3\frac{1}{2}$" LAG SCREW WITH WASHER
#8 x 3" Fh WOODSCREW
ARCH SUPPORT
I

a. **CROSS SECTION**
H
F
$\frac{1}{4}$" x 4" LAG SCREW WITH WASHER
$1\frac{1}{2}$

CROSS BARS

At this point the arbor is nearly complete. All that's left to add are the cross bars on top of the beams *(Fig. 12)*. These bars are notched to fit over the cross beams and are screwed in place (see photo below).

I started by cutting eight cross bars (J) to finished length (47") from 2x4 stock *(Fig. 12)*.

While these blanks are still square, the notches on the bottom edges of the bars can be laid out and cut *(Fig. 12)*.

To find the distance between these notches, I measured the distance between the cross beams. (My beams were 28$\frac{1}{4}$" apart.) The width of the notches in the cross bars equals the final thickness of the cross beams. (Mine were 4$\frac{1}{2}$" thick.) When laying out the notches, make sure they are the same distance from the ends. After the notches have been laid out they can be cut with a hand saw or a jig saw.

Note: Instead of laying out the notches on each cross bar separately, you can save some time by laying out and cutting the notches on a single bar first. Then use this bar as a template for laying out the others.

With the notches cut, the next thing to do is to bevel the ends of the bars *(Fig. 12b)*. Like the notches, I first laid out and cut the bevels on one bar and then used it as a template for the others. I attached a long auxiliary fence to my table saw's miter gauge to support the pieces during the cuts.

To complete the cross bars, $\frac{1}{8}$" roundovers are routed around all their edges *(Fig. 12a)*. Then drill pilot holes for screwing them to the cross beams. The bars are spaced 8" on centers (6$\frac{1}{2}$" apart) *(Fig. 12a)*. But before screwing the bars in place, I disassembled the arbor and gave it a few coats of finish (see the Finishing Tip at the top of the opposite page).

ARBOR INSTALLATION

After the parts of the arbor are finished, it's time to haul them out to your lawn or garden and reassemble them. Getting the site ready can be a project in itself. There are a number of ways to install the arbor. No matter how you do it, the key is to get everything level.

To install my arbor, I decided to use tubular paper concrete forms, concrete anchors, and L-brackets *(Fig. 13)*.

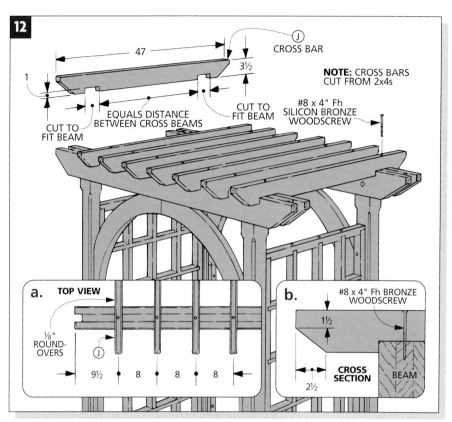

Once the notches are cut in the cross bars, they are screwed to the beams. To help space them evenly, I cut a piece of scrap to a length of 6$\frac{1}{2}$". After securing the first cross bar to the beam (Fig. 12a), put the scrap against it and position the next cross bar against the end of the scrap. Now screw the second cross bar in place. Simply repeat this process across one side of the arbor, then along the opposite side.

CONCRETE FORMS. The first thing to do is carefully stake out the location of the arbor. The ground here should be fairly level. But rather than trying to level the ground perfectly, I decided to pour concrete pads and make sure *they* were level. That's where the tubular concrete forms come in handy. These forms can be set so they end up level

with each other. (These forms can be found at most home centers.)

To check the forms, I placed a straight 8-foot-long 2x4 across a pair of forms and set a level on top of it. Check each form against the others until the forms are level in all four directions.

Note: If you live in an area that drops below freezing during the winter, make

When finishing an outdoor project, you want to protect the wood from moisture *and* sunlight. Fortunately, you have a couple of options.

The easiest choice is simply to paint the arbor. After all, a coat of a quality latex paint over an alkyd primer will provide a protective coat that will last for years with very little maintenance.

But I just couldn't bring myself to paint over the clear grain of the redwood. So to protect the arbor from sunlight without completely hiding the grain, I applied one coat of an exterior, semi-transparent stain. As an added benefit, it also evened out color variations in the wood.

It's easiest to apply the finish before the final assembly of the arbor (see photo). This also ensures better protection where the assemblies join together.

To get the stain into all the corners of the lattice screen and cross beams, I sprayed the stain on with a spray bottle. Then I wiped the excess off with a rag.

When the stain is completely dry, the arbor is ready for a top coat to provide additional protection. Here, the choice is

typically a spar varnish or a penetrating oil finish.

For this arbor, I chose an oil finish formulated for outdoor use. It isn't quite as durable as varnish (it will need an annual touch-up), but it's much easier to apply — and reapply when the arbor needs a fresh coat next year.

Especially on an outdoor project, you want to be sure you get good, complete coverage with your finish. So I carefully brushed on the oil instead of using a spray bottle.

sure you dig the holes deep enough that the concrete will be below the frost line.

ANCHORS. With the concrete poured and dried, the arbor can be set in place and fastened to the pads *(Fig. 13a)*. To do this, I used concrete anchors and L-brackets. There are a number of different expanding anchors available at home centers and hardware stores. The ones I used expanded when a pin was driven into them.

Have a helper assist you in moving the arbor onto the pads so you can mark the location of the holes for the brackets. (You'll need a hammer drill to drill the pilot holes for the anchors.)

To get the L-brackets to fit over the anchors, I had to enlarge the hole in each bracket *(Fig. 13a)*.

Then when the L-brackets are bolted down to the pads, the arbor can be moved back into place. Secure the arbor by fastening the L-brackets to the posts with lag screws. ◼

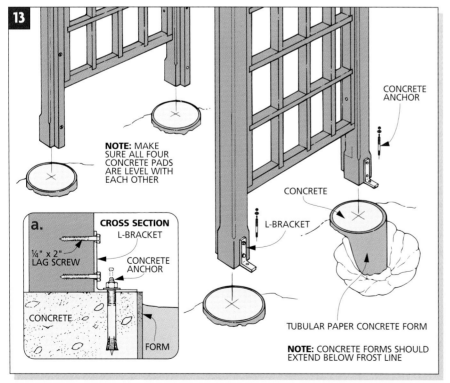

13

NOTE: MAKE SURE ALL FOUR CONCRETE PADS ARE LEVEL WITH EACH OTHER

a.

CROSS SECTION

L-BRACKET

¼" x 2" LAG SCREW

CONCRETE ANCHOR

CONCRETE

FORM

CONCRETE ANCHOR

CONCRETE

L-BRACKET

TUBULAR PAPER CONCRETE FORM

NOTE: CONCRETE FORMS SHOULD EXTEND BELOW FROST LINE

DESIGNER'S NOTEBOOK

Adding a bench transforms the Garden Arbor from an arched entryway into a peaceful destination. The simple design includes a quick way to install the back slats without cutting a series of mortises.

CONSTRUCTION NOTES:

■ When building the arbor, two of the arch supports (I) are cut to a length of 40" to make the back arch supports (K). This allows the bench to be mounted to the posts (refer to *Fig. 4*).

■ The first pieces to cut for the bench are the two side seat supports (L) and the center seat support (M) *(Fig. 1)*.

■ A curve is laid out and cut on one edge of each seat support. Refer to the Shop Tip on page 43 for more about this.

■ To accept a lag screw that secures the frame to the posts, drill a shank hole toward one end of each side seat support (L) (refer to *Fig. 3*).

■ Next, cut a front rail (N) and a rear rail (O) to size *(Fig. 1)*. To find the length of the front rail, measure between the two posts that the bench will be mounted to (48"). The length of the rear rail is 3" less than that of the front rail.

■ These five pieces can now be assembled into a frame *(Fig. 1)*.

■ Two curved braces (P) help support the bench (refer to *Fig. 3*). Start by cutting two blanks from a 2x8 *(Fig. 2)*.

■ To lay out the brace, place the flat edge of the arc template flush with one end and one edge of the blank *(Fig. 2)*. Cut the blank to rough shape, then sand to the line to bring it to final shape.

■ Drill a counterbored shank hole toward the front edge of each brace

ARBOR BENCH

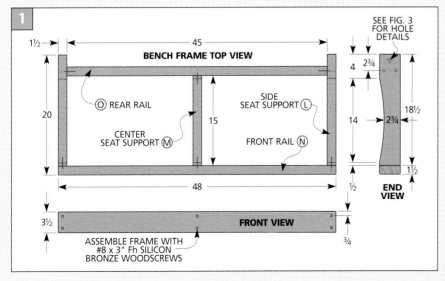

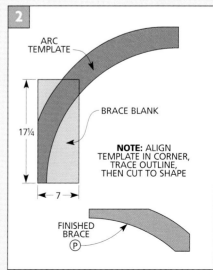

(Fig. 3). At the opposite end, drill a shank hole in the face for a lag screw.

■ To fasten the braces to the bench frame, align the rear edges of the braces with the back ends of the side seat supports (L) *(Fig. 3)*. Then drill pilot holes into the side seat supports and glue and screw the braces in place.

■ Now secure the frame to the arbor with lag screws *(Fig. 4)*.

■ Once the frame is fastened to the arbor, cut six 2½"-wide seat slats (Q) to fit between the lattice frames *(Fig. 3)*. (Mine were 50" long.)

■ Rout ⅛" roundovers on the long edges of each slat *(Fig. 3)*.

■ Screw the front slat to the frame so it overhangs the front rail (N) ½" *(Fig. 3)*. Space the remaining slats ¼" apart.

■ Work on the bench back starts by cutting two back rails (R) to length to fit between the lattice frames (50") *(Fig. 6)*.

■ Next, cut a 1"-wide rabbet 1" deep along each end to allow the rails to fit around the posts *(Figs. 7 and 8)*.

■ A ¼"-wide groove is then cut ½" deep in one edge of each back rail to accept a spline (T) *(Figs. 6 and 7)*.

■ Now cut seven back slats (S) from "one-by" stock *(Fig. 6)*.

■ Once the slats are cut to size, a ¼"-wide groove is cut in each end, centered on the thickness of the slat *(Fig. 7)*.

■ Assemble the back by gluing the splines into the rails, then gluing the slats between the rails *(Figs. 6 and 7)*.

■ Finally, screw the back assembly to the posts with the top edge 36" from the bottom edge of the posts *(Fig. 8)*.

MATERIALS LIST

CHANGED PARTS
I Arch Supports (2) 1½ x 1½ - 58

NEW PARTS
K Bk. Arch Sprts. (2) 1½ x 1½ - 40
L Sd. Seat Sprts. (2) 1½ x 3½ - 18½
M Ctr. Seat Sprts. (1) 1½ x 3½ - 15
N Front Rail (1)   1½ x 3½ - 48
O Rear Rail (1)   1½ x 3½ - 45
P Braces (2)   1½ x 7 - 17¼
Q Seat Slats (6)   ¾ x 2½ - 50
R Back Rails (2)   1½ x 3½ - 50
S Back Slats (7)   ¾ x 3½ - 9
T Splines (2)   ¼ x 1 - 48

HARDWARE SUPPLIES
(18) No. 8 x 1½" Fh woodscrews
(8) No. 8 x 2½" Fh woodscrews
(12) No. 8 x 3" Fh woodscrews
(6) ¼" x 3½" lag screws
(6) ¼" washers
Note: All woodscrews are silicon bronze.

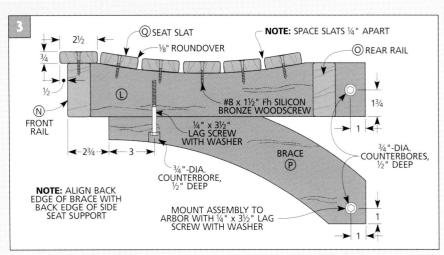

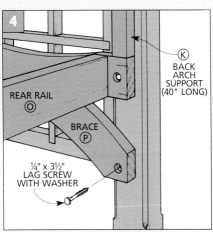

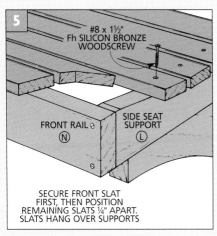

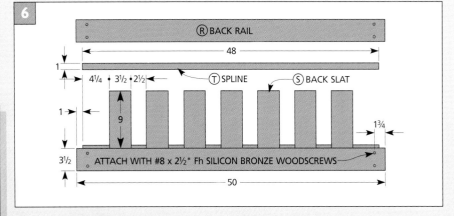

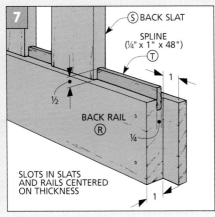

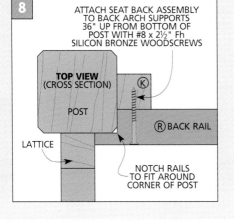

PATIO, DECK & PORCH

Today's house is not a home unless it has outdoor living space, like a patio, deck, porch, or balcony. The custom-made projects in this section make this space not only more attractive, but more enjoyable.

Planter boxes of various sizes are designed to suit every gardener's needs. The picnic table and benches — as sturdy as they are good looking — make a great gathering place to enjoy a cookout with family and friends. The patio table features a unique shape and joinery that will test your skills — plus it looks great anywhere. And the beautiful porch swing, with its curved back and slats, adds an old-fashioned touch to any porch or balcony.

Planter Boxes

Build this versatile Planter Box in one — or all — of the many variations. They fit nicely into any garden or patio arrangement, and each has an adjustable shelf to accommodate plants of different sizes.

One of the most interesting things about the design of this planter is its versatility. The basic planter is a square unit. But you can build one that's twice as wide to give it a different look. And by adding one with longer legs, you can create an attractive set. (The Designer's Notebook on the next page shows you how to build these variations.)

ADJUSTABLE SHELF. Another nice thing about this planter is its shelf. It's adjustable, so you can change the height to fit different-sized potted plants, moving it up or down as needed.

Also, the slats that make up the shelf have gaps between them, so rain water can't accumulate in the bottom and harm your plants — or the planter.

CONSTRUCTION. Since a planter has to be strong and stand up to the weather, I used water-resistant plastic resin glue in the mortise and tenon joints that connect the legs and rails.

The side slats have to be able to expand and contract with changes in humidity, so they aren't glued in place. They're held between the rails with tongue and groove joints. Or build a different version with raised panel sides. For more on how to do this, see the Designer's Notebook on page 94.

WOOD. I built the planter out of redwood. It's an attractive, straight-grained wood that's resistant to rot. Other woods that work well outdoors are western red cedar and northern white cedar. Or you could build one out of fir or pine, then paint it (see the inset photo above).

FINISH. To keep the redwood looking good throughout the year, I used a spar varnish and tung oil mixture to finish the Planter Boxes. For more on outdoor woods and finishes, see the Shop Info on page 48.

EXPLODED VIEW

OVERALL DIMENSIONS:
18⅝W x 18⅝D x 19½H

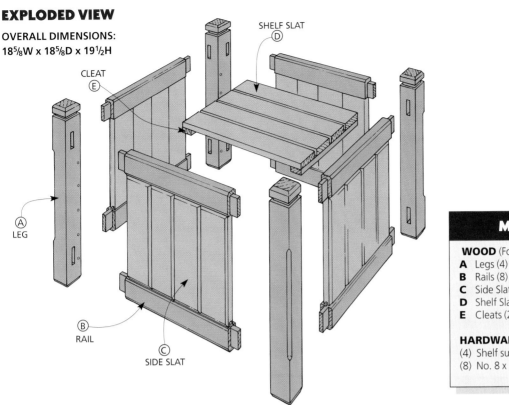

SHELF SLAT
(D)

CLEAT
(E)

(A)
LEG

(B)
RAIL

(C)
SIDE SLAT

MATERIALS LIST

WOOD (For one square planter)

A	Legs (4)	2¼ x 2¼ - 19½
B	Rails (8)	1¼ x 2½ - 16⅛
C	Side Slats (16)	¾ x 3½ - 11
D	Shelf Slats (4)	¾ x 3¾ - 13¾
E	Cleats (2)	¾ x 2½ - 15¾

HARDWARE SUPPLIES
(4) Shelf support pins
(8) No. 8 x 1¼" Fh woodscrews

DESIGNER'S NOTEBOOK

Add a bit of variety to the Planter Box by building it as a double unit, mid-height or tall version.

CONSTRUCTION NOTES:

■ To build the Double, Mid-Height, or Tall Planter Boxes simply change the lengths of the parts as shown. The only new parts will be the long rails (F) used on the Double Planter Box.

Note: As with the square Planter Box legs, always mark the top of the new legs, then lay out and make measurements for all of the mortises from that end (refer to *Fig. 2* on page 90).

MATERIALS LIST

CHANGED PARTS (For double planter)

B	Rails (4)	1¼ x 2½ - 16⅛
C	Side Slats (24)	¾ x 3½ - 11
D	Shelf Slats (8)	¾ x 3¾ - 13¾
E	Cleats (2)	¾ x 2½ - 29¾

NEW PARTS (For double planter)

F	Long Rails (4)	1¼ x 2½ - 30⅛

CHANGED PARTS (For mid-height planter)

A	Legs (4)	2¼ x 2¼ - 25½

CHANGED PARTS (For tall planter)

A	Legs (4)	2¼ x 2¼ - 31½

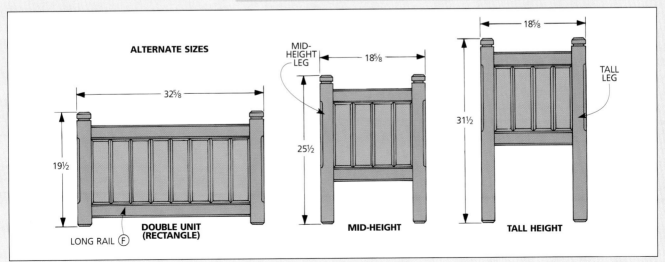

ALTERNATE SIZES

32⅝

19½

LONG RAIL (F)

DOUBLE UNIT
(RECTANGLE)

MID-HEIGHT LEG

18⅝

25½

MID-HEIGHT

18⅝

31½

TALL LEG

TALL HEIGHT

CUTTING DIAGRAM

4x4 (3½ x 3½) - 96 REDWOOD (10.6 Bd. Ft.)

A	A	A	A	

2x4 (1½ x 3½) - 72 REDWOOD (Two Boards @ 4 Bd. Ft. Each)

B	B	B	B	

1x6 (¾ x 5½) - 72 REDWOOD (3 Bd. Ft.)

D	D	D	D	E
				E

1x8 (¾ x 7¼) - 96 REDWOOD (5.3 Bd. Ft.)

C	C	C	C	C	C	C	C	
C	C	C	C	C	C	C	C	

LEGS

When I bought the posts for the legs, I learned something about redwood — 4x4 posts are rarely kiln dried. So there's a very good chance yours will still be wet. This means you'll have to do a few things differently before working with them.

WET REDWOOD. Working with very wet wood can be a real problem. So to avoid having the 4x4 posts twist or bend as they dried out, I dealt with the posts in three stages.

First, to speed up the drying time, I trimmed an equal amount of dry wood off all four faces. Then I rough cut each leg 2" longer than the finished length to allow for some checking on the ends of the 4x4 posts.

Next, I put the wood aside for a few days. (Don't be tempted to put it out in the sun, or hurry the process — that'll create more problems.)

Then after the posts had dried, I trimmed them again, this time to final dimensions. To make the pieces as straight as possible, you'll need to establish two flat sides that form a 90° angle.

SQUARE, FLAT SIDES. Begin by placing the flattest side of each piece against the rip fence. Now trim a narrow strip off the opposite side "A" (Step 1 in Fig. 1).

Note: Because the posts are too thick to cut all the way through in one pass, you'll have to turn the workpiece end for end and finish trimming the first strip with a second pass.

Next, to cut side "B", position side "A" down on the table and rip off another narrow strip, again in two passes (Step 2 in Fig. 1). Sides "A" and "B" should now be flat and 90° to each other.

CUT TO FINISHED SIZE. Now you're ready to cut the leg (A) to finished thickness. To do this, set the rip fence 2¼" from the blade. Then, with side "A" against the fence, rip a strip from side "C" (Step 3 in Fig. 1).

Make a final pass with side "B" against the fence (Step 4 in Fig. 1).

With the blanks cut square, trim the legs to finished length (Fig. 2).

LAY OUT AND CUT MORTISES. Now lay out the locations of four mortises on each leg (Fig. 2). The mortises are on the inside faces of each leg and are laid out exactly the same.

Note: To make it easier to keep things straight, mark the top of each leg and make all your measurements from that end (Fig. 2).

Next, use the drill press to bore out the mortises. Then square the ends and clean up the sides with a chisel.

DECORATIVE CUTS. After cleaning up the mortises I made a series of decorative cuts on the legs. Begin by cutting a ³⁄₈" dado (slot) around all four sides at the top ends of the legs (Fig. 3).

To make this continuous dado, first set your dado blade to cut ¼" deep. Then position the rip fence 1⅛" from the blade (Fig. 3a).

Note: Using an auxiliary fence on your miter gauge will give you better control of the leg, and also prevent chipout as you cut the dadoes (Fig. 3).

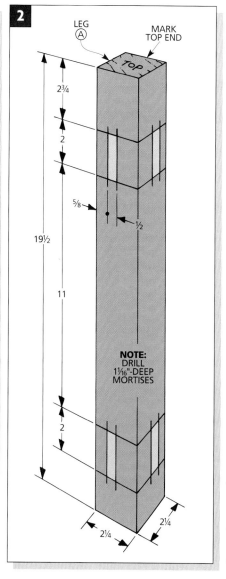

With the end of the leg butted to the fence, you can now cut the dadoes on all four sides of each leg.

STOPPED CHAMFER. The next step is to add the decorative "stopped" chamfers on the outside corner of each leg *(Fig. 4)*.

Note: The outside corner is the corner that is formed by the sides without mortises.

You could rout this chamfer with a handheld router. But since I was going to chamfer the top and bottom of the legs on the router table, I cut this stopped chamfer there, too.

Start by setting the height of the chamfer bit so it's $5/16"$ above the router table *(Fig. 5a)*. Then align the face of the fence so it's flush with the bearing on the bit.

To indicate the extremes of the stopped chamfer, I made two marks on each leg. The "start line" mark (5" from the top end) indicates where to plunge the leg to start the chamfer. The "stop line" mark ($15^1/2"$ from the top) indicates the stopping point. Then I made a reference mark on the router fence to indicate the centerpoint of the router bit.

Now turn on the router, and with a pivoting motion, plunge the leg against the fence so the start line on the leg lines up with the mark on the fence *(Fig. 5)*. Then slide the leg to the left. When the stop line on the leg lines up with the reference mark on the fence, stop and pivot the leg away from the fence *(Fig. 6)*.

TOP CHAMFERS. Once the corner chamfers are completed, you can cut the chamfers on the top end of each leg. This is also a $5/16"$-wide chamfer so you don't have to change the router bit *(Fig. 7a)*.

To make cutting the chamfers more accurate, I used a square piece of $3/4"$-thick plywood as a push block *(Fig. 7)*. The push block keeps the legs square to the router table fence, and helps prevent chipout on the back edge of the cut.

Now cut the chamfers on the top of each leg, holding the leg firmly to both the router table fence and the plywood push block. Again, feed the leg from right to left to cut the chamfer *(Fig. 7)*.

BOTTOM CHAMFERS. To prevent the legs from splintering when the planter box is dragged across the ground, I routed smaller chamfers on the bottom ends of the legs. To do this, set the height of the router bit to $3/16"$ *(Fig. 7a)*. Then rout the leg bottoms just as you did the tops.

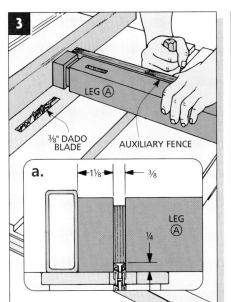

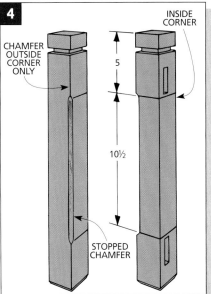

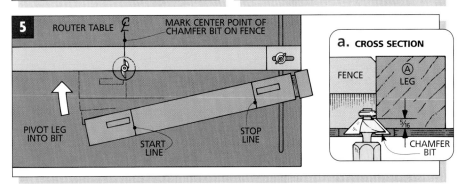

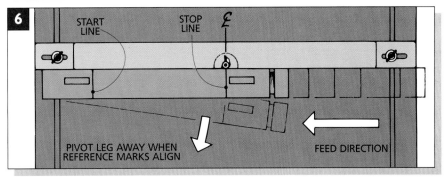

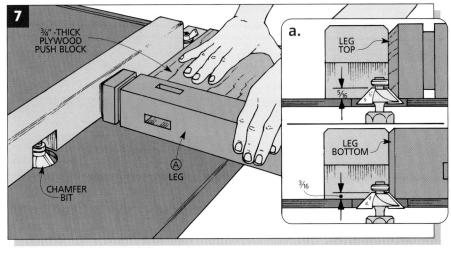

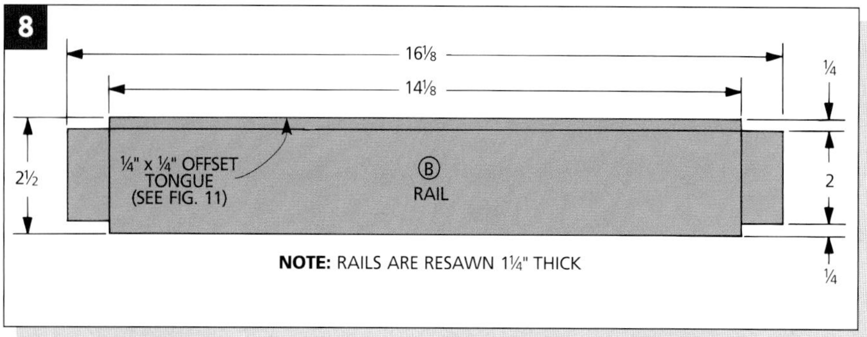
8
16⅛
14⅛
¼
2½
¼" x ¼" OFFSET TONGUE (SEE FIG. 11)
Ⓑ RAIL
2
¼
NOTE: RAILS ARE RESAWN 1¼" THICK

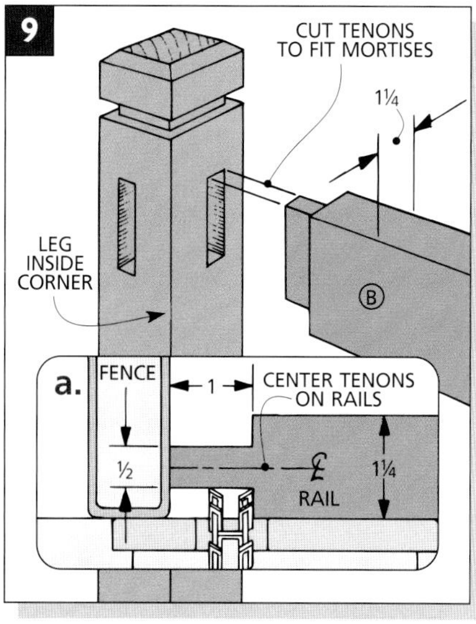
9
CUT TENONS TO FIT MORTISES
1¼
LEG INSIDE CORNER
Ⓑ
a.
FENCE
1
CENTER TENONS ON RAILS
½
℄
1¼
RAIL

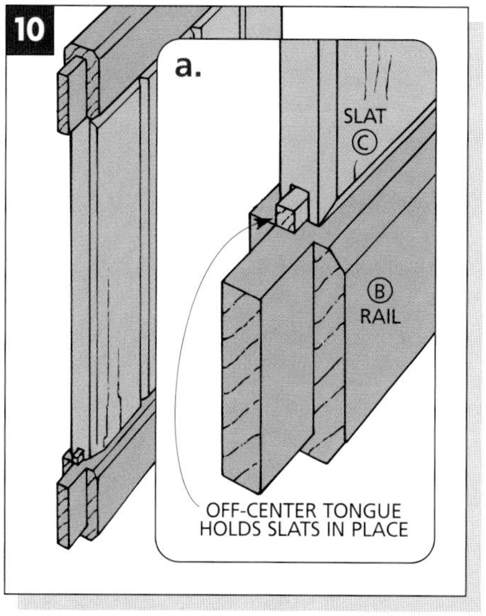
10
a.
SLAT Ⓒ
Ⓑ RAIL
OFF-CENTER TONGUE HOLDS SLATS IN PLACE

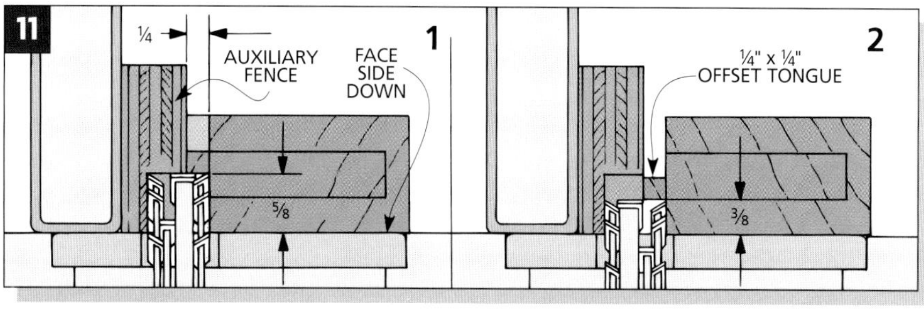
11
¼
AUXILIARY FENCE
FACE SIDE DOWN
1
⅝
¼" x ¼" OFFSET TONGUE
2
⅜

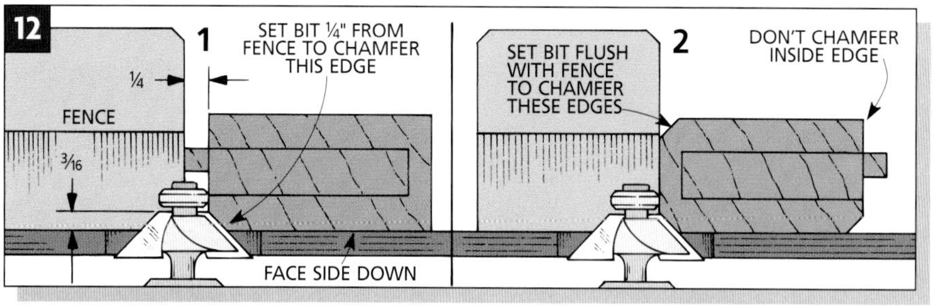
12
1
SET BIT ¼" FROM FENCE TO CHAMFER THIS EDGE
¼
FENCE
3⁄16
FACE SIDE DOWN
SET BIT FLUSH WITH FENCE TO CHAMFER THESE EDGES
2
DON'T CHAMFER INSIDE EDGE

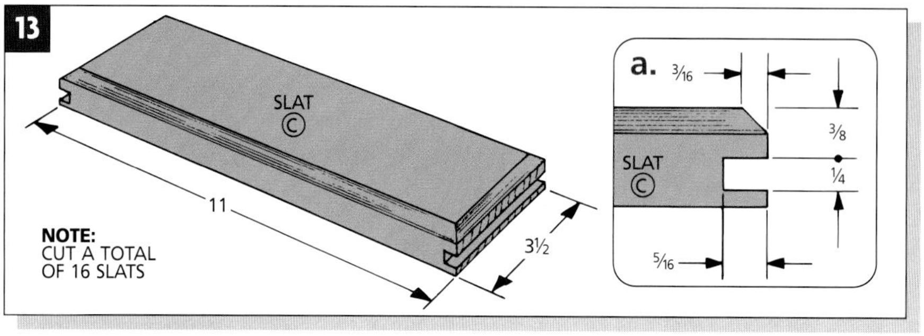
13
SLAT Ⓒ
11
3½
NOTE: CUT A TOTAL OF 16 SLATS
a. 3⁄16
⅜
¼
SLAT Ⓒ
5⁄16

SIDES

Once the legs are complete, you can start work on the sides. Each side consists of two rails and four slats held in place with tongue and groove joints.

RAILS. I started by resawing to 1¼" thick, enough 2x4 stock for the rails (B). Then cut eight rails to final width and length *(Fig. 8)*.

TENONS. The rails have a tenon on each end to fit the mortises in the legs. To set up the saw, position the rip fence as a stop so the *outside* edge of a dado blade is 1" from the fence *(Fig. 9a)*.

To create a centered tenon, first use a piece of scrap rail stock and sneak up on the final thickness of the tenon until it just fits the mortise. Then the tenons can be cut on the rails by making a series of passes over the dado blade.

The shoulders for the tenon can be cut by resetting the height of the dado blade to ¼". Then stand the workpiece on edge and make a series of passes over each edge of the rail top and bottom.

TONGUES. Once the tenons are cut on the rails, the saw can be set up to cut a tongue along one edge. This tongue holds the slats in place *(Fig. 10a)*. The ¼"-thick tongue is off-center on the thickness of the rail — it's set back ⅝" from the face.

To make the tongue, use a wood auxiliary fence to "bury" the dado blade, exposing only ¼" of the blade *(Fig. 11)*. Then raise the blade ⅝" above the table. Now, with the face side of the rail down, cut one side of the tongue *(Step 1 in Fig. 11)*. Then, lower the blade and cut the other side *(Step 2 in Fig. 11)*.

CHAMFER THE RAILS. The last step in making the rails is to chamfer three of the four edges (*not* the edge closest to the tongue). Chamfer the *other* edge on the tongue side with the fence set back ¼" from the bit *(Step 1 in Fig. 12)*. For the remaining edges, align the bearing flush with the fence *(Step 2 in Fig. 12)*.

SLATS. After the tongued rails are complete, the slats (C) can be made to fit between the rails *(Fig. 10)*. (There are four slats on each side.)

To determine the width of each slat, measure the shoulder-to-shoulder length of a rail (14⅛") and subtract ⅛" to allow for expansion. Then divide by four. My slats were 3½" wide *(Fig. 13)*.

Now cut them to length to equal the distance between the mortises on the legs. (Mine were 11" long.)

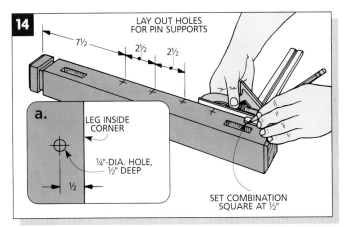

14 LAY OUT HOLES FOR PIN SUPPORTS

7½ 2½ 2½

a.
LEG INSIDE CORNER
¼"-DIA. HOLE, ½" DEEP
½
SET COMBINATION SQUARE AT ½"

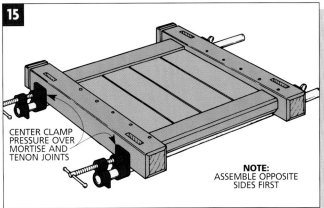

15
CENTER CLAMP PRESSURE OVER MORTISE AND TENON JOINTS

NOTE:
ASSEMBLE OPPOSITE SIDES FIRST

GROOVE THE SLATS. With the slats cut to size, you can now add an offset groove in the ends to fit the tongues on the rails *(Figs. 13 and 13a)*.

CHAMFER. To complete the side slats, chamfer all four edges on the face side.

PIN HOLES. Next, I laid out and drilled ¼" holes on each leg for pin supports.

The pins support an adjustable shelf (refer to *Fig. 17*). To position the holes, stand the legs up and mark the inside corner so the sets of holes will face each other (that is, mirrored sets). Then drill ½"-deep holes *(Fig. 14)*.

ASSEMBLE SIDES. The easiest way to assemble the planter is to first put together two of the side units, then connect these by adding rails and slats for the other sides.

Begin by applying glue to the tenons on the ends of two rails, and in the mortises in one leg. Insert the tenons, making certain the tongues on the rails face each other.

Next, slide (but don't glue) the slats onto the tongues of the rails. (The slats need room to move with changes in humidity.) Then apply glue to the other

two tenons and to the mortises of another leg, and fit the pieces together.

Next, clamp the side assembly together using two pipe clamps *(Fig. 15)*. Lay the assembly on the pipe clamps with the inside facing up. This way the clamp pressure will be centered directly on the mortise and tenon joints *(Fig. 15)*. Now, put together another side the same way.

ASSEMBLE THE PLANTER. Finish assembling the planter by connecting the two completed side units with the remaining rails and slats.

ADJUSTABLE SHELF

After completing the sides, work can begin on the adjustable shelf. It consists of four slats and two cleats *(Fig. 16)*.

CLEATS. Cut the cleats (E) to a width of 2½". To determine the length of the cleats (E), measure the distance on the inside of the planter from side slat to side slat and subtract ⅜" for clearance. (This made my cleats 15¾" long.)

SLATS. Next, cut the shelf slats (D). To allow water to run off between the slats, I left ¼" gaps between each one *(Fig. 16)*.

So, to determine the width of each slat, subtract ¾" from the length of the cleat (for the three ¼" gaps). Then divide this measurement by four (for the four slats). In my case, this made each slat 3¾" wide *(Fig. 16)*.

To determine the length of the slats, I measured from the drilled side of one post to the drilled side of the opposite post and subtracted ⅜" for easy clearance. (Mine were 13¾" long.)

ASSEMBLY. I completed the shelf assembly by screwing the cleats to the shelf slats. The screws go through the cleats and are centered on the width of each slat *(Fig. 16a)*.

To put the shelf in place, tip one end down into the planter. Then set the ends of the cleats on the shelf pins and simply allow the other end of the shelf to drop into place *(Fig. 17)*.

FINISH. To finish the planter, I used an equal mixture of spar varnish and tung oil (see the Shop Info on page 48). It seals the wood and darkens it only slightly so the deep red tones of the redwood remain visible. It also builds up a soft sheen after two coats. ∎

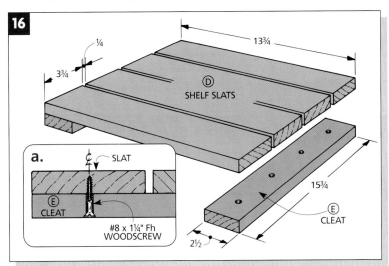

16
¼
3¾
13¾
Ⓓ
SHELF SLATS

a.
SLAT
Ⓔ CLEAT
#8 x 1¼" Fh WOODSCREW
15¾
Ⓔ CLEAT
2½

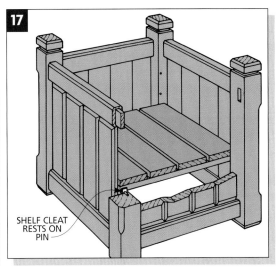

17
SHELF CLEAT RESTS ON PIN

DESIGNER'S NOTEBOOK

The addition of raised panels definitely dresses up the look of the Planter Box sides. The panels lend a more sophisticated style to the boxes without interfering with their flexible design.

CONSTRUCTION NOTES:

■ The Raised Panel Planter Boxes described here are built using the standard height legs *(Fig. 1)*. Each planter can be built with the middle or tall height legs if desired. Refer to the Designer's Notebook on page 89 for ideas on how this can be done.

■ Begin by squaring up and cutting the legs (A) to length as before.

■ Then lay out and cut the mortises for the rails *(Fig. 2)*.

■ To simplify construction, I decided to rout a groove in the legs and add a spline (K) to the groove. The spline, in effect, becomes a tongue on the leg, which will match the size and position of the tongues on the rails (B) (refer to *Fig. 4*).

■ To add the ¼"-deep groove to the legs, set up a ¼" straight bit in a table-mounted router. Then position the fence to align the bit with the inside edge of the mortise *(Figs. 2 and 3)*.

■ After the fence has been set to rout the groove, you'll need to lower the workpiece over the bit starting the cut inside the upper leg mortise. Then rout along the fence, stopping when you reach the opposite mortise *(Fig. 3)*.

■ Once the groove has been added, rout the decorative cuts and chamfers.

■ The next step is to rip a ¼"-thick, ½"-wide piece of stock for the spline. Then cut the splines to length (mine were 11") and glue them in place in the grooves centered between the mortises *(Fig. 4)*.

■ When you've completed the legs, rip and crosscut the rails (B) to size adding the tenons, tongues, and chamfers.

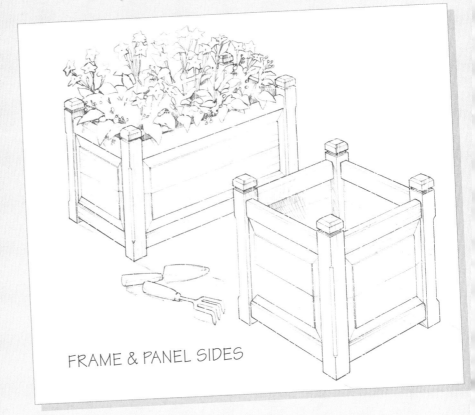

FRAME & PANEL SIDES

■ Now work can begin on the raised panels (J). First, glue up the blanks from ¾"-thick stock *(Fig. 5)*.

■ To size the panels, I first measured the frame opening, then subtracted ⅛" to allow for expansion. (My panels were 10⅞" wide and 14" long.) Once the glue has fully dried, the edges on each of the blanks can be beveled to create the raised panels.

■ To do this, attach an 8"-tall auxiliary fence to the rip fence and tilt the table saw blade to 5°. Then raise the saw blade to a height of 1½" *(Figs. 6 and 7)*.

■ Begin by cutting the bevels on the end grain edges first. This way any chipout that may occur will be removed when the face grain edges are cut.

■ Make the cut in two passes, moving the rip fence slightly between passes.

MATERIALS LIST

NEW PARTS FOR SINGLE UNIT

J	Single Panels (4)	¾ x 10⅞ - 14
K	Splines (8)	½ x ¾ - 11

NEW PARTS FOR DOUBLE UNIT

J	Single Panels (2)	¾ x 10⅞ - 14
K	Splines (8)	½ x ¾ - 11
L	Double Panels (2)	¾ x 10⅞ - 28

Note: Do not need part C.

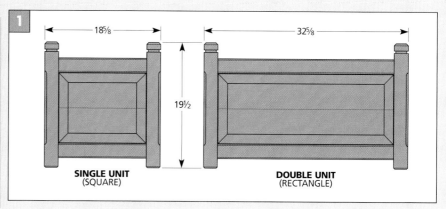

1

18⅝

32⅝

19½

SINGLE UNIT
(SQUARE)

DOUBLE UNIT
(RECTANGLE)

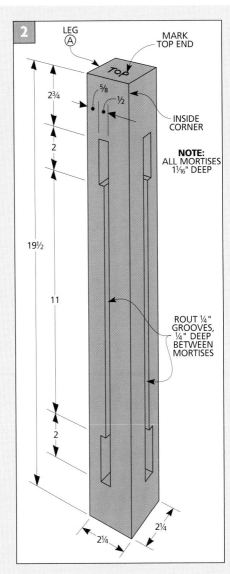

2

LEG Ⓐ

MARK TOP END

TOP

INSIDE CORNER

⅝

½

2¾

2

19½

11

NOTE: ALL MORTISES 1¹⁄₁₆" DEEP

ROUT ¼" GROOVES, ¼" DEEP BETWEEN MORTISES

2

2¼

2¼

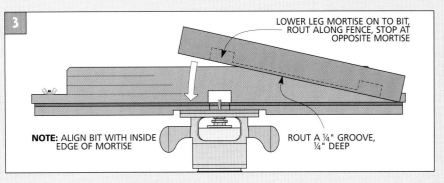

3

LOWER LEG MORTISE ON TO BIT, ROUT ALONG FENCE, STOP AT OPPOSITE MORTISE

NOTE: ALIGN BIT WITH INSIDE EDGE OF MORTISE

ROUT A ¼" GROOVE, ¼" DEEP

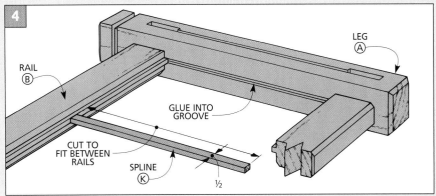

4

RAIL Ⓑ

LEG Ⓐ

GLUE INTO GROOVE

CUT TO FIT BETWEEN RAILS

SPLINE Ⓚ

½

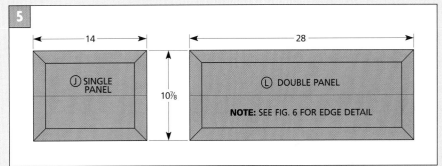

5

14

28

10⅞

Ⓙ SINGLE PANEL

Ⓛ DOUBLE PANEL

NOTE: SEE FIG. 6 FOR EDGE DETAIL

The idea is to remove most of the waste on the first pass, then to remove any burn or swirl marks that might remain with the second pass.

Note: Cut the bevels on *all* four edges of *all* of the panels before moving the rip fence to make the second pass.

■ If needed, use a sanding block with a beveled edge to finish sand the saw marks and the undercut shoulders.

■ Then, I use a ¼" straight bit in the router table to rout the centered grooves along the edges of the panel to fit over the rail and leg tongues *(Fig. 6)*. The top groove on each panel is ⁵⁄₁₆" deep, while the side and bottom grooves are ³⁄₁₆" deep *(Figs. 8a and 8b)*. This will allow for expansion, while spacing the panel evenly within the frame.

■ Finally, it's best to assemble opposite sides first, then connect them by adding rails and panels for the other sides. Add a bead of silicone caulk in the top grooves when adding the panels (but no glue).

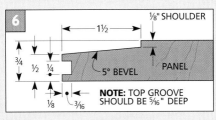

6

⅛" SHOULDER

1½

¾

½

¼

5° BEVEL

PANEL

⅛

³⁄₁₆

NOTE: TOP GROOVE SHOULD BE ⁵⁄₁₆" DEEP

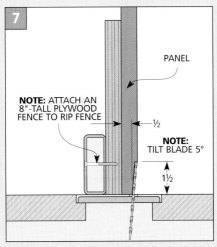

7

PANEL

NOTE: ATTACH AN 8"-TALL PLYWOOD FENCE TO RIP FENCE

½

NOTE: TILT BLADE 5°

1½

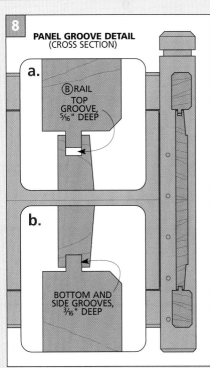

8

PANEL GROOVE DETAIL (CROSS SECTION)

a.

Ⓑ RAIL TOP GROOVE, ⁵⁄₁₆" DEEP

b.

BOTTOM AND SIDE GROOVES, ³⁄₁₆" DEEP

Picnic Table

As sturdy as it is good looking, this set features splined miter joints on the table and bench tops to keep them flat. The simple design of all three pieces means construction moves along quickly.

All it took was a few warm days to remind me of the picnic table and benches I'd been planning to build. What I had in mind was a simple, straightforward design. Something I could knock out in a few days. Yet it needed to have a solid base and be sturdy enough to last for years.

To make the table and benches easy to build, the joinery on each one is identical. Strong mortise and tenon joints keep the bases from racking. And splined miter joints ensure that the tops will stay flat.

WOOD. I used redwood for the table top and bench tops. The straight, even grain of this outdoor wood makes it a perfect choice for a long, flat surface like a picnic table. But when building the bases, I used Douglas fir. It's an excellent choice for outdoor furniture where something less expensive than redwood will do. And since the leg assemblies are painted, I didn't need to worry about covering up a more attractive wood grain.

SPLINED MITERS. The table and bench tops consist of mitered frames. The frames surround the redwood planks which make up the surface of the table and bench. Since the pieces are joined together at an angle, the end grain is hidden. But gluing end grain to end grain produces a weak bond, so I used splines to add strength to this common form of joinery. For more on how to construct splined miter joints, see the Technique article beginning on page 102.

MORTISE AND TENONS. The sturdy legs for the table and bench base look like they're made from 4x4 lumber. But in fact, I just used "two-by" material and added dadoes and rabbets to form "mortises" for the rails.

FINISH. No matter how strong the joints are, the table and benches still need protection from the weather. I applied an outdoor oil to the redwood tops and several coats of paint to the bases. (For more on redwood and outdoor finishes, see pages 35 and 48.)

DESIGN OPTIONS. If you don't have the space for a full-size Picnic Table, you can make a square table with two short benches to match. See the Designer's Notebook on page 104 for more on how to do this.

EXPLODED VIEW

OVERALL DIMENSIONS:
Table 72W x 35³/₈D x 30H
Bench 72W x 15¹/₈D x 17H

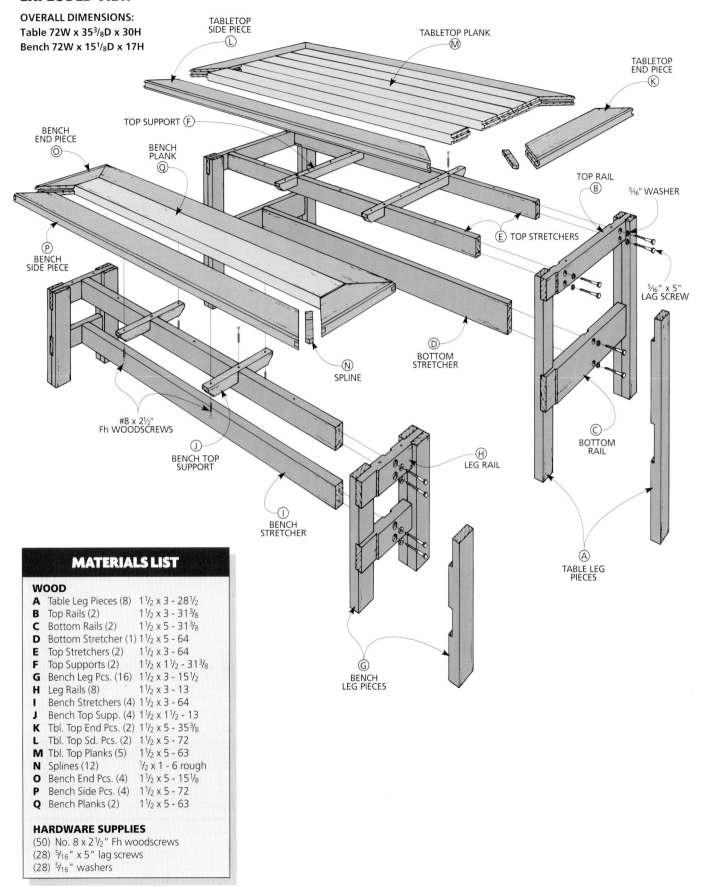

TABLETOP SIDE PIECE — L

TABLETOP PLANK — M

TABLETOP END PIECE — K

TOP SUPPORT — F

BENCH END PIECE — O

BENCH PLANK — Q

TOP RAIL — B

⁵/₁₆" WASHER

E — TOP STRETCHERS

⁵/₁₆" x 5" LAG SCREW

P — BENCH SIDE PIECE

D — BOTTOM STRETCHER

BOTTOM RAIL — C

#8 x 2¹/₂" Fh WOODSCREWS

N — SPLINE

J — BENCH TOP SUPPORT

LEG RAIL — H

I — BENCH STRETCHER

G — BENCH LEG PIECES

A — TABLE LEG PIECES

MATERIALS LIST

WOOD

A	Table Leg Pieces (8)	1¹/₂ x 3 - 28¹/₂
B	Top Rails (2)	1¹/₂ x 3 - 31³/₈
C	Bottom Rails (2)	1¹/₂ x 5 - 31³/₈
D	Bottom Stretcher (1)	1¹/₂ x 5 - 64
E	Top Stretchers (2)	1¹/₂ x 3 - 64
F	Top Supports (2)	1¹/₂ x 1¹/₂ - 31³/₈
G	Bench Leg Pcs. (16)	1¹/₂ x 3 - 15¹/₂
H	Leg Rails (8)	1¹/₂ x 3 - 13
I	Bench Stretchers (4)	1¹/₂ x 3 - 64
J	Bench Top Supp. (4)	1¹/₂ x 1¹/₂ - 13
K	Tbl. Top End Pcs. (2)	1¹/₂ x 5 - 35³/₈
L	Tbl. Top Sd. Pcs. (2)	1¹/₂ x 5 - 72
M	Tbl. Top Planks (5)	1¹/₂ x 5 - 63
N	Splines (12)	¹/₂ x 1 - 6 rough
O	Bench End Pcs. (4)	1¹/₂ x 5 - 15¹/₈
P	Bench Side Pcs. (4)	1¹/₂ x 5 - 72
Q	Bench Planks (2)	1¹/₂ x 5 - 63

HARDWARE SUPPLIES

(50) No. 8 x 2¹/₂" Fh woodscrews
(28) ⁵/₁₆" x 5" lag screws
(28) ⁵/₁₆" washers

CUTTING DIAGRAM

2x8 (1½ x 7¼) - 96 DOUGLAS FIR (Two Boards @ 10.7 Bd. Ft. Each)

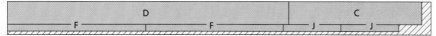

A	A	G	G
A	A	G	G

2x8 (1½ x 7¼) - 96 DOUGLAS FIR (Two Boards @ 10.7 Bd. Ft. Each)

H	H	I
H	H	I

2x8 (1½ x 7¼) - 96 DOUGLAS FIR (10.7 Bd. Ft.)

G	G	G	G	B
G	G	G	G	B

2x8 (1½ x 7¼) - 96 DOUGLAS FIR (10.7 Bd. Ft.)

D	C
F	F	J	J

2x8 (1½ x 7¼) - 96 DOUGLAS FIR (10.7 Bd. Ft.)

E	C
E	J	J

2x6 (1½ x 5½) - 96 REDWOOD (8 Bd. Ft.)

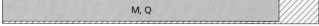

K	K

2x6 (1½ x 5½) - 96 REDWOOD (Two Boards @ 8 Bd. Ft. Each)

L

2x6 (1½ x 5½) - 96 REDWOOD (Four Boards @ 8 Bd. Ft. Each)

P	O

2x6 (1½ x 5½) - 72 REDWOOD (7 Boards @ 6 Bd. Ft. Each)

M, Q

The table consists of two end assemblies that are connected with stretchers at the top and bottom *(Fig. 1)*. I also added a pair of supports for the top. They span the upper stretchers and give strength to the table top.

END ASSEMBLIES. Each end assembly is made up of a pair of sturdy legs that are held together with a rail at the top and bottom *(Fig. 2)*. To simplify the mortise and tenon joinery, each leg is built up from two table leg pieces (A).

I began by cutting a dado near the middle and a rabbet at the top of each piece. This way you form "mortises" for the rails when the legs are glued up.

RAILS. Each pair of legs is connected by a narrow top rail (B) and a wide bottom rail (C). To do this, I cut a 3"-long tenon on the end of each rail to fit the mortises *(Figs. 2a and 2b)*. And to accept the stretchers, there are two shallow dadoes in the top rail and a single dado centered on the bottom rail.

For easier assembly, two counterbored shank holes are drilled in each dado *(Fig. 1a)*. And counterbored shank holes drilled from the bottom of the rails will be used to attach the top to the base assembly (refer to *Fig. 2* and *Fig. 10a* on page 101).

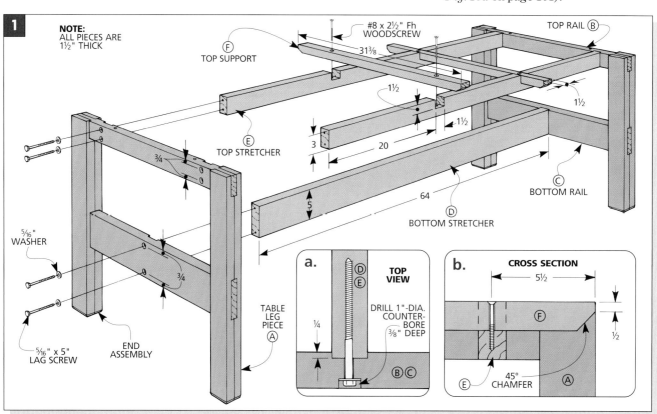

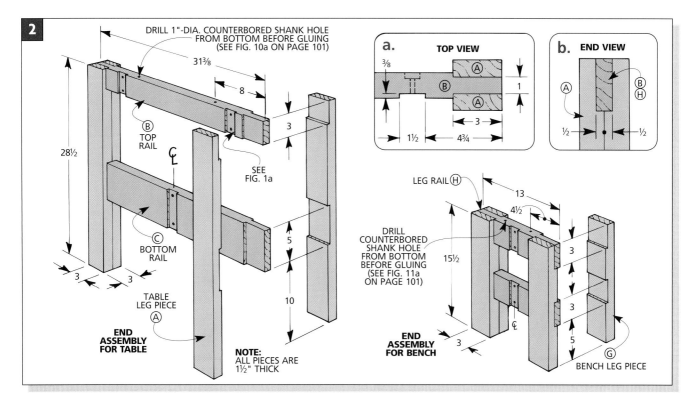

2

DRILL 1"-DIA. COUNTERBORED SHANK HOLE FROM BOTTOM BEFORE GLUING (SEE FIG. 10a ON PAGE 101)

31⅜

8

3

B TOP RAIL

28½

SEE FIG. 1a

C BOTTOM RAIL

5

3 3

TABLE LEG PIECE

A

10

END ASSEMBLY FOR TABLE

NOTE: ALL PIECES ARE 1½" THICK

a. TOP VIEW

⅜

A

B

A

1

3

1½ 4¾

b. END VIEW

A

B H

½ ½

LEG RAIL H

13

4½

DRILL COUNTERBORED SHANK HOLE FROM BOTTOM BEFORE GLUING (SEE FIG. 11a ON PAGE 101)

15½

3

3

5

END ASSEMBLY FOR BENCH

3

G

BENCH LEG PIECE

Now it's just a matter of gluing up each end assembly. To provide plenty of working time (and protect against moisture), I used slow-curing epoxy. (For more on epoxies and other types of glues, refer to the Shop Info on page 48.)

STRETCHERS. To hold the end assemblies together, I added a bottom stretcher (D) and two top stretchers (E) *(Fig. 1)*. After cutting a pair of notches in each top stretcher to accept the supports (added next), the stretchers can be attached to the end assemblies with lag screws *(Fig. 1a)*.

TOP SUPPORTS. All that's left to complete the base is to add two top supports (F). To provide some extra knee room, I added a 45° chamfer to each end of the supports *(Fig. 1b)*. Finally, glue and screw the supports so that the ends are flush with the leg assemblies *(Fig. 1b)*.

BENCH BASE

The bases for the two benches are built the same way as the table base. But the size and number of parts is just a little bit different.

The biggest difference will be that the leg pieces (G) are shorter (see the End Assembly for Bench in *Fig. 2*). And unlike the table base, the two rails (H) that end up joining the legs together are both the same width *(Fig. 2)*.

Another difference is that the end assemblies are held together with two stretchers (I) instead of three *(Fig. 3)*. Both stretchers are the same width. Here again, two notches will accept the chamfered top supports (J). Finally, glue and screw the supports so that the ends are flush with the leg assemblies *(Fig. 3a)*.

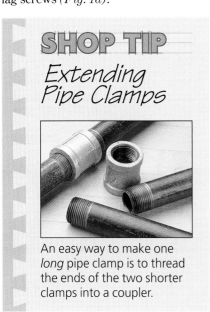

SHOP TIP

Extending Pipe Clamps

An easy way to make one *long* pipe clamp is to thread the ends of the two shorter clamps into a coupler.

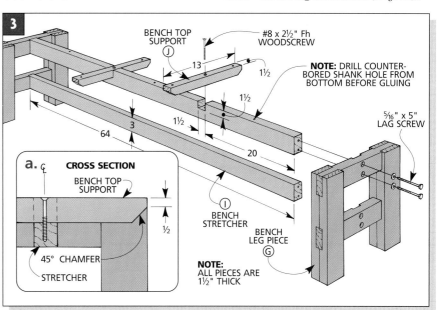

3

BENCH TOP SUPPORT J

#8 x 2½" Fh WOODSCREW

13

1½

NOTE: DRILL COUNTER-BORED SHANK HOLE FROM BOTTOM BEFORE GLUING

1½

3

1½

64

20

⁵⁄₁₆" x 5" LAG SCREW

a. CROSS SECTION

BENCH TOP SUPPORT

½

45° CHAMFER STRETCHER

I BENCH STRETCHER

BENCH LEG PIECE G

NOTE: ALL PIECES ARE 1½" THICK

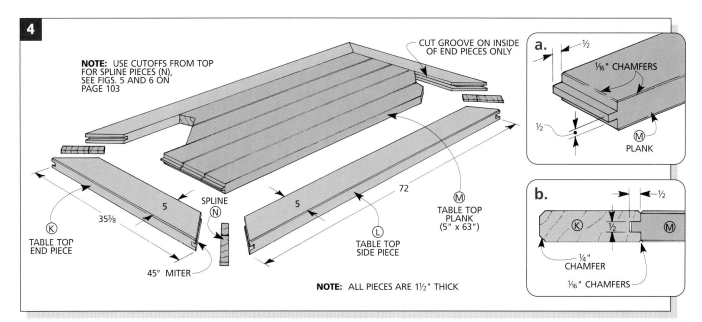

4

NOTE: USE CUTOFFS FROM TOP FOR SPLINE PIECES (N), SEE FIGS. 5 AND 6 ON PAGE 103

CUT GROOVE ON INSIDE OF END PIECES ONLY

a. ½ ¹/₁₆" CHAMFERS ½ Ⓜ PLANK

72

5

5

SPLINE Ⓝ

35⅜

Ⓚ
TABLE TOP END PIECE

45° MITER

Ⓛ
TABLE TOP SIDE PIECE

Ⓜ
TABLE TOP PLANK (5" x 63")

NOTE: ALL PIECES ARE 1½" THICK

b. ½ Ⓚ ½ Ⓜ ¼" CHAMFER ¹/₁₆" CHAMFERS

TABLE TOP

Now that the base assemblies have been completed, you can turn your attention to the table top. It consists of a mitered frame that surrounds several wood planks *(Fig. 4)*.

FRAME. The frame is made up of two table top end pieces (K) and two table top side pieces (L) that are mitered at a 45° angle *(Fig. 4)*. To strengthen the miter joints, they're held together with wood splines. These splines fit in grooves that are routed in the end of each frame piece. (For more on making splined miters, refer to the Technique article on page 102.)

Note: While you're set up to cut the table top side pieces (L), go ahead and cut the four bench side pieces (P) also (refer to *Fig. 9*).

In addition to the grooves for the splines, you'll need to rout two other grooves of the same size to accept the tongues on the planks that are cut next. These grooves are on the inside edge of each end piece (K, O) *(Fig. 4)*.

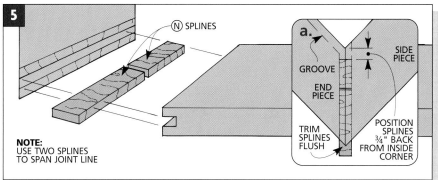

5

Ⓝ SPLINES

a. SIDE PIECE GROOVE END PIECE TRIM SPLINES FLUSH POSITION SPLINES ¾" BACK FROM INSIDE CORNER

NOTE: USE TWO SPLINES TO SPAN JOINT LINE

PLANKS. With the frame complete, the next step is to cut the planks (M) to length *(Fig. 4)*. Rabbeting the top and bottom ends of each plank forms a tongue that fits into the grooves in the table top end pieces *(Fig. 4a)*.

Note: Again, take the time now to cut two extra planks (Q) for the bench top assemblies (refer to *Fig. 9*).

CHAMFER. While I was at it, I routed a decorative chamfer (¹/₁₆") around the top and bottom edges of the table top and bench planks and the inside edges of all the frame pieces *(Fig. 4b)*.

SPLINES. Before assembling the table top, you'll need to make the splines (N). I found it easiest to use the cutoffs from the top for this. But since these pieces are too narrow to span the length of the joint line, you'll need to butt two small splines together *(Fig. 5)*.

ASSEMBLY. Now you're ready to assemble the table top. Even after dry-assembling and checking the fit, gluing up a large project like this can be a real challenge. So to make things easier, I decided to assemble the table top in stages *(Figs. 6, 7, and 8)*.

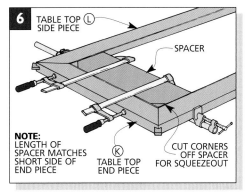

6

TABLE TOP Ⓛ SIDE PIECE

SPACER

NOTE: LENGTH OF SPACER MATCHES SHORT SIDE OF END PIECE

Ⓚ TABLE TOP END PIECE

CUT CORNERS OFF SPACER FOR SQUEEZEOUT

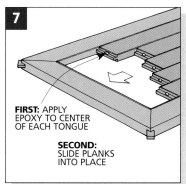

7

FIRST: APPLY EPOXY TO CENTER OF EACH TONGUE

SECOND: SLIDE PLANKS INTO PLACE

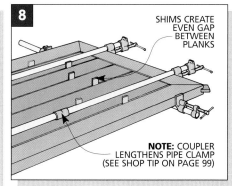

8

SHIMS CREATE EVEN GAP BETWEEN PLANKS

NOTE: COUPLER LENGTHENS PIPE CLAMP (SEE SHOP TIP ON PAGE 99)

Start by epoxying the corners at one end of the frame, using two splines per corner to span the joint line. Then clamp a spacer to the end of the frame and position another clamp across the sides to keep the corners square *(Fig. 6)*.

Note: There are a few things to watch for here. To avoid filling the grooves that the planks fit into, the splines are set back from the inside corner *(Fig. 5a)*. And I also cut the corners off the spacer. This will allow for any squeeze out *(Fig. 6)*.

Once the frame assembly has completely dried, apply epoxy to the *center* of each tongue and slide each of the table top planks (M) into place at the end of the frame *(Fig. 7)*.

Now, using shims to create an even ($^1/_{16}$") gap between the planks, simply glue and clamp the opposite end of the frame in place *(Fig. 8)*.

After trimming the splines flush with a hand saw and sanding the edges smooth, there's just one more thing to do. That's to "break" the sharp edges on the top and bottom edges of the table by routing $^1/_4$" chamfers *(Fig. 4b)*.

BENCH TOPS

The two tops for the benches are built the same way as the table top. The only difference is that they're smaller.

While the bench end pieces (O) are quite a bit shorter than the ends of the table top, the bench side pieces (P) are exactly the same length *(Fig. 9)*.

Here again, the mitered frame for each benchtop is held together with splines. And a tongue on the end of a single plank (Q) fits into a groove in each end piece.

ASSEMBLY

At this point, all that's left to do is to attach the tops of the table and the benches to the base assemblies.

TABLE. The easiest way to position the table top is to place it upside down on the floor and center the base assembly on top of it *(Fig. 10)*.

After drilling counterbored shank holes in each stretcher (E) and countersunk shank holes through the top supports (F), simply screw the top in place using woodscrews *(Figs. 10a and 10b)*.

Installing screws in the holes drilled earlier in the top rails (B) secures the ends of the frame.

BENCHES. Now it's just a matter of attaching the two bench tops. They're screwed to the bases using the same procedure as with the table top *(Fig. 11)*.

CHAMFER. There's one last thing to do. To prevent the legs from splintering when moving the table and benches, I sanded slight chamfers on the bottom edges of the legs *(Figs. 10 and 11)*.

FINISH. To preserve the natural look of the redwood and protect it from the elements, I wiped on an outdoor oil finish. (You'll need to renew this type of finish regularly.) For more on how to do this, see the Finishing Tip on page 122. The table base and bench bases are protected with several coats of an alkyd primer and a quality latex paint. ∎

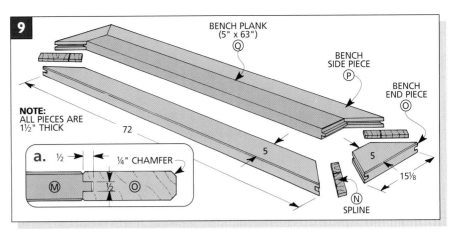

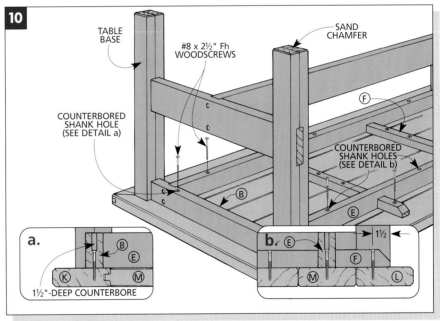

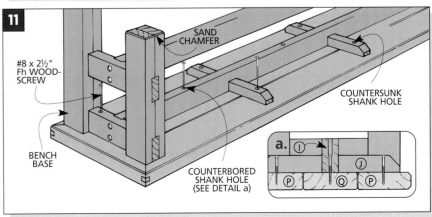

TECHNIQUE .... *Splined Miters*

'Ve always thought of a miter joint as something of a mixed bag. Since the pieces are joined together at an angle, the end grain is hidden. But gluing end grain to end grain produces a weak joint.

SPLINE. Fortunately, all that's needed to strengthen a miter joint is a simple spline. This is just a strip of wood that's glued into a groove cut in the angled end of each piece (see the photo at right). With a spline, you get a larger glue surface. And this creates a stronger surface-to-surface glue joint.

SLOT CUTTER. A quick way to cut the grooves for the splines is to use a router and a slot cutter bit (see the Shop Tip at left). Depending on the length of the pieces, I use two different approaches.

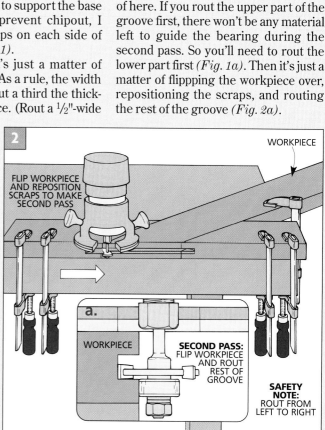

LONG PIECES. Since long pieces can be awkward to handle (like the pieces in the Picnic Table), it's easiest to clamp them to the bench and use the router in a hand-held position *(Figs. 1 and 2)*.

The problem is the tip of the miter doesn't provide much support for the router base. And when the bit cuts through, it's likely to chip out the edge of the workpiece. So to support the base of the router and prevent chipout, I clamp mitered scraps on each side of the workpiece *(Fig. 1)*.

GROOVE. Now it's just a matter of routing the groove. As a rule, the width of the groove is about a third the thickness of the workpiece. (Rout a ½"-wide groove in 1½"-thick stock for example.) And the depth of the groove always matches its width.

To ensure the groove is centered on the thickness of the workpiece, the idea is to rout it in two passes — flipping the workpiece between each one.

Note: I use a slot cutter that's smaller than the width of the groove.

There is one other thing to be aware of here. If you rout the upper part of the groove first, there won't be any material left to guide the bearing during the second pass. So you'll need to rout the lower part first *(Fig. 1a)*. Then it's just a matter of flippping the workpiece over, repositioning the scraps, and routing the rest of the groove *(Fig. 2a)*.

SHOP TIP
Slot Cutter

A slot cutter bit makes quick work of routing a groove for a spline. And different size bearings let you adjust the depth of cut. Use it in a hand-held router or mount it in your router table, depending on the size of the workpiece.

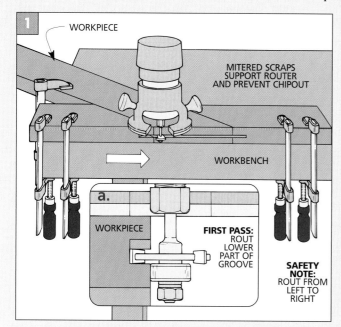

1 WORKPIECE

MITERED SCRAPS SUPPORT ROUTER AND PREVENT CHIPOUT

WORKBENCH

a. WORKPIECE

FIRST PASS: ROUT LOWER PART OF GROOVE

SAFETY NOTE: ROUT FROM LEFT TO RIGHT

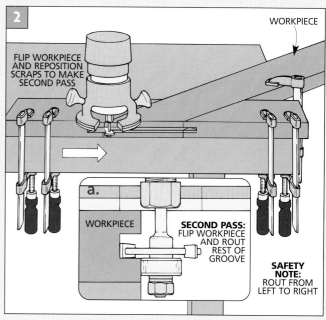

2 WORKPIECE

FLIP WORKPIECE AND REPOSITION SCRAPS TO MAKE SECOND PASS

a. WORKPIECE

SECOND PASS: FLIP WORKPIECE AND ROUT REST OF GROOVE

SAFETY NOTE: ROUT FROM LEFT TO RIGHT

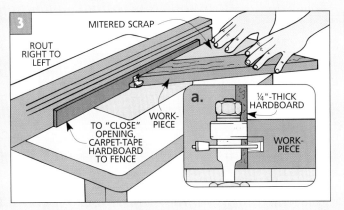

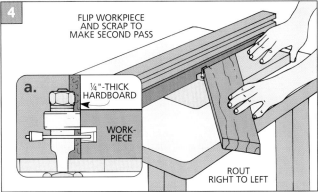

SHORT PIECES. When routing a groove in a short workpiece, I find it's quicker and easier to use the router table *(Figs. 3 and 4).*

The basic idea is the same. The groove is routed in two passes *(Figs. 3a and 4a).* And using a mitered scrap as a push block reduces chipout. To prevent the tip of the miter from catching, I carpet-tape a piece of hardboard to the fence to reduce the size of the opening. (For details about doing this, see the Shop Tip below right.)

SPLINES

Once you've routed the grooves, the next step is to cut the splines.

GRAIN. The important thing here is the direction of the grain in the spline.

To provide the most strength, the grain should run perpendicular to the joint line (see photos on previous page).

SIZE. You also need to consider the size of the spline.

What you want is to cut the spline to thickness so it fits snug in the groove. But not so tight that it squeezes out all the glue. And to the ensure the workpieces draw tightly together, it's cut to length (width) so it doesn't "bottom out" in the grooves.

Finally, to allow for trimming, I usually cut the spline from a block of wood that's wider than the length of the joint.

Note: When working with wide pieces like those on the Picnic Table, you can butt two small splines together.

CUT SPLINES. An easy way to make the splines is to use a scrap from the

project you're working on and cut it on the table saw. Start by setting the rip fence to the desired thickness of the spline *(Fig. 5a).*

Then raise the saw blade 1/8" higher than the length (width) of the spline and cut several kerfs. Now, after repositioning the fence and then lowering the blade so it just cuts into the kerf, you can cut each spline from the block *(Fig. 6a).* Be sure to saw the block so that the spline falls away from the saw blade *(Fig. 6).* Use a zero-clearance insert to keep the pieces from falling through.

ASSEMBLY. Now it's just a matter of applying glue to the splines and grooves and clamping the pieces together. When the glue dries, trim the splines flush and sand them smooth (see the inset photo).

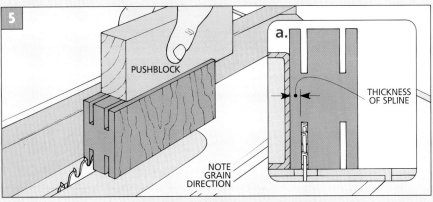

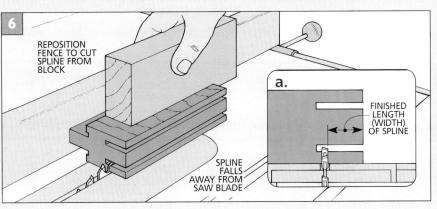

SHOP TIP
Zero Clearance Insert

A 1/4" hardboard auxiliary fence with notches cut in it prevents the tip of the mitered piece from catching on the opening in the fence.

DESIGNER'S NOTEBOOK

This Square Picnic Table will be the envy of every visitor to your patio or balcony. The changes made to the table make it accessible from all sides, so it fits in those spaces where a larger table can't.

CONSTRUCTION NOTES:

■ Designed for compact spaces and small areas, such as an apartment balcony, the Square Picnic Table uses the same mortise and tenon style joinery for the table and bench bases. But now, instead of stretchers connecting the leg assemblies, I added half laps to the two top rails. This design changes the orientation of the legs (they're now at a 45° angle to the table top), making the table look less bulky. This also allows you to sit at all four sides of the table, since there are no lower rails or stretchers to bump your legs on.

Although four benches would easily fit around this table, I liked the look of just two benches.

■ Start building the Square Picnic Table by constructing the criss-cross style table base assembly *(Fig. 1)*. The rails are slightly longer and wider than before (4" x 43"). But the leg assemblies are built similar to the larger Picnic Table.

■ Start by cutting the rabbets at the top of each leg piece (A) to form the "mortise," and then add the tenons on each end of the rails (B). But now instead of cutting dadoes for stretchers into the top rails, I added half laps.

■ To do this, I use the table saw to cut a centered dado or "notch" in each of the rails. The notches are cut $1^1/_2$" wide to

SQUARE PICNIC TABLE

match the width of the rails and just deep enough for the top edges of the rails to line up flush once the leg assemblies are complete.

■ Before assembling the legs and rails, it's best to drill the two shank holes near the ends of each rail for screws used to mount the top *(Fig. 1)*. The holes are

centered on the rails and drilled from the bottom edge. Later I add $1/_4$" x $4^1/_2$"-long hex head bolts and washers that thread into inserts added to the underside of the table top (refer to *Fig. 4*).

Note: Build one leg assembly with the top rail notch facing down and with the other notch facing up *(Fig. 1)*.

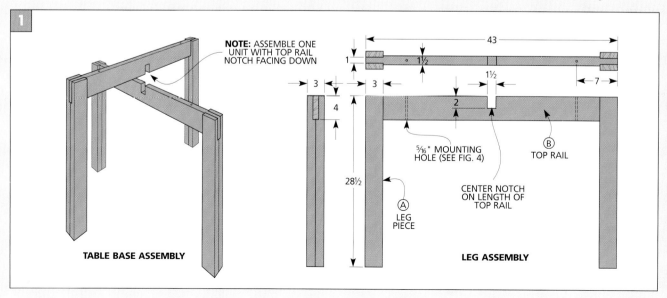

1

TABLE BASE ASSEMBLY

NOTE: ASSEMBLE ONE UNIT WITH TOP RAIL NOTCH FACING DOWN

43

1

$1^1/_2$

$1^1/_2$

3

3

4

2

7

$^5/_{16}$" MOUNTING HOLE (SEE FIG. 4)

Ⓑ TOP RAIL

$28^1/_2$

Ⓐ LEG PIECE

CENTER NOTCH ON LENGTH OF TOP RAIL

LEG ASSEMBLY

■ Finally, glue the two leg assemblies together making sure to keep them square to each other.

■ Once the table base assembly is complete, begin on the bench base assemblies. The only change is in the length of the bench stretchers (I). They're now 24" long *(Fig. 2)*.

■ Add the rabbets at the tops and the dadoes near the middle of the leg pieces (G). Then tenons are cut on the ends of each leg rail (H) to fit the mortises.

■ Next you can cut dadoes centered on each of the rails for the stretcher (I).

■ Drill counterbored shank holes through the upper bench rails before assembling the bench base *(Fig. 2)*.

■ Now, begin work on the smaller table top and bench tops. Once again, they consist of mitered frames that surround the table and bench planks *(Fig. 3)*.

■ The frame for the table top is made up of four top end pieces (K) that are mitered at a 45° angle *(Fig. 3)*.

■ To strengthen the miter joints, you need to use splined miters. (For more on making splined miters, see the Technique article on pages 102 and 103.)

■ As before, rout grooves on the inside edges of two of the top end pieces (K).

■ Next rip and crosscut the top planks (M) to length and rout the tongues that fit in the grooves in the end pieces.

■ Finally, build the bench top as before, using the bench end pieces (O), with the shortened bench side pieces (P), and the bench plank (Q) *(Fig. 3)*.

■ All that's left now is to attach the top to the table base using the threaded inserts and the hex head bolts and washers *(Fig. 4)*. The bench bases are attached with lag screws.

MATERIALS LIST

CHANGED PARTS

A	Leg Pieces (8)	$1\frac{1}{2}$ x 3 - $28\frac{1}{2}$
B	Top Rails (2)	$1\frac{1}{2}$ x 4 - 43
I	Bench Stretchers (4)	$1\frac{1}{2}$ x 3 - 24
K	Top End Pieces (4)	$1\frac{1}{2}$ x 5 - $35\frac{3}{8}$
M	Top Planks (5)	$1\frac{1}{2}$ x 5 - $26\frac{3}{8}$
P	Bench Side Pcs. (4)	$1\frac{1}{2}$ x 5 - 32
Q	Bench Planks (2)	$1\frac{1}{2}$ x 5 - 23

Note: Do not need parts C, D, E, F, J, and L.

HARDWARE SUPPLIES

(8) No. 8 x $2\frac{1}{2}$" Fh woodscrews
(4) $\frac{1}{4}$" x $4\frac{1}{2}$" hex head bolts
(4) $\frac{1}{4}$" washers
(16) $\frac{5}{16}$" x 5" lag screws
(16) $\frac{5}{16}$" washers
(4) $\frac{1}{4}$-20 threaded inserts

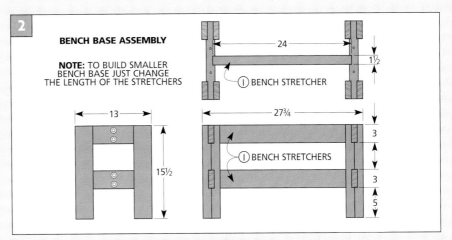

2

BENCH BASE ASSEMBLY

NOTE: TO BUILD SMALLER BENCH BASE JUST CHANGE THE LENGTH OF THE STRETCHERS

24

$1\frac{1}{2}$

(I) BENCH STRETCHER

13

$15\frac{1}{2}$

$27\frac{3}{4}$

(I) BENCH STRETCHERS

3

3

5

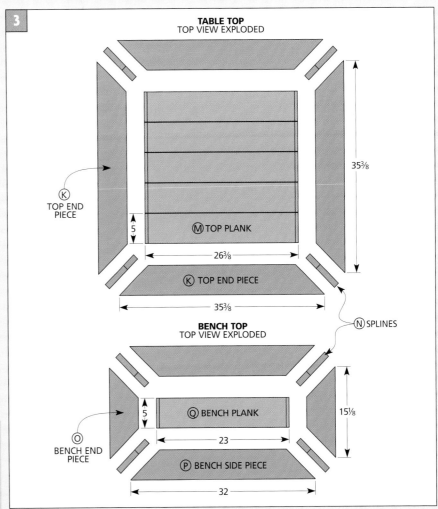

3

TABLE TOP
TOP VIEW EXPLODED

(K) TOP END PIECE

$35\frac{3}{8}$

5

(M) TOP PLANK

$26\frac{3}{8}$

(K) TOP END PIECE

$35\frac{3}{8}$

(N) SPLINES

BENCH TOP
TOP VIEW EXPLODED

5

(Q) BENCH PLANK

$15\frac{1}{8}$

(O) BENCH END PIECE

23

(P) BENCH SIDE PIECE

32

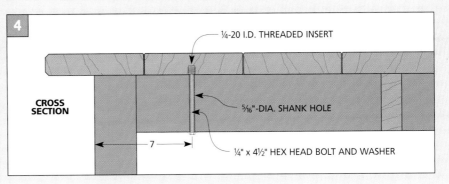

4

$\frac{1}{4}$-20 I.D. THREADED INSERT

CROSS SECTION

$\frac{5}{16}$"-DIA. SHANK HOLE

7

$\frac{1}{4}$" x $4\frac{1}{2}$" HEX HEAD BOLT AND WASHER

Patio Table

Even though its joinery is similar to what you'd find in an indoor table, this project has one feature a dining room table doesn't — a removable top for easy storage in the winter.

This Patio Table isn't shaped like most picnic tables, and it's not built like one either. The top and base use three types of joints: lap joints, mortise and tenons, and splined miters. Not the kind of joinery you'd expect to find in an outdoor project.

But the great thing is that all the joints can be built using just a table saw and a router.

MITERS. Although you'll get to try your hand at a variety of joinery, the main challenge comes in accurately cutting the miters for the frame around the top. With sixteen miters to cut, each one has to be exact. Any error gets multiplied when the frame is assembled.

So the secret is to take your time and make a test frame from scrap wood first. Then, when you're done, you'll have an outdoor table that's built with the craftsmanship of indoor furniture.

SUPPLIES. I used Clear All Heart redwood for the table base and top frame. (See the Shop Info article on page 35 for more on redwood grades.) I made the top slats of western red cedar — they add contrast and hold down the cost.

The main joints in the table have no hardware. They're assembled with moisture-resistant glue. Keeper strips and screws hold the top slats in place. The top itself is secured to the base with threaded inserts and machine bolts (making it easy to store the table in the winter).

ROUND TOP. If you'd like to try your hand at a slightly different technique used to build a round table top, refer to the Designer's Notebook on page 113.

FINISH. I finished the table with a mixture of spar varnish and tung oil (refer to Shop Info on page 48).

EXPLODED VIEW

OVERALL DIMENSIONS:
48¼W x 48¼D x 29H

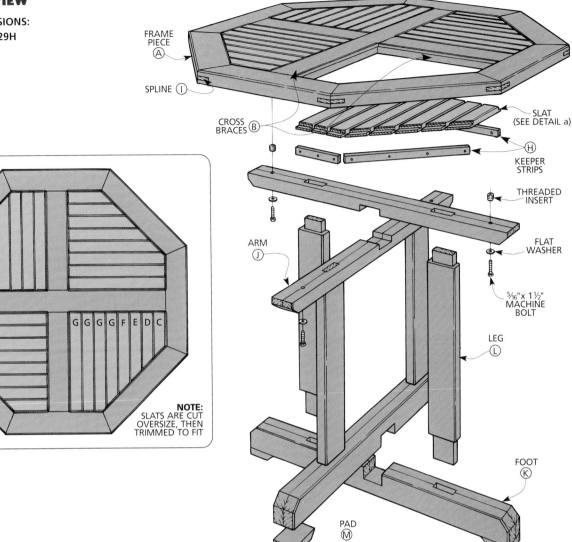

FRAME
PIECE
(A)

SPLINE (I)

CROSS
BRACES (B)

SLAT
(SEE DETAIL a)

(H)

KEEPER
STRIPS

THREADED
INSERT

FLAT
WASHER

ARM
(J)

⁵⁄₁₆" x 1½"
MACHINE
BOLT

LEG
(L)

FOOT
(K)

PAD
(M)

a.

G G G G F E D C

NOTE:
SLATS ARE CUT
OVERSIZE, THEN
TRIMMED TO FIT

MATERIALS LIST

WOOD

A	Frame Pieces (8)	1½ x 4 - 20
B	Cross Braces (2)	1½ x 4 - 46¼
C	Slats (4)	¾ x 2⅛ - 9 rough
D	Slats (4)	¾ x 2⅛ - 12 rough
E	Slats (4)	¾ x 2⅛ - 14 rough
F	Slats (4)	¾ x 2⅛ - 17 rough
G	Slats (16)	¾ x 2⅛ - 19 rough
H	Keeper Strips (4)	⅜ x ¾ - 45 rough
I	Splines (8)	½ x 6 - 4 rough
J	Arms (2)	1⅜ x 2¾ - 42
K	Feet (2)	2¾ x 3 - 42
L	Legs (4)	1½ x 4 - 26¾
M	Pads (4)	¾ x 2¾ - 4

HARDWARE SUPPLIES

(40) No. 6 x 1" Fh woodscrews
(16) No. 8 x 1¼" Fh woodscrews
(4) ⁵⁄₁₆" threaded inserts
(4) ⁵⁄₁₆" x 1½" machine bolts w/ washers
(64) ⅝" wire brads

CUTTING DIAGRAM

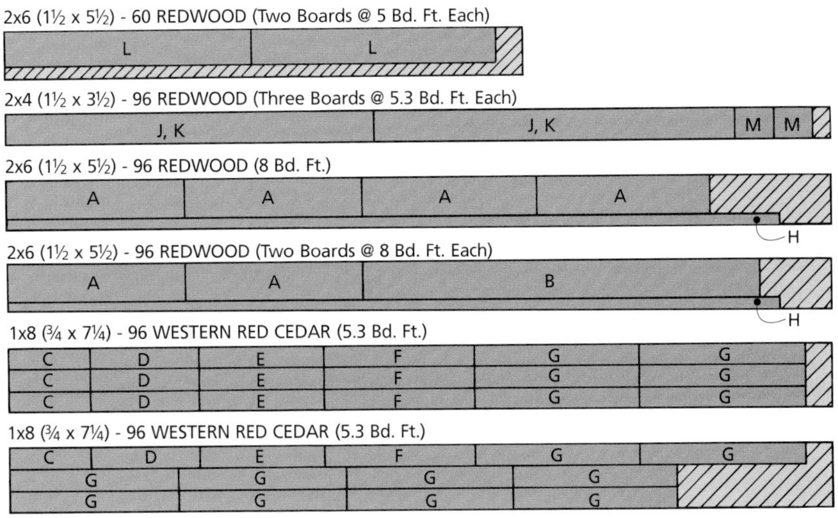

2x6 (1½ x 5½) - 60 REDWOOD (Two Boards @ 5 Bd. Ft. Each)

L	L

2x4 (1½ x 3½) - 96 REDWOOD (Three Boards @ 5.3 Bd. Ft. Each)

J, K	J, K	M	M

2x6 (1½ x 5½) - 96 REDWOOD (8 Bd. Ft.)

A	A	A	A	

H

2x6 (1½ x 5½) - 96 REDWOOD (Two Boards @ 8 Bd. Ft. Each)

A	A	B	

H

1x8 (¾ x 7¼) - 96 WESTERN RED CEDAR (5.3 Bd. Ft.)

C	D	E	F	G	G
C	D	E	F	G	G
C	D	E	F	G	G

1x8 (¾ x 7¼) - 96 WESTERN RED CEDAR (5.3 Bd. Ft.)

C	D	E	F	G	G
G	G	G	G	
G	G	G	G	

The top of the table is an eight-sided frame joined with splined miters.

To strengthen the frame, a pair of interlocking cross braces is added. These create four openings that are later filled with slats.

FRAME PIECES. Start work on the top by cutting eight frame pieces (A) from a 2x6 to rough lengths of 22". Then rip these to finished width (4") *(Fig. 1)*.

MITERS. To check that the miter gauge is set at the exact angle, I first made a series of test cuts on eight pieces of 4"-wide scrap plywood.

Then, to guarantee that all the pieces were identical in length, I attached an auxiliary fence to my miter gauge and clamped a stop block to this fence.

Once the test pieces form a perfect octagon, miter all eight frame pieces to length *(Fig. 1)*.

KERFS AND SPLINES. To strengthen the joints, I used $1/2$"-thick splines. The splines fit in kerfs centered on the thickness of the frame pieces *(Fig. 1a)*. I cut these kerfs on the table saw using a dado blade and a special jig (see the Shop Jig below).

Next, make the splines by resawing

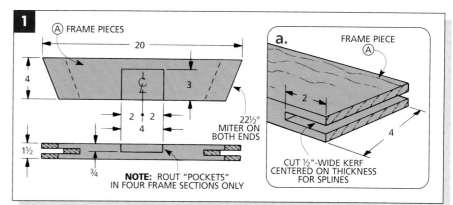

enough stock to fit the kerfs. Then cut the splines to width and length (refer to *Fig. 4* on next page).

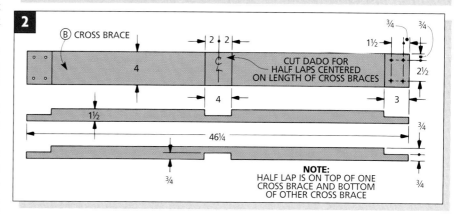

Note: For maximum strength, orient the grain of the spline across the frame's joint line.

SHOP JIG .... *Kerfing Jig*

The frame sections of the table top are mitered, then joined with splines that fit in kerfs. But they're not just any splines — these splines are $1/2$" thick and 4" long. Which means cutting kerfs with a $1/2$"-wide dado blade set to cut 2" deep.

With that much blade exposed I wanted my hands in a safe position, but still in control of the workpiece. This jig securely supports the workpiece as it runs vertically along the rip fence.

MAKING THE JIG. Two of the pieces for this jig are cutoffs from the already-mitered frame sections. They support the workpiece and help prevent chipout. The other two parts of the jig are plywood strips that hold the jig together and create a "pocket" for the workpiece.

To make the kerfing jig, glue the two plywood sides to the mitered cutoffs with a third cutoff temporarily held in place as a spacer *(Fig. 1)*.

USING THE JIG. To cut a kerf on the end of a mitered workpiece, raise the saw blade to the desired depth. Then position the jig against the rip fence and adjust the fence so the blade is roughly centered on the thickness of the jig *(Fig. 2)*.

To ensure the kerfs are centered on the thickness, cut each kerf in two passes. Just turn the jig around backwards for the second pass (without removing the workpiece) *(Fig. 3)*.

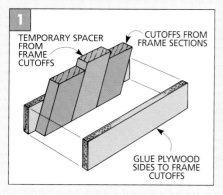

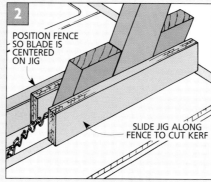

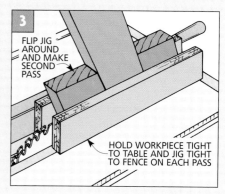

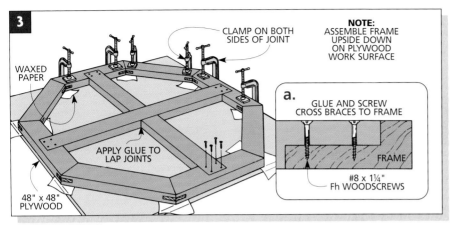

3

CLAMP ON BOTH SIDES OF JOINT

NOTE: ASSEMBLE FRAME UPSIDE DOWN ON PLYWOOD WORK SURFACE

WAXED PAPER

APPLY GLUE TO LAP JOINTS

48" x 48" PLYWOOD

a. GLUE AND SCREW CROSS BRACES TO FRAME

FRAME

#8 x 1¼" Fh WOODSCREWS

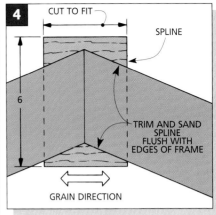

4

CUT TO FIT

SPLINE

6

TRIM AND SAND SPLINE FLUSH WITH EDGES OF FRAME

GRAIN DIRECTION

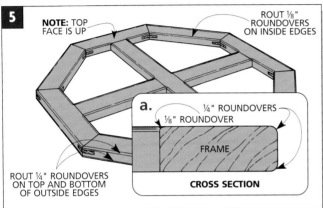

5

NOTE: TOP FACE IS UP

ROUT ⅛" ROUNDOVERS ON INSIDE EDGES

a. ¼" ROUNDOVERS ⅛" ROUNDOVER

FRAME

CROSS SECTION

ROUT ¼" ROUNDOVERS ON TOP AND BOTTOM OF OUTSIDE EDGES

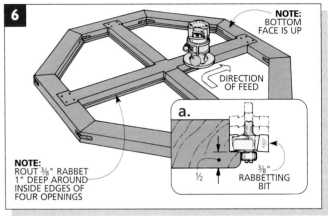

6

NOTE: BOTTOM FACE IS UP

DIRECTION OF FEED

NOTE: ROUT ⅜" RABBET 1" DEEP AROUND INSIDE EDGES OF FOUR OPENINGS

a. ½ ⅜" RABBETTING BIT

POCKETS. The next step is to cut "pockets" on the underside of four of the frame sections to receive the cross braces (refer to *Figs. 1 and 3*). I roughed them out using a router, to within ⅛" of the layout lines. Then I cleaned up to the lines with a chisel.

CROSS BRACES

To make the cross braces (B), first dry-assemble the frame and measure between the extremes of each pocket. Then cut two pieces of 2x6 to this length and also to final width.

HALF LAPS. Now lay out and cut half lap joints on the ends and center of each cross brace *(Fig. 2)*.

Note: The center half lap is cut on the top of one cross brace and the bottom of the other.

ASSEMBLY. I assembled the top upside down on a half sheet of plywood *(Fig. 3)*. Spread some plastic resin glue in each saw kerf, then add the splines. (See the Shop Info article on page 48 for more on outdoor glues.)

Clamp the frame pieces to the plywood as you work your way around the table. Then glue and screw the cross braces into the pockets *(Fig. 3a)*.

TRIM SPLINES. Once the glue dries, you can trim, then sand the splines flush with the inside and outside edges of the frame *(Fig. 4)*.

With the top frame assembled, the next step is to round over the edges.

ROUNDOVERS. To round over the outside edges of the frame, I used a ¼" roundover bit, making sure to rout in a counter-clockwise direction *(Fig. 5)*.

Note: To remove the track left by the router bearing (sometimes it's not obvious until finish is applied), see the Shop Tip at right.

For the top inside edges of the top frame — and also the top edges of the cross braces — I used a ⅛" roundover bit, routing this time in a clockwise direction *(Fig. 5)*.

RABBETS. When the top slats are added, they're held in place by a series of keeper strips attached to the underside of the frame (refer to *Fig. 9* on page 110). The slats rest on a ledge that's formed by routing a ⅜"-wide rabbet along the bottom inside openings of the frame *(Fig. 6)*.

Make at least two passes to rout the 1"-deep rabbet, leaving a ½"-thick ledge to support the slats *(Fig. 6a)*. Then square up the corners with a chisel.

SHOP TIP

Router Bearing Tracks

After rounding over the table top frame, I noticed a shallow "track" left by the router bit bearing. A line of wood fibers in the redwood had been compressed.

To restore the compressed wood fibers to their original shape, I use a damp cloth and a hot iron (see drawing).

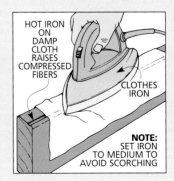

HOT IRON ON DAMP CLOTH RAISES COMPRESSED FIBERS

CLOTHES IRON

NOTE: SET IRON TO MEDIUM TO AVOID SCORCHING

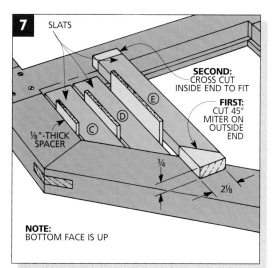

7
SLATS

SECOND:
CROSS CUT
INSIDE END TO FIT

FIRST:
CUT 45°
MITER ON
OUTSIDE
END

E

D

C

1/8"-THICK
SPACER

3/4

2 1/8

NOTE:
BOTTOM FACE IS UP

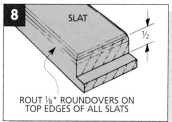

8
SLAT

1/2

ROUT 1/8" ROUNDOVERS ON
TOP EDGES OF ALL SLATS

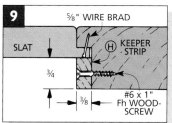

9
5/8" WIRE BRAD

SLAT

H KEEPER
STRIP

3/4

3/8

#6 x 1"
Fh WOOD-
SCREW

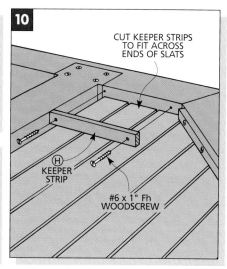

10
CUT KEEPER STRIPS
TO FIT ACROSS
ENDS OF SLATS

H KEEPER
STRIP

#6 x 1" Fh
WOODSCREW

TOP SLATS

Each of the four openings in the table top contains eight slats. The slats start out as blanks of differing lengths that are individually cut to fit.

RIP SLATS TO WIDTH. But before you can do this, the top slats (C, D, E, F, and G) will need to fit into the frame openings with equal 1/8"-wide spacing between them *(Fig. 7)*. To determine how wide each slat should be, first measure across the widest part of the opening.

Then, to allow for nine 1/8"-wide gaps, subtract 1 1/8" from this measurement. Finally, divide this figure by eight to obtain the desired width of the slats. (In my case, this was 2 1/8".)

Now, cut enough stock to finished width for eight of the slats (refer to detail 'a' in the Exploded View on page 107).

Then simply repeat this procedure for the other three openings.

CUT TO ROUGH LENGTH. With the stock for the slats ripped to uniform width, they can be cut to length. To minimize waste, I started by first cutting them to five different rough lengths (refer to parts C, D, E, F, and G in the Materials List on page 107).

MEASURE AND FIT. The procedure for cutting the slats to finished length is the same for each of the four openings. So for each opening, first cut a 45° miter across the outside end of the five shortest slat blanks (refer to *Fig. 7* and detail 'a' in the Exploded View on page 107).

Next, position the slats over the opening with a 1/8"-thick temporary spacer positioned on each side of each slat. Now make a pencil mark on the inside end of all eight slats to indicate

where it meets the edge of the cross-brace *(Fig. 7)*. Then cross-cut each slat to finished length at the pencil mark.

RABBETS. The slats should fit in the openings now, but they won't be flush with the top surface of the table frame. To get them flush, cut rabbets on the ends of each slat *(Figs. 8 and 9)*. I cut the rabbets with a dado blade on the table saw.

ROUNDOVERS. Now round over all four top edges of each slat with a 1/8" roundover bit in the router table.

Note: The bearing on the router bit has to be removed for routing the rabbeted ends (see the Shop Tip below).

INSTALL THE SLATS. Next, to maintain a uniform space between the slats, I tacked them in place, one at a time, through the rabbeted ends *(Fig. 9)*. Position the spacers between each slat as they are tacked down *(Fig. 7)*.

SHOP TIP . . . . *Removing a Router Bearing*

I needed to round over the rabbeted ends of the top slats. But the bearing prevented the cutter from making contact with the workpiece *(Fig. 1)*.

So I took the bearing off the bit by removing the screw that holds it in place *(Fig. 2)*.

Note: On some router bits you can't remove the bearing — it holds the cutter in place.

Without a bearing, you have to use an edge guide or a router table with a

fence to guide the work. On the slats, I used the router table.

But there was another problem — the throat opening on the fence is too wide for the slats. So the corner of the workpiece can get hung up in the opening.

To get around this problem, I made an auxiliary fence from hardboard with a smaller opening. Then I clamped this to the router table fence *(Fig. 3)*.

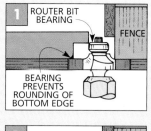

1 ROUTER BIT
BEARING

FENCE

BEARING
PREVENTS
ROUNDING OF
BOTTOM EDGE

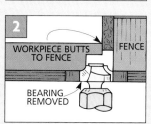

2
WORKPIECE BUTTS
TO FENCE

FENCE

BEARING
REMOVED

3 CLAMP

HARDBOARD
AUXILIARY FENCE
WITH NARROW
THROAT

KEEPER STRIPS. When all the slats have been tacked in place, rip the keeper strips (H) to a finished width of ³/₄" (*Fig. 9*). Then cut each keeper strip to fit, and screw them under the slats (*Fig. 10*).

Note: Don't glue the keeper strips in place. That way it's no problem to replace damaged or broken slats later.

TABLE BASE

When the table top is complete, work can begin on the base. The base has four legs joined to cross-shaped arm (top) and foot assemblies.

I started by making the arms (J) and feet (K) from three identical blanks.

Each blank is made from two 2x4s that are glued together (*Fig. 11*). Start by planing one face of each 2x4 to provide a clean, flat, gluing surface.

There's a trick to forming the mortises in each blank. Before gluing the planed faces together, I cut notches across each face (*Fig. 11*). Then, when the pieces are glued together, the notches will form mortises (*Fig. 11a*).

Note: To help keep the dadoes aligned during glue-up, I fill the mortises with temporary "tenons."

After the pieces are glued together, rip the assembly to 3" wide (*Fig. 12*).

FEET

Now set one blank aside and begin working on the two blanks for the feet.

HALF LAPS. The two feet (K) are joined into a cross shape with half lap joints (refer to *Fig. 17* on page 112). I make identical "self-centering" half laps by using the rip fence as a stop and an auxiliary fence screwed to the miter gauge.

To make the half laps, lay out the position of the notch centered on the length of one foot blank (*Fig. 12a*).

Then, to cut the notches, make two cuts on each piece, turning the piece end for end between cuts. Then clean out the waste between the first two cuts with additional passes.

CHAMFERS. When you're finished cutting the notches that form the half laps on the foot blanks, lay out and cut a decorative chamfer on the top end of each foot (*Figs. 13 and 13a*).

Note: The chamfers are cut with the half lap notch *down* on one foot, and the half lap notch *up* on the other (*Fig. 12*).

PADS. To keep the table feet dry, I glued pads (M) to the bottom ends of each foot (*Figs. 14 and 14a*).

ASSEMBLE FEET. With the pads in place, the feet can now be assembled into a cross-shaped unit. I used plastic resin glue and clamps. Finally, I soften the upper edges and outside ends of the feet with a ¹/₄"-dia. roundover bit.

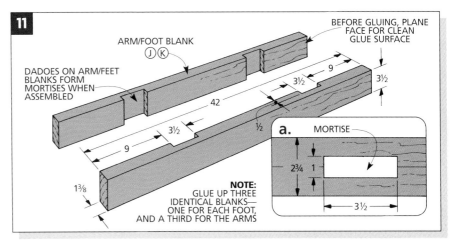

11 ARM/FOOT BLANK (J)(K) — BEFORE GLUING, PLANE FACE FOR CLEAN GLUE SURFACE — DADOES ON ARM/FEET BLANKS FORM MORTISES WHEN ASSEMBLED — 42 — 9 — 3½ — 3½ — 9 — 3½ — ½ — 1³/₈ — **NOTE:** GLUE UP THREE IDENTICAL BLANKS—ONE FOR EACH FOOT, AND A THIRD FOR THE ARMS

a. MORTISE — 2³/₄ — 1 — 3½

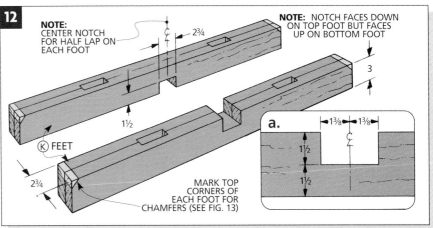

12 **NOTE:** CENTER NOTCH FOR HALF LAP ON EACH FOOT — 2³/₄ — **NOTE:** NOTCH FACES DOWN ON TOP FOOT BUT FACES UP ON BOTTOM FOOT — 3 — (K) FEET — 1½ — 2³/₄ — MARK TOP CORNERS OF EACH FOOT FOR CHAMFERS (SEE FIG. 13)

a. 1³/₈ — 1³/₈ — 1½ — 1½

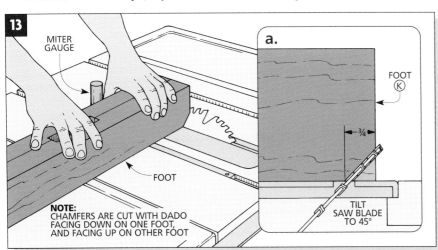

13 MITER GAUGE — FOOT — **NOTE:** CHAMFERS ARE CUT WITH DADO FACING DOWN ON ONE FOOT, AND FACING UP ON OTHER FOOT

a. FOOT (K) — ³/₄ — TILT SAW BLADE TO 45°

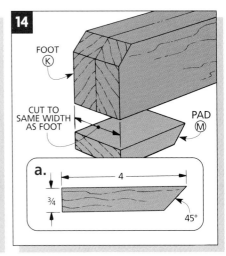

14 FOOT (K) — CUT TO SAME WIDTH AS FOOT — PAD (M)

a. 4 — ³/₄ — 45°

ARMS

To make the arms, start by ripping the remaining glued-up blank into two 1$\frac{3}{8}$"-thick pieces. Rip the first to finished size, then rip the other to match the first.

Note: You'll have to make two passes to rip each arm *(Figs. 15a and 15b)*.

HALF LAPS. To cut the notches that form the half lap joint, first lay out the position of the notch centered on the length of one of the arms *(Fig. 15)*. Then cut the notches using the same procedure as on the feet.

CHAMFER. The next thing to do is to add a 45° chamfer across the end of each arm. Again, orient the chamfers in relation to the center half laps *(Fig. 15)*.

ASSEMBLE AND ROUND OVER. Now glue and clamp the arms together at the lap joint. Complete the arms by routing roundovers on the lower edges *(Fig. 17)*.

LEGS

To make the legs, cut four lengths of 2x6 to finished dimensions *(Fig. 16)*.

TENONS. After the legs are cut to size, the tenons can be cut on each end of the legs *(Fig. 16)*.

Note: Since the arms and feet are different thicknesses, the tenons for the legs are different lengths *(Fig. 16)*.

To cut the tenons, I made a shoulder cut on each piece with the end of the leg butted to the rip fence. Then I made multiple passes to complete the tenon.

Before assembling the base, rout $\frac{1}{4}$" roundovers on the edges (but not the tenons) of all four legs *(Fig. 17)*.

ASSEMBLE THE BASE. To assemble the table base, first glue the legs, one at a time, into the mortises in the feet assembly *(Fig. 17)*. Then glue the arm assembly onto the top ends of the legs.

ATTACH TOP. With the table base assembled, the table top can be attached.

Begin by drilling a counterbore and shank hole centered on the width and near the end of each arm *(Fig. 17)*.

THREADED INSERTS. Now place the top and base upside down and center the arms on the cross braces. Make a mark through each shank hole for the location of a hole for a threaded insert *(Fig. 18)*. Then drill holes for the inserts *(Fig. 18a)*.

INSTALL INSERTS. With all the holes drilled, install the threaded inserts in the cross braces. Finally, attach the base to the top with machine bolts *(Fig. 18a)*. ■

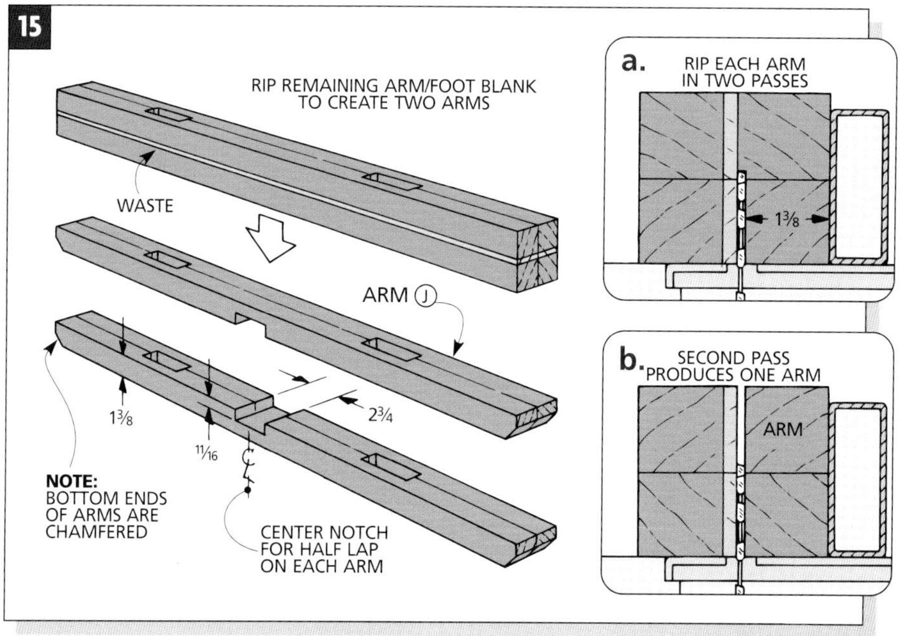
15
RIP REMAINING ARM/FOOT BLANK TO CREATE TWO ARMS
WASTE
ARM (J)
1 3/8
11/16
2 3/4
NOTE: BOTTOM ENDS OF ARMS ARE CHAMFERED
CENTER NOTCH FOR HALF LAP ON EACH ARM
a. RIP EACH ARM IN TWO PASSES
1 3/8
b. SECOND PASS PRODUCES ONE ARM
ARM

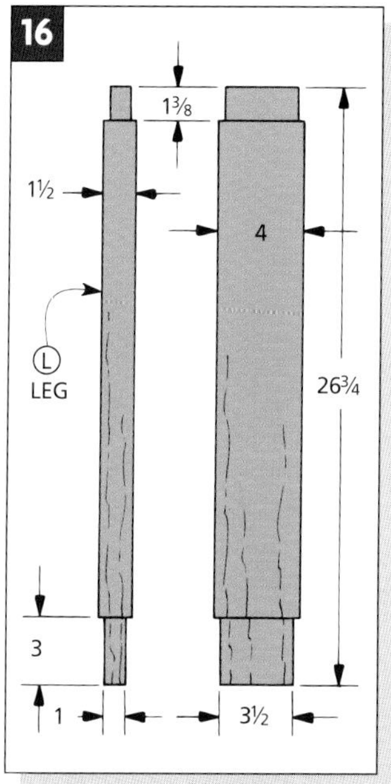
16
1 3/8
1 1/2
4
(L) LEG
26 3/4
3
1
3 1/2

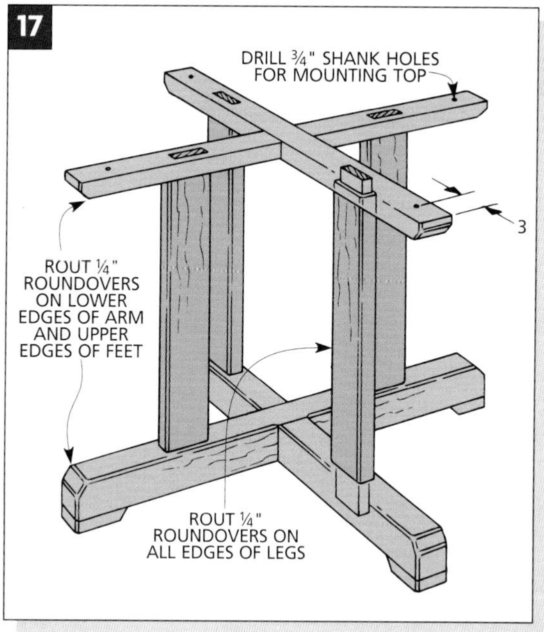
17
DRILL 3/4" SHANK HOLES FOR MOUNTING TOP
3
ROUT 1/4" ROUNDOVERS ON LOWER EDGES OF ARM AND UPPER EDGES OF FEET
ROUT 1/4" ROUNDOVERS ON ALL EDGES OF LEGS

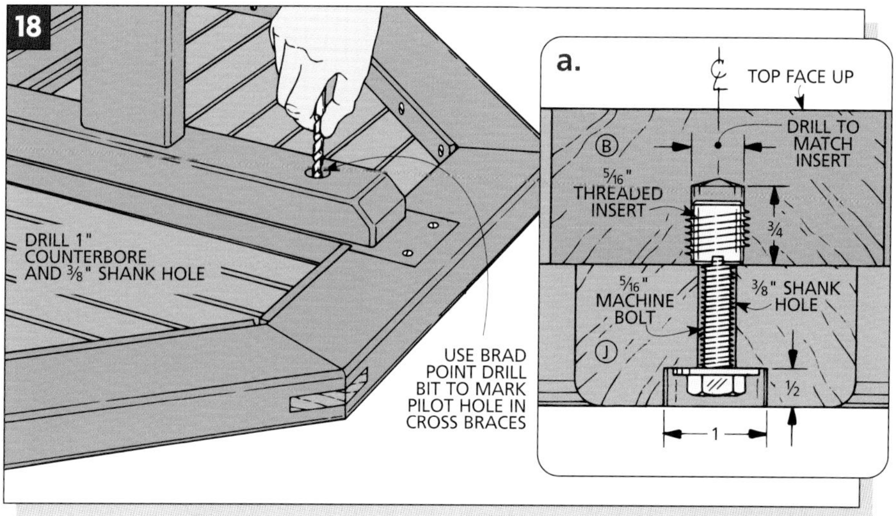
18
DRILL 1" COUNTERBORE AND 3/8" SHANK HOLE
USE BRAD POINT DRILL BIT TO MARK PILOT HOLE IN CROSS BRACES
a.
TOP FACE UP
(B)
DRILL TO MATCH INSERT
5/16" THREADED INSERT
3/4
5/16" MACHINE BOLT
3/8" SHANK HOLE
(J)
1/2
1

DESIGNER'S NOTEBOOK

This Cafe Table features the same sturdy base and solid construction as the larger Patio Table. But instead of an eight-sided design, it has a round top for a more continental appearance.

CONSTRUCTION NOTES:

■ To build the Cafe Table you'll need to start by constructing the trammel jig used to make the top round.

The jig is easy to make (it looks like a large clock pendulum). All you'll need is some ¼" hardboard and a nail *(Fig. 1)*.

■ But before you can use it, a few slight changes are made to the table frame.

■ The frame still has eight pieces with a 22½° miter cut on each end *(Fig. 2)*. But first the frame pieces (A) are ripped from 2x6 stock to a width of 5¼" and then rough cut to 24" long.

■ Once the frame pieces are mitered and cut to length *(Fig. 2)*, add the splined miters and assemble the frame.

■ Cut the "pockets" in the frame and add a temporary cross brace. Set the trammel jig to cut a 25" radius *(Fig. 3)*.

■ To use the jig, begin by routing in a counterclockwise direction with a ¼" straight bit. Rout in ¼"-deep passes until halfway through, then flip the frame and rout through to the other side *(Fig. 4)*. Finally, add ¼" roundovers to the outside edges of the table.

CAFE TABLE

MATERIALS LIST

CHANGED PARTS
A Frame Pieces (8) ¾ x 5¼ - 24 rough

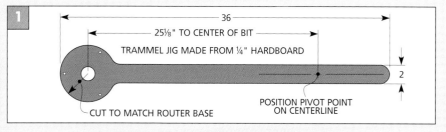

1
36
25⅛" TO CENTER OF BIT
TRAMMEL JIG MADE FROM ¼" HARDBOARD
2
CUT TO MATCH ROUTER BASE
POSITION PIVOT POINT ON CENTERLINE

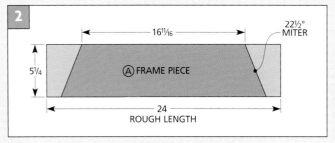

2
16¹¹⁄₁₆
22½° MITER
5¼
(A) FRAME PIECE
24
ROUGH LENGTH

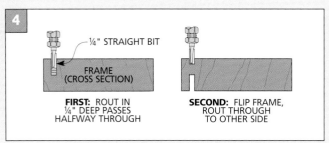

4
¼" STRAIGHT BIT
FRAME (CROSS SECTION)
FIRST: ROUT IN ¼" DEEP PASSES HALFWAY THROUGH
SECOND: FLIP FRAME, ROUT THROUGH TO OTHER SIDE

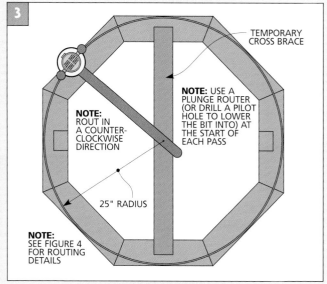

3
TEMPORARY CROSS BRACE
NOTE: USE A PLUNGE ROUTER (OR DRILL A PILOT HOLE TO LOWER THE BIT INTO) AT THE START OF EACH PASS
NOTE: ROUT IN A COUNTER-CLOCKWISE DIRECTION
25" RADIUS
NOTE: SEE FIGURE 4 FOR ROUTING DETAILS

Porch Swing

The arched back and the curve of the seat make this swing attractive as well as comfortable. A ladder-like frame underneath provides a solid foundation and a sturdy structure from which to hang the swing.

While the design of this Porch Swing was progressing, there were a couple of elements I really liked. The arched back gives the swing a graceful look, almost like an English garden bench. It also makes the swing more of a challenge to build.

Just as important as appearance, I wanted the swing to be strong. Some swings are suspended entirely by the arms. But this one is held up by a unique hanging system using eye bolts attached to the front and rear rails (see photo above). The rails also support the seat and are slightly longer than the seat slats to provide clearance for the chains.

The seat slats are strengthened by seat supports that connect the rails.

This makes the seat as solid as the floor in a new home.

JOINERY AND MATERIAL. The swing's strength is also affected by the material and joinery used. For the wood parts of the swing I used red oak — plenty strong to hold a couple of adults. And for extra strength, the back of the swing is built with mortise and tenon joints.

But instead of drilling a lot of mortises, I used a simpler technique. I start with one long groove in the upper and lower back rails, then use short filler strips to create the mortises.

COMFORT. Strength is important in a project that's going to support the weight of a person swinging. But comfort should also be part of the design.

So, to make the seat of the swing comfortable, there's a gentle curve on the top edge of the seat supports. This way, the slats follow the contour of your body.

Finally, all the edges of every piece of wood that your body will touch have been softened by sanding, or rounded over with a router.

ALTERNATE BACK PANEL. For a swing with a "country" look, you can build it with a decorative panel in the back. This option is shown in the Designer's Notebook on page 123.

FINISH. Any project that spends time outdoors needs a water resistant finish. I decided to use an outdoor oil finish on the Porch Swing. See the Finishing Tip on page 122 for more on this.

EXPLODED VIEW

OVERALL DIMENSIONS:
$58^{3}/_{4}$W x 24D x $24^{3}/_{4}$H

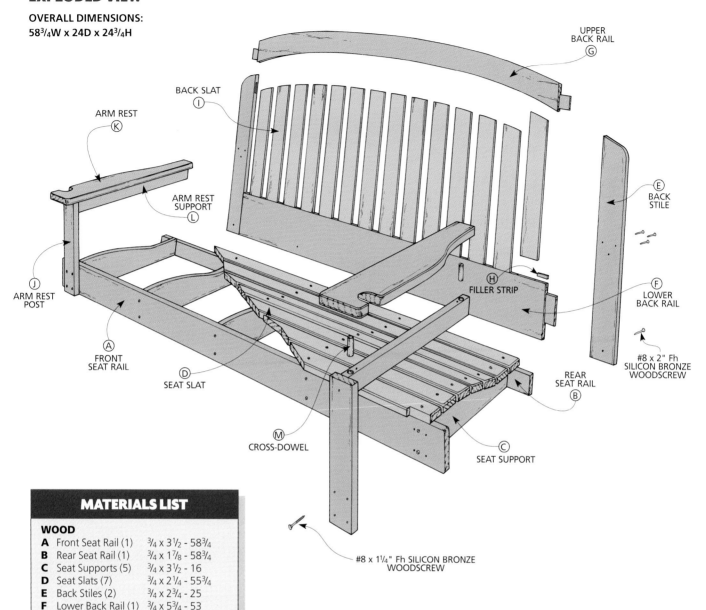

UPPER BACK RAIL — G

BACK SLAT — I

ARM REST — K

ARM REST SUPPORT — L

ARM REST POST — J

FRONT SEAT RAIL — A

SEAT SLAT — D

CROSS-DOWEL — M

FILLER STRIP — H

BACK STILE — E

LOWER BACK RAIL — F

#8 x 2" Fh SILICON BRONZE WOODSCREW

REAR SEAT RAIL — B

SEAT SUPPORT — C

#8 x $1^{1}/_{4}$" Fh SILICON BRONZE WOODSCREW

MATERIALS LIST

WOOD

A	Front Seat Rail (1)	$^{3}/_{4}$ x $3^{1}/_{2}$ - $58^{3}/_{4}$
B	Rear Seat Rail (1)	$^{3}/_{4}$ x $1^{7}/_{8}$ - $58^{3}/_{4}$
C	Seat Supports (5)	$^{3}/_{4}$ x $3^{1}/_{2}$ - 16
D	Seat Slats (7)	$^{3}/_{4}$ x $2^{1}/_{4}$ - $55^{3}/_{4}$
E	Back Stiles (2)	$^{3}/_{4}$ x $2^{3}/_{4}$ - 25
F	Lower Back Rail (1)	$^{3}/_{4}$ x $5^{3}/_{4}$ - 53
G	Upper Back Rail (1)	$^{3}/_{4}$ x $6^{1}/_{2}$ - 53
H	Filler Strips (30)	$^{3}/_{8}$ x $^{1}/_{2}$ - $1^{1}/_{4}$
I	Back Slats (14)	$^{3}/_{8}$ x $2^{1}/_{4}$ - $17^{1}/_{2}$ rgh.
J	Arm Rest Posts (2)	$^{3}/_{4}$ x $2^{1}/_{4}$ - 11
K	Arm Rests (2)	$^{3}/_{4}$ x 4 - 21
L	Arm Rest Supps. (2)	$^{3}/_{4}$ x $1^{1}/_{2}$ - $19^{1}/_{8}$
M	Cross-Dowels (4)	$^{1}/_{2}$ dowel - $1^{3}/_{8}$

HARDWARE SUPPLIES

(8) No. 8 x $1^{1}/_{4}$" Fh bronze woodscrews
(35) No. 8 x $1^{1}/_{2}$" Fh bronze woodscrews
(37) No. 8 x 2" Fh bronze woodscrews
(4) $^{5}/_{16}$" x 3" screw eyes
(2) $^{5}/_{16}$" x 4" eye bolts
(2) $^{5}/_{16}$" x 6" eye bolts
(4) $^{5}/_{16}$" hex nuts
(4) $^{5}/_{16}$" washers
2/0 Tenso chain (length determined by location of swing)
(4) Chain connectors
(2) $^{3}/_{4}$" S-hooks

CUTTING DIAGRAM

$^{3}/_{4}$ x 6 - 96 OAK (4 Bd. Ft.)

A	E
B	E

$^{3}/_{4}$ x 4 - 96 OAK (2.7 Bd. Ft.)

C	C	C	C	C

$^{3}/_{4}$ x 5 - 96 OAK (3 boards @ 3.3 Bd. Ft. Each)

D	I	I
D	I	I

$^{3}/_{4}$ x 3 - 96 OAK (2 Bd. Ft.)

D	I

$^{3}/_{4}$ x $6^{1}/_{2}$ - 96 OAK (4.7 Bd. Ft.)

G	K	L
		L
		H

$^{3}/_{4}$ x 6 - 96 OAK (4 Bd. Ft.)

F	K	J
		J

The seat of the swing starts out as a frame. It's built like a ladder with curved "rungs" (seat supports) *(Fig. 1)*.

The seat supports reinforce the frame, but that's not all they do. The curved top edge of each support is a design feature that makes the seat conform to the shape of your body. So the swing is not only strong, it's comfortable to sit in, too.

The rails are a key to the strength of the suspension system. Some swings are suspended only by the arms. This puts a strain on several weaker joints. The chains used to hang this Porch Swing are attached to eye bolts that run through the rails. So the swing and its occupants are supported from below (refer to *Fig. 26* on page 122).

SEAT RAILS. Start by cutting the front seat rail (A) and the rear seat rail (B) to the same finished length *(Fig. 1)*.

Then the front rail can be ripped to finished width and the rear rail ripped to a rough width of 2" *(Fig. 2)*.

The next step is to drill a $5/16$"-dia. hole for an eye bolt through each end of each rail *(Figs. 2 and 2a)*.

Note: Unless you have an extra-long drill bit, the holes in the front rail have to be drilled from both sides.

After all four holes have been drilled in the rails, the rear seat rail can be ripped to finished width. To do this, adjust the angle of the saw blade to cut a 10° bevel along the top edge of the rail *(Fig. 3)*.

Note: There's a good reason for ripping this bevel. On a typical porch swing, water and debris can accumulate in the crack between the seat and back. The bevel turns this crack into a

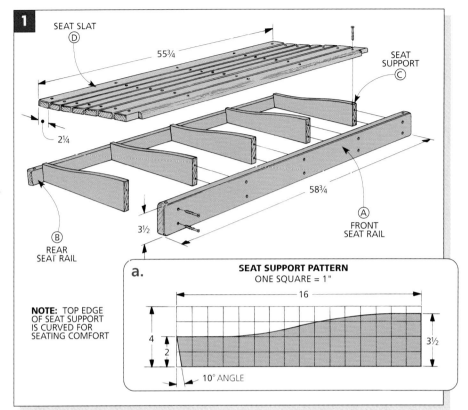

1

SEAT SLAT Ⓓ — $55\frac{3}{4}$ — SEAT SUPPORT Ⓒ

$2\frac{1}{4}$

Ⓑ REAR SEAT RAIL

$3\frac{1}{2}$

$58\frac{3}{4}$

Ⓐ FRONT SEAT RAIL

NOTE: TOP EDGE OF SEAT SUPPORT IS CURVED FOR SEATING COMFORT

a. SEAT SUPPORT PATTERN
ONE SQUARE = 1"

16 — 4 — 2 — $3\frac{1}{2}$ — 10° ANGLE

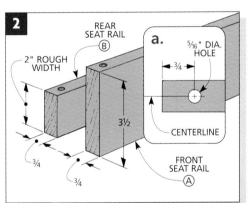

2 REAR SEAT RAIL Ⓑ

2" ROUGH WIDTH

a. $5/16$" DIA. HOLE — $3/4$ — CENTERLINE

$3\frac{1}{2}$

$3/4$ — $3/4$

FRONT SEAT RAIL Ⓐ

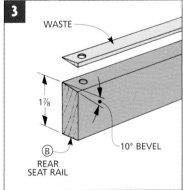

3 WASTE

$1\frac{7}{8}$ — 10° BEVEL

Ⓑ REAR SEAT RAIL

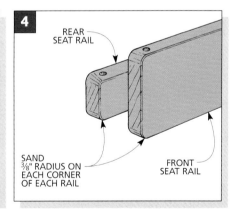

4 REAR SEAT RAIL

SAND $3/8$" RADIUS ON EACH CORNER OF EACH RAIL

FRONT SEAT RAIL

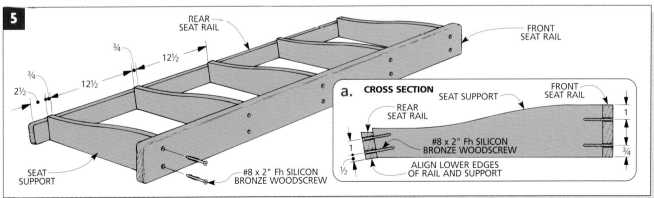

5 REAR SEAT RAIL

$3/4$ — $12\frac{1}{2}$ — $3/4$ — $12\frac{1}{2}$

$2\frac{1}{2}$

FRONT SEAT RAIL

a. CROSS SECTION

SEAT SUPPORT

REAR SEAT RAIL

FRONT SEAT RAIL

1

#8 x 2" Fh SILICON BRONZE WOODSCREW

1 — $3/4$

$1/2$ — ALIGN LOWER EDGES OF RAIL AND SUPPORT

SEAT SUPPORT

#8 x 2" Fh SILICON BRONZE WOODSCREW

channel, so water and dirt flow out more easily (refer to *Fig. 20a* on page 120).

Now, before moving on to the seat supports, round the corners of both seat rails by sanding a ³⁄₈" radius on each *(Fig. 4)*. Then soften all the edges of the rails with a sanding block.

SEAT SUPPORTS

The seat rails are connected by five seat supports (C) *(Fig. 1)*. These support the seat slats and also strengthen the seat assembly.

To make the seat slats conform better to the human body, there's a gentle curve along the top edge of the seat supports. And there's a simple way to cut these curves so they're all identical.

SEAT SUPPORTS. To make the supports, start by cutting a blank for each of the five seat supports (C) *(Fig. 1a)*.

Next, transfer the curve shown in the pattern onto one of the blanks *(Fig. 1a)*. It's not important that the curve be perfect. Only that it have a smooth shape.

Then cut along the curved line, and sand the curve smooth. Use the *first* seat support as a template to lay out the curve on the remaining four blanks.

Finally, a 10° miter can be cut across the back end of each support to establish the angle of the back assembly *(Fig. 1a)*.

ASSEMBLY. Now the frame of the seat is ready to be assembled. To do this, install a pair of silicon bronze woodscrews through the front and back rails into each of the seat supports *(Fig. 5a)*.

Note: Drill countersunk shank holes for all the screws (see the Shop Tip at right). For more on outdoor woodscrews, see the Shop Info on page 79.

SEAT SLATS

Complete the seat assembly by making the seven seat slats. Start by cutting the seat slats (D) to finished dimensions *(Figs. 6 and 8)*. Then roundovers are routed on the edges of these pieces for comfort and to prevent splinters *(Fig. 6)*.

A larger roundover (³⁄₈") is routed along the top front edge of the front slat *(Fig. 7)*. And notches on the front corners of the slat make room for the arm posts added later *(Fig. 7)*.

ATTACH SLATS. Now attach the front slat to the seat frame so it overhangs the front seat rail by ¹⁄₂" — the same as the depth of the notch *(Fig. 8b)*.

Note: All the slats should be centered on the frame from left to right. On my swing, this means the slats overhang the outside seat supports by 1" on each end *(Fig. 8a)*.

Also note that the screw holes

SHOP TIP
Silicon Bronze Screws

Silicon bronze woodscrews are rustproof, but the heads are easily twisted off. So drill pilot and shank holes, and avoid over-tightening them.

COUNTERSINK SCREW SO HEAD IS BELOW SURFACE

¹⁄₈"-DIA. PILOT HOLE, FULL DEPTH

³⁄₁₆"-DIA. SHANK HOLE

#8 x 2" Fh SILICON BRONZE WOODSCREW

should be drilled so they align with the centers of the seat supports *(Fig. 8)*.

Then attach the rear slat the same as the front — but this slat overhangs the seat supports (C) by ¹⁄₂" *(Fig. 8b)*.

The third slat is centered between the front and rear slats *(Figs. 8 and 8b)*. Then attach the four remaining slats.

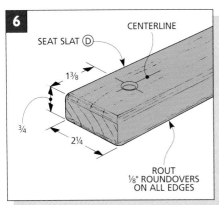

6
SEAT SLAT Ⓓ
CENTERLINE
1³⁄₈
³⁄₄
2¹⁄₄
ROUT ¹⁄₈" ROUNDOVERS ON ALL EDGES

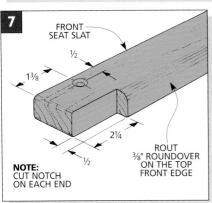

7
FRONT SEAT SLAT
¹⁄₂
1³⁄₈
2¹⁄₄
¹⁄₂
ROUT ³⁄₈" ROUNDOVER ON THE TOP FRONT EDGE
NOTE: CUT NOTCH ON EACH END

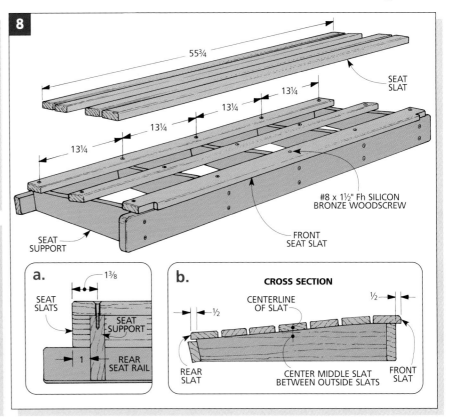

8
55³⁄₄
SEAT SLAT
13¹⁄₄
13¹⁄₄
13¹⁄₄
13¹⁄₄
#8 x 1¹⁄₂" Fh SILICON BRONZE WOODSCREW
SEAT SUPPORT
FRONT SEAT SLAT

a.
1³⁄₈
SEAT SLATS
SEAT SUPPORT
1
REAR SEAT RAIL

b.
CROSS SECTION
¹⁄₂
CENTERLINE OF SLAT
¹⁄₂
REAR SLAT
CENTER MIDDLE SLAT BETWEEN OUTSIDE SLATS
FRONT SLAT

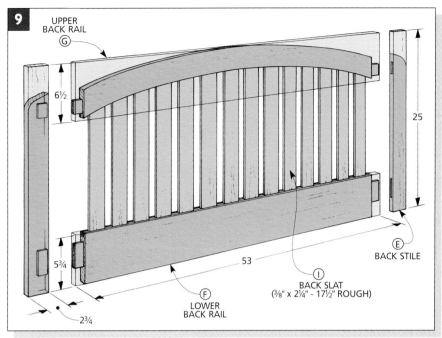

9

UPPER BACK RAIL (G)

6½

25

53

BACK SLAT (⅜" x 2¼" - 17½" ROUGH)

5¾

2¾

LOWER BACK RAIL (F)

(E) BACK STILE

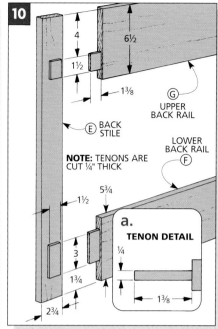

10

4

1½

6½

1⅜

(G) UPPER BACK RAIL

(E) BACK STILE

LOWER BACK RAIL (F)

NOTE: TENONS ARE CUT ¼" THICK

1½

5¾

3

1¾

2¾

a.
TENON DETAIL

¼

1⅜

BACK ASSEMBLY

Building the arched back of the swing can be a challenge. But if you break it down into a few steps, it will go smoothly.

BACK FRAME. The back assembly is just a big frame that holds the back slats. I started by cutting the two back stiles (E) to the same width and length *(Fig. 9)*. The tops of the stiles will be cut off later.

RAILS. Start by cutting both rails the same length, then rip the lower back rail (F) to finished width *(Fig. 9)*. But the upper back rail (G) starts out wider because of the curved shape.

JOINERY. Now, begin work on the joinery by laying out the mortises and tenons on the stiles and rails *(Figs. 10 and 10a)*. The Shop Tip below explains how to cut the off-center tenons.

CUT ARCS. After the joints have been cut, dry-assemble the frame and lay out the top arc on the rail and across the stiles *(Fig. 11)*. See the Technique at right for tips on laying out parallel curves. Then cut this arc and sand it smooth (with the frame still assembled).

GROOVES FOR SLATS. The back slats for the Porch Swing fit between the upper and lower rails. They fit in the

SHOP TIP . . . . *Off-Center Tenons*

The back of the Porch Swing is held together with mortise and tenon joints. But the tenons on the upper back rail weren't built with the usual procedure.

Actually, they started out normally. I cut the cheeks of the tenons on the table saw.

But the top edge of the tenon is too tall to be cut with the table saw. The top of the tenon is 4" from the top of the blank. (An ordinary table saw blade can only be raised 3½".) And it has to be extra wide to allow for the curve of the

upper back rail *(Fig. 1)*.

So to solve this problem, just cut both edges of the tenon with a coping saw.

First, lay out the edges of the tenons, taking the dimensions directly from the mortise *(Fig. 1)*.

Next, remove most of the

waste with the coping saw *(Fig. 2)*, staying outside the lines. Then use a chisel to trim the top and bottom edges until the tenon fits into the mortise *(Fig. 3)*.

Finally, clean up the shoulders so the stile pulls tight to the rail *(Fig. 3)*.

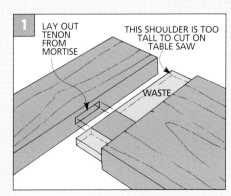

1

LAY OUT TENON FROM MORTISE

THIS SHOULDER IS TOO TALL TO CUT ON TABLE SAW

WASTE

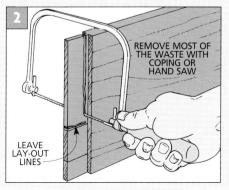

2

REMOVE MOST OF THE WASTE WITH COPING OR HAND SAW

LEAVE LAY-OUT LINES

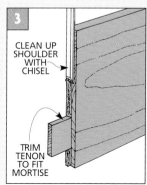

3

CLEAN UP SHOULDER WITH CHISEL

TRIM TENON TO FIT MORTISE

frame like tenons in mortises. But instead of drilling a lot of mortises, I used a much simpler technique.

ROUT GROOVES. The mortises start as long grooves cut on the inside (facing) edges of the back rails *(Fig. 12a)*. Then, I fill the grooves with short filler strips to create a series of mortises.

I use a slot cutter to form the grooves *(Fig. 12)*. Each centered, $3/8$"-wide groove is routed in two passes.

LOWER MORTISES. Next, lay out the position of the back slats on the top edge of the lower rail *(Fig. 13)*. Then transfer the marks to the front face of the rail.

FILLER STRIPS. Now the filler strips for the mortises can be cut. To do this, start with a long strip of wood the same thickness as the width of the groove.

Then rip the strip so it's slightly wider than the depth of the groove *(Fig. 13a)*.

Now cut this long strip into $1^1/4$"-long filler strips (H) *(Fig. 13a)*. Then, when the strips are glued in the grooves at $2^1/4$" intervals, mortises are created for the back slats *(Fig. 13)*.

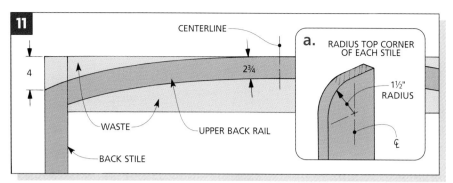

11
CENTERLINE
4
$2^3/4$
WASTE
UPPER BACK RAIL
BACK STILE

a. RADIUS TOP CORNER OF EACH STILE
$1^1/2$" RADIUS

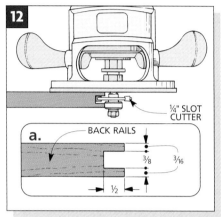

12
$1/4$" SLOT CUTTER

a. BACK RAILS
$3/8$
$3/16$
$1/2$

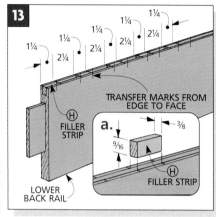

13
$1^1/4$ $1^1/4$ $1^1/4$ $1^1/4$ $1^1/4$ $1^1/4$ $1^1/4$
$2^1/4$ $2^1/4$ $2^1/4$ $2^1/4$ $2^1/4$
TRANSFER MARKS FROM EDGE TO FACE
FILLER STRIP
LOWER BACK RAIL

a. $3/8$
$9/16$
FILLER STRIP

TECHNIQUE .... *Parallel Curves*

The curved rail on the back of the Porch Swing is a nice touch. But making the top and bottom curves parallel was a problem.

TOP CURVE. The top curve for the back is quite large, but it's easy to lay out. The only thing unusual is that it

spans across three pieces. So first, I dry-assembled the rails and stiles *(Fig. 1)*. Then to form the curve, I used a long strip of $1/4$"-thick hardboard.

ENDS. The curve should end 4" down from the top edge of the assembly. To hold the hardboard strip in place, add two nails near the outside edges *(Fig. 1)*.

CENTER. The center of the curve is held in place with a simple wooden block. Center the block on the top rail and clamp it in place so the top of the strip is flush with the edge of the rail blank.

Now the curve can be drawn, following the top edge of the hardboard *(Fig. 1)*. Then the next step is to cut the curve and sand it smooth.

BOTTOM CURVE. With the top curve complete, I had to figure a way to draw

the bottom one so it was parallel with the top. To do this, I used a scribing jig.

SCRIBING JIG. This jig is a scrap piece of hardboard and two finish nails *(Fig. 2)*. (It's a good idea to drill pilot holes for the nails so the hardboard won't split.)

Set the jig on the upper back rail with the finish nails resting against the top curve. Then trace this curved edge on the underside of the jig *(Fig. 3)*.

TRIM TO FIT. Next measure down $2^3/4$" from the center of the curve and cut the scribing jig to this length *(Fig. 4)*.

DRAW CURVE. At this point, the bottom curve can be laid out. Simply scribe a line as you slide the jig along the top edge of the rails. Now you can cut and sand the bottom curve to shape just like the curve on top.

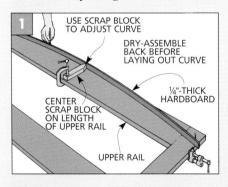

1
USE SCRAP BLOCK TO ADJUST CURVE
DRY-ASSEMBLE BACK BEFORE LAYING OUT CURVE
$1/4$"-THICK HARDBOARD
CENTER SCRAP BLOCK ON LENGTH OF UPPER RAIL
UPPER RAIL

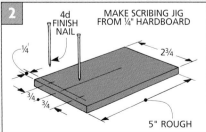

2
4d FINISH NAIL
MAKE SCRIBING JIG FROM $1/4$" HARDBOARD
$1/4$
$2^3/4$
$3/4$ $3/4$
5" ROUGH

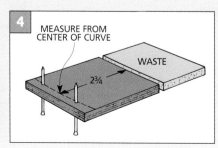

3
TRACE CURVE ON JIG
CURVED EDGE OF UPPER BACK RAIL

4
MEASURE FROM CENTER OF CURVE
WASTE
$2^3/4$

The slats in the back of the Porch Swing fit in a series of mortises. But they're not cut in the usual way. They start out as one long groove. Evenly-spaced filler strips "plug" the groove to form the mortises.

UPPER MORTISES. To create the mortises on the upper rail, start by transferring the marks from the lower rail using a framing square *(Fig. 14)*. Then glue the filler strips into this groove *(Fig. 15)*.

Note: Because the rail is curved and the marks are straight, one end of each filler strip should be trimmed off using a sharp chisel *(Fig. 15a)*.

Now the filler strips can be trimmed to fit perfectly flush *(Fig. 16)*. Then lightly sand the edges of the rails *(Fig. 17)*.

BACK SLATS. Next, rip the back slats (I) from a $3/8$"-thick blank to fit each mortise. In my case, all the blanks are $2^1/4$" wide and are cut to a rough length of $17^1/2$" *(Fig. 18)*.

CURVED CUTS. Now cut the slats to finished length. Because the top rail is curved, the length of the slats varies depending on their location in the frame.

So to mark the slats the correct length, rest them on a piece of scrap clamped to the lower rail *(Fig. 18)*. The scrap should be clamped 1" lower than the rail to allow for both mortises. Trace the curve of the upper rail on each slat *(Fig. 18)*. Then cut them to length along the curved line.

Finally, the frame can be assembled with the slats in the mortises, but only glue the tenons in the stiles. The slats are *not* glued in the rails.

Before attaching the back to the seat assembly, round over the outside edges of the frame *(Fig. 19)*. Then attach the back assembly to the seat. I used glue and screws through the rear seat rail and into the seat supports *(Figs. 20 and 20a)*.

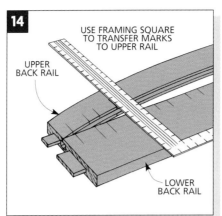

14 USE FRAMING SQUARE TO TRANSFER MARKS TO UPPER RAIL
UPPER BACK RAIL
LOWER BACK RAIL

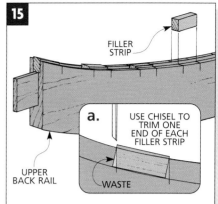

15 FILLER STRIP
a. USE CHISEL TO TRIM ONE END OF EACH FILLER STRIP
UPPER BACK RAIL
WASTE

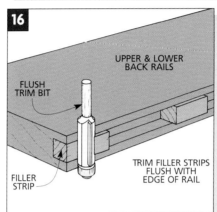

16 UPPER & LOWER BACK RAILS
FLUSH TRIM BIT
TRIM FILLER STRIPS FLUSH WITH EDGE OF RAIL
FILLER STRIP

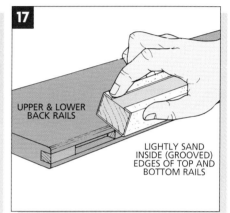

17 UPPER & LOWER BACK RAILS
LIGHTLY SAND INSIDE (GROOVED) EDGES OF TOP AND BOTTOM RAILS

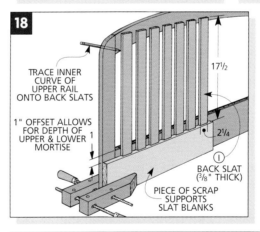

18 TRACE INNER CURVE OF UPPER RAIL ONTO BACK SLATS
1" OFFSET ALLOWS FOR DEPTH OF UPPER & LOWER MORTISE
$17^1/2$
$2^1/4$
BACK SLAT (I) ($3/8$" THICK)
PIECE OF SCRAP SUPPORTS SLAT BLANKS

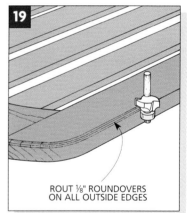

19 ROUT $1/8$" ROUNDOVERS ON ALL OUTSIDE EDGES

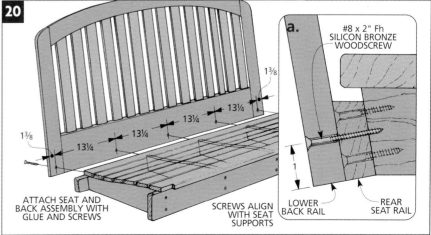

20 ATTACH SEAT AND BACK ASSEMBLY WITH GLUE AND SCREWS
$1^3/8$
$13^1/4$
$13^1/4$
$13^1/4$
$13^1/4$
$1^3/8$
SCREWS ALIGN WITH SEAT SUPPORTS
a. #8 x 2" Fh SILICON BRONZE WOODSCREW
$1^3/8$
1
LOWER BACK RAIL
REAR SEAT RAIL

Each arm assembly consists of an arm post, an arm rest, and an arm rest support *(Fig. 21)*. I started building the assemblies by making the posts.

ARM POST. Each arm post (J) is simply a short piece of stock attached to the front of the swing. The width of the post equals the width of the notch in the front seat rail (2¼") *(Figs. 21 and 24a)*.

The length of the post determines the height of the arm rest. I found that an 11"-long post produces a comfortable height for the arm rest.

After cutting the posts to finished width and length, they can be screwed and glued to the front seat rail *(Fig. 21)*.

Note: The bottom of the posts should be flush with the bottom of the front seat rail *(Fig. 24a)*.

ARM REST. The arm rest is another gently curved workpiece, with a wide area at the front. The back is about as wide as your elbow.

Begin work on the arm rest (K) by first cutting a blank to rough dimensions (4" wide and 21" long) *(Fig. 22)*.

Next, draw the curved shape along the side toward the back of the blank, and lay out the circular notch toward the front *(Fig. 22)*. (The notch provides clearance for a screw eye that will guide the chain past the arm rest.)

Before cutting this profile, cut the arm rest to finished length with a 10° bevel across the back end *(Fig. 23)*. This angle matches the tilt of the back.

Note: When it's attached, the arm rest should overhang the front post 1".

Now, the arm rest can be cut to shape. Then sand a ¼" radius on each front corner. And round over all the edges with a ⅛" roundover bit. (Don't round over the beveled ends.)

ARM REST SUPPORT. Before installing the arm rest, I added an arm rest support (L). Rip it to finished width and cut it to length with a 10° miter across the end. The length of the support equals the distance from the front post to the back stile *(Fig. 23)*. (Mine was 19⅛" long.)

Next, drill two holes into the bottom edge for a pair of cross-dowels (M) *(Fig. 23)*. These give the woodscrews at the front and rear more to grab onto than just the end grain of the support.

After gluing in the cross-dowels, glue and screw the support to the arm rest *(Fig. 23)*, and install this assembly to the swing *(Fig. 24)*.

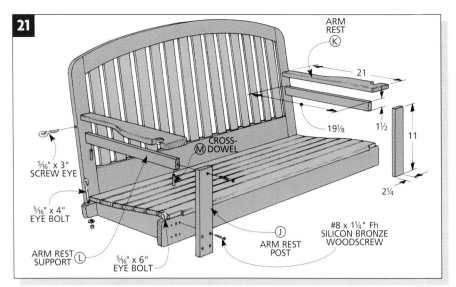

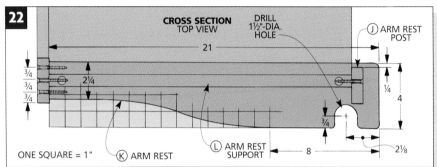

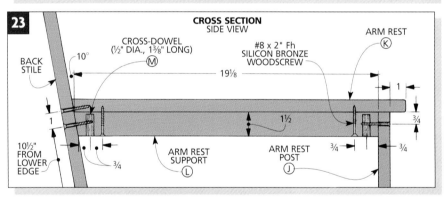

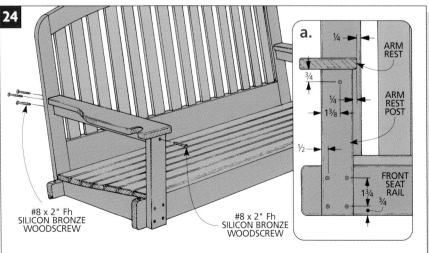

HANGING SYSTEM

Now that the swing is complete, all that's left is to install the hanging system. This includes the eye screws, eye bolts, and a heavy-duty chain.

Note: All the hardware, including the chain, should be available at most hardware stores and home centers. (Refer to the Sources on page 126 for information on where to find the silicon bronze woodscrews that are needed.)

FINISH. Before installing the hardware, it's a good idea to give the swing a couple coats of a good outdoor finish. (See the Finishing Tip below right for more information on the preparing your workpiece and applying an oil finish.)

SCREW EYES AND EYE BOLTS. After the finish has had time to dry, drill a ¼" pilot hole, 2" deep in the bottom of each notch that was cut earlier in the arm rest *(Fig. 25a)*. Then install screw eyes into these pilot holes.

Next, two more pilot holes are centered and drilled 13" from the bottom of the back stile *(Fig. 25)*. This allows you to install the screw eyes the same way in the back stiles.

Finally, secure the 4" eye bolts through the pre-drilled holes in the rear seat rail. And the 6" eye bolts are installed in the holes already in the front seat rail *(Fig. 25)*.

Once all this is done, the swing can be hung *(Fig. 26)*.

What's the best height to hang the Porch Swing? Here you'll have to experiment. Just keep in mind that the swing should be suspended high enough that your feet don't drag as you swing and low enough that you can still push off with your toes.

Also, by hanging the swing so the front is higher than the back, you won't feel like you're being pitched out as you swing forward *(Fig. 26)*. ■

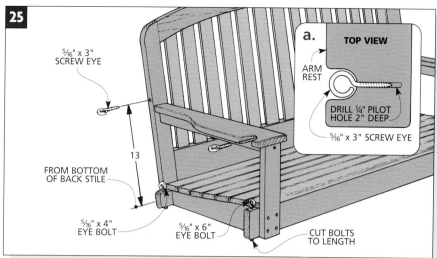

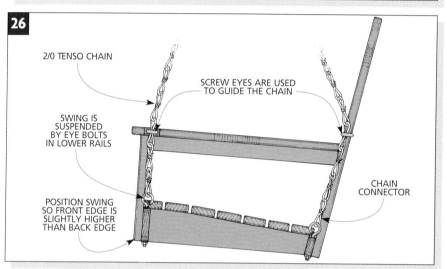

FINISHING TIP . . . . . *Outdoor Oil*

Any project that will spend time outdoors needs a weatherproof finish. An exterior paint or spar varnish would give the protection needed. But no outdoor finish lasts forever, so for the Porch Swing, I decided to use a finish that is easy to renew on an annual basis.

I used an oil finish that is actually a tung oil with UV and mildew inhibitors added.

Because of the additives, outdoor oils act as *both* a water repellent and wood preserv- ative. And they're easy to maintain — just add a fresh coat as needed.

Just as you would indoor furniture, it's best to prepare the workpiece properly by sanding up to 120-grit and then cleaning with a tack cloth.

Be sure to soak the wood around joints and end grain. Coat it thoroughly and wipe off any excess. Then let it sit a couple days and dry completely before applying another coat.

One thing to remember when applying an oil finish: don't attempt to build up several coats — it cures too soft.

Oil finishes don't protect by forming a thick coat between the wood and the surrounding environment as other finishes do. That's why renewing them is important.

Note: Always leave oily rags hanging over the edge of a worktable to dry before disposing of them. Heat can build up in a pile of oily rags and ignite a fire.

DESIGNER'S NOTEBOOK

Here's another version of the swing with panel-style slats and diamond-shaped decorative cutouts. The straight rails make the back much easier to build and the cutouts give the swing a country feel.

CONSTRUCTION NOTES:

■ Start by cutting two back stiles (E) to the same width and length from ³/₄" stock *(Fig. 1)*.

■ Next, lay out and cut the mortises for the rails on the back stiles *(Fig. 1)*. Then add ¹/₂" roundovers to the top corners of each back stile.

■ Now the upper back rail (G) can be cut to size *(Fig. 1)*. Since there will no longer be an arc in the upper rail it is now only 2³/₄" wide.

Note: The lower back rail (F) will be the same width as before.

■ Next, cut a centered ³/₈" groove, ¹/₂" deep in the bottom edge of the upper back rail (G) and the top edge of the lower back rail (F) *(Fig. 1)*.

■ This groove holds the diamond back slats (I). The slats need to be planed or resawn from ³/₄" stock to ³/₈" thick.

■ Now cut the slats to length *(Fig. 2)*. They'll have to be slightly shorter than the space between the grooves in the back rails. (Mine were 15⁷/₁₆".)

■ Next, the decorative cutouts can be added. Since there are only fourteen slats, I laid out the diamonds and held two slats together (like a sandwich), so I could cut the diamonds at the band saw.

Note: It's best to gang all fourteen slats together to mark the diamond cutouts. This helps assure that when the slats are installed, the cutouts will line up horizontally across the seat back *(Fig. 1)*.

■ Finally, assemble the seat back, beginning with the middle two slats. I placed a bead of silicone caulk in the bottom groove before adding the slats. Center them on the rails and work your way out, leaving ¹/₁₆" between each slat.

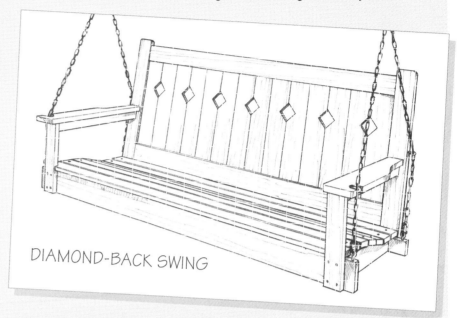

DIAMOND-BACK SWING

MATERIALS LIST

CHANGED PARTS

E	Back Stiles (2)	³/₄ x 2³/₄ - 24
G	Upper Back Rail (1)	³/₄ x 2³/₄ - 53
I	Back Slats (14)	³/₈ x 3¹/₂ - 15⁷/₁₆

Note: Do not need part H.

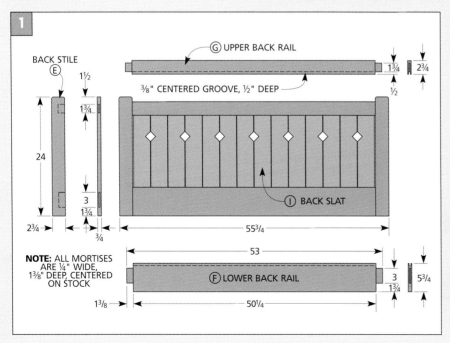

1

BACK STILE
(E)

1½

(G) UPPER BACK RAIL

1¾   2¾

³/₈" CENTERED GROOVE, ½" DEEP

½

24

(I) BACK SLAT

3
1¾

2¾   ³/₄   55³/₄

NOTE: ALL MORTISES ARE ¼" WIDE, 1³/₈" DEEP, CENTERED ON STOCK

53

(F) LOWER BACK RAIL

3
1¾   5³/₄

1³/₈   50¹/₄

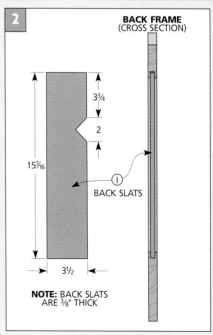

2   BACK FRAME
(CROSS SECTION)

3¾

2

15⁷/₁₆

(I)
BACK SLATS

3½

NOTE: BACK SLATS ARE ³/₈" THICK

Mortise and tenon joints fall into that category of "inventions civilizations are built on." Like the wheel, the lever, and the inclined plane.

Okay, so I'm exaggerating a bit, but in woodworking, there isn't any joint that's as versatile, strong, or long-lasting as the mortise and tenon.

VERSATILE. The mortise and tenon typically joins pieces at right angles. So it's a simple solution for many woodworking applications — like when you're building a frame. (I used mortises and tenons on the back of the Porch Swing.) Or when connecting two legs with a stretcher. (See the Redwood Bench on pages 38-49).

And for special applications, the mortise and tenon has a number of variations. For instance, there are through, twin, and keyed mortise and tenons. But these don't require new skills. They simply apply the basic joint to a new situation.

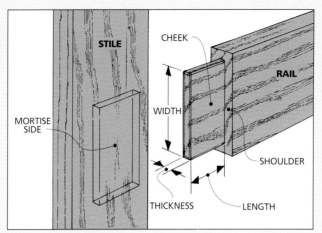

MECHANICAL STRENGTH. Besides being versatile, the mortise and tenon joint is strong. The obvious reason for this is mechanical. The tenon fits into the mortise like a handle fits in the head of a hammer.

To maximize this strength, I follow the "one-third rule." The thickness of the tenon is one-third the thickness of the mortised workpiece. This way, each

side of the mortise is as thick as the tenon. There is no "weak link."

GLUE STRENGTH. Mechanical strength isn't the only thing a mortise and tenon has going for it. It's a very strong *glue* joint as well. The cheeks of the tenon create large face grain surfaces that contact the face grain sides of the mortise. As long as the mating pieces fit snug, the glue joint will be strong.

EASY TO MAKE. For as strong as it is, a mortise and tenon joint is easy to make. All it requires is a drill press, a chisel to square the ends, and a table saw. The hardest part is cutting multiple mortise and tenon joints identically so that they make a square frame.

The trick here is to follow a certain procedure and to use standard settings and fences to minimize any variations between the joints.

MORTISE

I always prefer to drill the mortise first. Then I cut the tenon to fit. A mortise is limited by the size of your drill bits. But you can sneak up on the size of the tenon with the table saw. And it's easier to shave a tenon smaller than it is to chop a mortise bigger.

But even though I drill the mortise first, I lay it out based on the finished size of the tenon. And since a tenon that's centered on the thickness of a workpiece is easier to cut, I usually center the mortise on its workpiece as well (see *Step 1* below).

SET FENCE. A centered mortise is a simple operation on the drill press. Start by adding a fence so the workpiece is roughly centered under the bit. Then set the depth of the hole. I always drill the hole a little deeper than the finished length of the tenon. This way, the shoulders of the tenon pull tight against the mortised workpiece.

Note: To set the bit dead center, start with a piece of scrap that's the same thickness as your workpiece *(Step 1)*. Drill a shallow hole. Then flip the test piece around and drill a second

hole in the same location. If necessary, adjust the fence and repeat the procedure. When the two holes align, the bit will be perfectly centered.

DRILL MORTISE. To drill the mortise, start with the end holes *(Step 2)*.

Note: I drill these holes just inside the lay-out lines.

The next step is to remove the waste between the end holes and clean the sides *(Step 2)*.

CLEAN MORTISE. When the mortise has been drilled, all that's left is to square up the corners with a chisel *(Step 3)*.

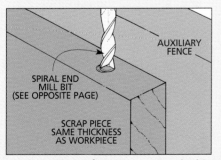

1 *Use a piece of scrap to center the bit. Place the scrap against the fence and drill a shallow hole. Then flip it around to see if the second hole matches the first.*

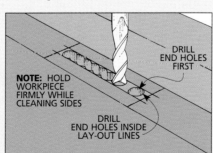

2 *Drill end holes first, then remove waste with overlapping holes. To clean sides, lower bit in 1/4" increments and slide the piece back and forth.*

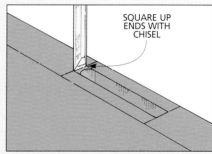

3 *If you want a mortise with square corners, start by chopping straight down at the ends. Then clean up the corners by paring down on the sides of the mortise.*

TENON

Cutting tenons on the table saw allows you to sneak up on their final size. Adding an auxiliary fence helps prevent chipout, and the rip fence acts as a stop for cutting the tenon to desired length.

TWO STEPS. The tenon is cut in two steps. First, form the cheeks *(Steps 1-4)*. Then when a corner just fits the mortise, cut the tenon to width *(Step 5)*.

PROCEDURE. The procedure for both of these steps is the same. First, set the height of the blade *(Steps 1 and 5)*. Then make two test cuts, flipping the piece between passes.

Note: Test the cuts only on the very end of the piece *(Steps 2 and 5)*. Then if the cuts are off, they can be corrected without making another workpiece.

When each test cut fits, the rest of the tenon can be cut *(Steps 4 and 5)*.

ASSEMBLY TIPS. If you have problems getting the joint together, there are some things you can do *(Step 6)*. First, to allow the tenon to slip more easily into the mortise, I chamfer the ends of the tenon.

Also, if there are gaps between the pieces when they're assembled, you can often get a tighter fit by undercutting the shoulders of the tenon with a chisel.

Finally, to avoid messy squeeze-out, apply glue only to the cheeks of the tenon near the ends. The glue spreads out as the tenon is pushed into the mortise.

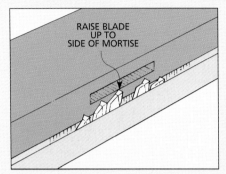

1 To set the height of the blade, place the mortised piece flat on the table. Raise the blade so the highest tooth lines up with the side of the mortise.

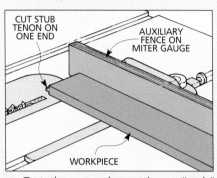

2 Test the setup by cutting a "stub" tenon on the end of the piece. Just attach an auxiliary fence to the miter gauge and make one pass for each cheek.

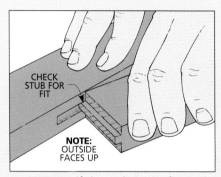

3 Now see if the stub tenon fits in the mortise. (Make sure the outside faces of both pieces are up.) If it's too tight, raise the blade and test the fit again.

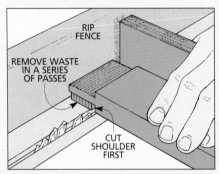

4 Set rip fence so distance to the outside of the blade equals the length of the tenon. Then cut the shoulder making repeated passes to remove waste.

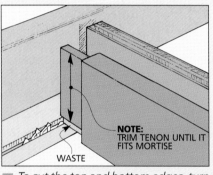

5 To cut the top and bottom edges, turn the workpiece on edge and sneak up on the cuts until the width of the tenon matches the length of the mortise.

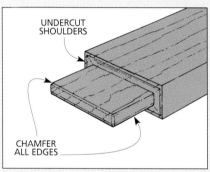

6 To allow tenon to slip into mortise and provide room for excess glue, chamfer all the edges. Plus, undercut the shoulders with a chisel to ensure a tight fit.

SPIRAL END MILL BIT

A spiral end mill bit is especially designed to cut mortises. (For information on where to find these bits, see the Sources on page 126.) Its spiral cutting edge has an "up-cut" design. So unlike Forstner bits, the chips are pulled up out of the mortise. This eliminates heat build-up and clogging. But the longer cutting edge also makes for a cleaner cut, so the sides of the mortise end up much smoother.

A clean cut is also the result of higher speed. Because these bits are designed to run in a router, I set the drill press at its highest speed setting (between 3000 and 5000 RPM).

PROCEDURE. Drilling a mortise with an end mill bit is just like drilling one with a regular drill bit. First, drill the holes at each end. Then drill overlapping holes between them.

But to clean up the sides of the mortise, the end mill bit has a definite advantage. As a router bit, it's also designed to cut side to side. So you can slide the workpiece "through" the bit.

A couple of words of caution. Don't clean up the entire face of the sides at one time. Instead, lower the bit 1/4" and slide it back and forth. Then lower the bit another 1/4" and so on. Also, be sure to keep a firm grip on the workpiece when sliding it sideways. The mill bit can grab a little as it removes the waste.

With a spiral end mill bit, chips are pulled up out of the workpiece.

One thing we take into consideration when designing projects is whether the hardware is commonly available. Most of the supplies for the projects in this book can be found at local hardware stores or home centers, but sometimes you may have to order hardware through the mail. If so, we've tried to find reputable sources with toll-free phone numbers (see right).

Woodsmith Project Supplies also offers hardware for some projects (see below).

WOODSMITH PROJECT SUPPLIES

At the time this book was printed, the following project supply kits and hardware were available from *Woodsmith Project Supplies*. The kits include hardware, but you must supply any lumber, plywood, or finish. For current prices and availability, call toll free:

1-800-444-7527

Bird Feeder
(pages 52-59)
Hardware kit.............No. 7106200

This kit includes the following:
(12) No. 8 x 1" brass Fh woodscrews
(42) 1" escutcheon pins
(24) No. 17 x $^3/_8$" copper tacks
(1) $^1/_4$"-dia. x $1^3/_4$" quick release pin
(1) $1^1/_8$" I.D. washer
(4 sheets) Copper foil 12" x 19"
(1 bag) Fish scale shingles
(1 bag) Square cut cedar shingles
(2) $^1/_8$" acrylic panels, 6" x 12"

Porch Swing
(pages 114-125)
Silicon bronze screws
......................................No. 798100

This kit includes the following screws for the Porch Swing:
(10) No. 8 x $1^1/_4$" Fh
(40) No. 8 x $1^1/_2$" Fh
(40) No. 8 x 2" Fh
Note: These are square drive screws that require a square drive screwdriver or bit for your driver.

KEY: TL09

MAIL ORDER SOURCES

The most important "tools" you may have in your shop are your mail order catalogs. The ones listed below are filled with supplies that can't be found at a local hardware store or home center. You should be able to find many of the supplies for the projects in this book in one or more of these catalogs.

THE WOODSMITH STORE

2625 Beaver Avenue
Des Moines, IA 50310
800-835-5084
Our own retail store with tools, jigs, hardware, books, and finishing supplies. We don't have a catalog, but we do send out items mail order.

ROCKLER WOODWORKING & HARDWARE

4365 Willow Drive
Medina, MN 55340
800-279-4441
www.rockler.com
A catalog of hardware and accessories, including plug cutting drill bits and spiral and slot cutting router bits.

WOODCRAFT

560 Airport Industrial Park
P.O. Box 1686
Parkersburg, WV 26102-1686
800-225-1153
www.woodcraft.com
This catalog has all kinds of hardware. You'll also find outdoor glues and finishes, plus a full line of drill bits, flush trim, spiral, and slot cutting router bits.

MCFEELY'S SQUARE DRIVE SCREWS

P.O. Box 11169
Lynchburg, VA 24506-9963
800-443-7937
www.mcfeelys.com
All kinds of screws, fasteners, square drive drill bits, and related hardware for indoor and outdoor projects. They specialize in screws with a square recess in the head to provide more driving power.

Note: The information below was current when this book was printed. Time-Life Books and August Home Publishing do not guarantee these products will be available nor endorse any specific mail order company, catalog, or product.

WOODWORKER'S SUPPLY

1108 North Glenn Road
Casper, WY 82601
800-645-9292
A good selection of outdoor hardware, glues, and finishes. You'll also find plug cutting drill bits, as well as spiral and slot cutting router bits.

CALIFORNIA REDWOOD ASSOCIATION

405 Enfrente Drive, Suite 200
Novato, California 94949
888-225-7339
www.calredwood.org
For information on availability of Clear All Heart Redwood, including links to retail and mail order sources throughout the United States.

LEE VALLEY TOOLS LTD.

P.O. Box 1780
Ogdensburg, NY 13669-6780
800-871-8158
www.leevalley.com
Several catalogs offering shelf supports, brushes, drill bits, outdoor and indoor screws, and glue.

CONSTANTINE'S

2050 Eastchester Road
Bronx, NY 10461
800-223-8087
www.constantines.com
Find hardware, outdoor glues (including epoxy and plastic resins), plug cutting drill bits, finials, brass screws, and other outdoor fasteners.

MCMASTER-CARR SUPPLY CO.

600 County Line Road
Elmhurst, IL 60126
630-833-0300
www.mcmaster.com
Supplier of copper sheeting.

AUGUST HOME
PUBLISHING COMPANY

President & Publisher: Donald B. Peschke
Executive Editor: Douglas L. Hicks
Creative Director: Ted Kralicek
Senior Graphic Designer: Chris Glowacki
Associate Editor: Craig L. Ruegsegger
Assistant Editors: Joseph E. Irwin, Joel Hess
Graphic Designers: Vu Nguyen, April Walker Janning, Stacey L. Krull
Design Intern: Heather Boots

Designer's Notebook Illustrator: Mike Mittermeier
Photographer: Crayola England
Electronic Production: Douglas M. Lidster
Production: Troy Clark, Minniette Johnson
Project Designers: Ken Munkel, Kent Welsh
Project Builders: Steve Curtis, Steve Johnson
Magazine Editors: Terry Strohman, Tim Robertson
Contributing Editors: Vincent S. Ancona, Jon Garbison, Bryan Nelson
Magazine Art Directors: Todd Lambirth, Cary Christensen
Contributing Illustrators: Harlan Clark, Mark Higdon, David Kreyling, Roger Reiland, Kurt Schultz, Cinda Shambaugh, Dirk Ver Steeg

Director of Finance: Mary Scheve
Controller: Robin Hutchinson
Production Director: George Chmielarz
Project Supplies: Bob Baker
New Media Manager: Gordon Gaippe

For subscription information about
Woodsmith and *ShopNotes* magazines, please write:
August Home Publishing Co.
2200 Grand Ave.
Des Moines, IA 50312
800-333-5075
www.augusthome.com/customwoodworking

Woodsmith® and *ShopNotes*® are registered trademarks of August Home Publishing Co.

The photo on page 35 courtesy of the California Redwood Association.

©2000 August Home Publishing Co.
All rights reserved. No part of this book may be reproduced in any form or by any electronic or mechanical means, including information storage and retrieval devices or systems, without prior written permission from the publisher, except that brief passages may be quoted for reviews.

First Printing. Printed in U.S.A.

School and library distribution by Time-Life Education, P.O. Box 85026, Richmond, Virginia 23285-5026.

TIME LIFE BOOKS

Time-Life Books is a division of Time Life Inc.
Time–Life is a trademark of Time Warner Inc. and affiliated companies.

TIME LIFE INC.
Chairman and Chief Executive Officer: Jim Nelson
President and Chief Operating Officer: Steven Janas
Senior Executive Vice President and Chief Operations Officer: Mary Davis Holt
Senior Vice President and Chief Financial Officer: Christopher Hearing

TIME-LIFE BOOKS
President: Larry Jellen
Senior Vice President, New Markets: Bridget Boel
Vice President, Home and Hearth Markets: Nicholas M. DiMarco
Vice President, Content Development: Jennifer L. Pearce

TIME-LIFE TRADE PUBLISHING
Vice President and Publisher: Neil S. Levin
Senior Sales Director: Richard J. Vreeland
Director, Marketing and Publicity: Inger Forland
Director of Trade Sales: Dana Hobson
Director of Custom Publishing: John Lalor
Director of Rights and Licensing: Olga Vezeris

OUTDOOR PROJECTS: DECK, LAWN & GARDEN
Director of New Product Development: Glen B. Ruh
Marketing Director: Nancy L. Gallo
Senior Editor: Linda Bellamy
Director of Design: Kate L. McConnell
Project Editor: Terrell D. Smith
Technical Specialist: Monika Lynde
Page Makeup Specialist: Jennifer Gearhart
Production Manager: Virginia Reardon
Quality Assurance: Jim King and Stacy L. Eddy

LIBRARY OF CONGRESS CATALOGING-IN-PUBLICATION DATA
Outdoor projects : deck, lawn & garden / by the editors of Time-Life Books and Woodsmith magazine.
   p. cm. – (Custom woodworking)
   Includes index.
   ISBN 0-7835-5958-5
   1. Outdoor furniture. 2. Garden ornaments and furniture–Design and construction. 3. Woodwork. I. Time-Life Books. II. Woodsmith (Des Moines, Iowa) III. Series.

   TT197.5.O9 O9823 2001
   684.1'8–dc21

                                                    00-048924

10 9 8 7 6 5 4 3 2 1
X X X X X X X X